TRANSGENERATIONAL FAMILY THERAPY

Transgenerational Family Therapy

Stuart Lieberman

CROOM HELM LONDON

©1979 Stuart Lieberman
Croom Helm Ltd, 2-10 St. John's Road, London SW11

British Library Cataloguing in Publication Data

Lieberman, Stuart
    Transgenerational family therapy.
    1. Family psychotherapy
    I. Title
    616.8'915   RC488.5

    ISBN 0-85664-776-4

Printed in Great Britain by
Biddles Ltd, Guildford, Surrey

CONTENTS

To the Mizuses, the Liebermans
and the hybrids they produced

PREFACE

This book is not intended as an introductory text for family therapy training. It is meant to redress the balance of previous works on family therapy which have, by and large, undervalued the importance of transgenerational influences upon the family member. I intend to put the transgenerational view about families; although I realise that there are other equally important foci of interest in regard to family functioning. I hope that readers interested in family therapy, whether psychiatrists, psychologists, social workers, nurses or any other member of the helping professions will gain a better understanding of the profound influences which extended family members and the family of origin have on the course of development of nuclear families and individual family members.

The book has two separate emphases. The first is more theoretical and explores the definitions, antecedents and theory of transgenerational influence. The second is clinically oriented and explores the therapeutic use of the concepts introduced in section one. The reader is expected to have sufficient grasp of the concepts to be able to apply them to the clinical material presented in later chapters. For this reason I have deliberately omitted exhaustive theoretical explanations of the therapeutic work.

It is my hope that the material in this book will also provide practical guidance to those professionals ready and willing to take the risk of working with their patients or clients in a new way. For this reason I have particularly emphasised the use of the geneogram. It is a simple workable technique whose use can provide structure and understanding for beginning family therapists.

Throughout the numerous clinical examples and diagrams provided in this book, facts which could identify family members have been altered or omitted. The omission of certain names, dates or alteration of specific details has been done in such a way that, while preserving confidentiality, the underlying dynamics and meaning have been preserved.

ACKNOWLEDGEMENTS

I am grateful to my wife and children for allowing me to withdraw from family life in the evenings during the past year while writing. My wife has also provided a practical and critical view of the content and presentation of the material in this book which has been especially helpful.

Special thanks are due to Mrs J. Lambert who has undertaken the tedious task of typing the bulk of the manuscript and offered several useful suggestions. I also wish to thank Mrs J. Lake for her help in typing the last chapter and for the time and energy she has given additionally towards the completion of this project. To Alan Jones I must add my thanks for the Artwork and geneograms which he produced at very short notice.

I am very grateful to my colleagues in the Institute of Family Therapy (London) for their patience with me during the period in which this book was written. I also wish to thank Dr R. Skynner for providing a trusting setting in Britain for me to teach and learn family therapy. To all of my colleagues at the Institute I owe a great debt for sharing their work and thoughts with me as well as sharing themselves.

Finally, I wish to acknowledge the important role which Dr N. Paul played in the development of my work in family therapy. Much of what is written has its origin in his thinking and his work.

1 INTRODUCTION

Time present and time past are both perhaps present in time
future and time future contained in time past

T.S. Eliot, 'Burnt Norton', 1941

Definitions

Family therapy differs from other psychological and environmental
treatments in its perception of the family as an organism which is
made up of individuals closely bound by their interactions. It imposes an
ecological framework which assumes that the mutual relationship
between family members and their environment is a pivotal area of
intervention. This definition encompasses a seminal conceptual shift
from the understanding of illness and pathology in individual psychological terms to that of the interactions between individuals in close
emotional relationships. This shift of focus from intrapsychic to ecologic
carries implications as profound as that which the Viennese neurologist,
Sigmund Freud, pioneered when he recognised hysteria as a psycho-
logically caused disorder rather than one physically caused. In family
therapy, an assumption is made that the whole is equal to the product
of its parts rather than the sum and cannot be fully explained by means
of theories that describe the parts separately.

Families are those individuals bound by blood or marriage who,
through their culture, make up a kinship. The family is in the broadest
sense a kinship of three or four generations interrelated like the tiers of a
wedding cake. At the top and smallest layer are the remains of the eldest
generation, below which are arrayed several larger layers until the base is
reached wherein are contained numerous nuclear families. The nuclear
family includes mother, father, and children and forms the substrate
upon which many family therapists restrict their field of activity. For
example, conjoint family therapy is usually defined as the treatment of
the nuclear family in regular sessions attended by all family members.
The therapeutic focus is the troubled family interaction within the
session. The curative treatment involves changing those destructive interactions which occur in the family so as to mutually benefit all of the
family members. Some conjoint family therapists would occasionally
include important extended family members such as grandparents, but
concentration on the narrowed substrate of the nuclear family imposes a
useful boundary for many of the problems which are family based. An

13

eight-year-old boy with a school phobia required only two conjoint nuclear family sessions. The parents' conflicting desires had previously prevented them from exercising the mutual parental guidance and control necessary to allow the child freedom from anxiety while at school. Family therapy may take other forms, however, in order to meet the needs of the family and its problems.

Transgenerational theory and analysis address the circumstances arising when the interactions of the nuclear family members are inexplicable and uncorrectable in the session without recourse to the other tiers of the family cake. Transgenerational analysis is a dissection of the transmission of family culture in its broadest sense from one generation to the next encompassing those patterns, styles, customs, secrets, myths, and problems which determine the uniqueness of a family.

Transgenerational theory focuses on the dimension of time within family systems in an attempt to catalyse the present through the use of the past. It can bring a thorough understanding to the present family quandary leading to a more elegant solution to the unresolved family problem. The transgenerational approach connects the present nuclear family quandary with the past as far back as four or five generations, as well as to the living past in the form of the present extended family. It is a wide-angle view which gains in breadth what it may lose in detailed study of the current interactions and communications.

The Family as a Client

In order to understand why the family, whether defined narrowly or broadly, can be treated as a client or patient, it is necessary to understand the reasons for the very existence of family life. Families exist for reasons. Although attempts have been made to envisage civilisations without families, these visions have remained the province of gothic predictive works such as *1984* and *Brave New World.* There have been no serious attempts to totally eliminate the family as an institution.

Families exist initially out of biological requirements. Men and women attach themselves to each other and have children, all of whom must be fed, clothed, sheltered, raised and acculturated. The closeness of relationships between the various family building blocks are variables which allow for the diverse family arrangements which exist in different cultures. Husbands and wives may meet only for sexual contact or they may be inseparably bound for a lifetime. Children may be raised by either mother or father living together, or separately. Roles are assigned to family members by utility at first and later by tradition. The roles are based on the constraints of the physical and social environment in a pattern constructed over millenia which has had to alter and adjust to the exigencies of new discoveries, social changes and environmental alterations. The family's basic aim is to survive and reproduce itself. Viewed organismically, any influence which attempts to destroy a family or prevent it from procreating will be resisted. Failure of that resistance will result in the death of the family as it was constituted. In times of extreme hardship, family members needed to co-operate in order to eat, be protected from the elements and allow enough energy free to bear offspring in order to continue the family. This cohesive force of co-operation was a selective force for survival in that those family members who followed their own individual proclivities contrary to the family and kinship would become outcasts with less chance of survival.

In most Western civilisations the basic biological requirements are plentiful. Secondary goals of family life assume a greater relevance, while individuality is relatively less dangerous to the family member. Secondary goals can be subsumed under the term acculturation. The provision of the culture of a family as codified in the beliefs, practices and verbal and non-verbal patterns becomes a unifying force in the family. Acculturation encompasses religious beliefs, ethics, standards of conduct, and the learning of emotional expressivity. Family culture is passed from one generation to another in this way and the sums of individual family cultures are passed on as community heritage. Where family and community culture is static and unchanging the older generations' accumulated wisdom will remain valid and will be valued by succeeding generations.

Family quandaries develop when the aims of the family are thwarted. Four different areas may be involved in the development of a quandary. Failure to meet basic needs such as food, clothing and shelter will cause stress and tension within the relationships of a family. Here the quandary is generated through conflict between the family and its physical environment. Individual proclivities of family members which conflict with the family culture will generate tension in the relationships and cause the development of a quandary. Here, the quandary is generated through conflict between the family and one of its members. The social milieu in which the family exists may radically differ from that of the entire family as in immigrants and minority races or religions. Here the quandary is generated through conflict between the family and the community culture. Finally, in cultures which rapidly change their social rules, the older generation is no longer valued for its attempts to pass on obsolete wisdom to the younger generation within the same family. Here the quandary is generated between one generation of the family and another.

I have not at any point mentioned individual pathology. The family quandary differs qualitatively from individual problems although it encompasses them. Unfortunately, despite efforts at developing an objective taxonomy of family dysfunction, most family therapists still classify families by the problems of the identified patient such as the schizophrenic family, the anorexic family or the phobic family. It was upon the family quandary that therapists slowly began to focus their therapeutic interventions, as a basic redefinition of the therapeutic task. The concern with relatedness as opposed to the inner subjective life is responsible for the diversity of techniques and methods of treatment found in the family therapy movement.

The Field of Family Therapy

Family therapy is a relatively young discipline originating in the late 1940s in the United States where three independent research teams were studying the family relationships of schizophrenics. Eventually, these teams developed treatment methods based on their understanding of the families they were studying and began to apply them to those families. (By 1957, the family researchers had discovered each other through presentations of work at the American Orthopsychiatric Association and the American Psychiatric Association.)The therapeutic aspects of the family research were raised incidentally but a national impetus had been stimulated.[1] In the ferment that followed, therapists such as Ackerman, Bell, and Satir who had independently been practising family therapy became better known. The arena of family therapeutics expanded rapidly.)

In Britain, little actual work on the development of family therapy occurred until the late 1950s and early 1960s when Scott,[2] Howells,[3] and Skynner,[4] were independently developing their own approaches. Skynner initially based his treatment of the family as a whole on his training as a group analyst, conceiving of the family as a 'natural' group as opposed to a 'stranger' group. Out of this beginning and coupled with his work as a child psychiatrist he eventually saw the need for the establishment of an introductory course teaching family and marital therapy which was begun in 1972 at the Institute of Group Analysis in London. The teachers on this course were from various disciplines and theoretical backgrounds, brought together by their interest and work in family therapy. Realising their common interests, a process was initiated which led to the establishment of the first international association devoted to family therapy in 1976; the Association for Family Therapy. Walrond-

Skinner established a Family Institute in Cardiff in 1971, the first setting devoted wholly to family therapy practice.

The 'unstructured state of chaos' which Bowen wrote about when describing the state of family therapy in 1971 no longer exists. The development of 'schools' of family therapy has not yet occurred but there are dimensions along which family therapists group themselves, based on either their theoretical orientations, their activity, or their conceptual focus in their family work. Transgenerational analysis introduces a fourth dimension, the attention to the effects of time on the family and its quandary. Stein[5] has organised the various therapists into groups based on their adherence to one of three theoretical orientations. Crowe[6] would include a fourth orientation, based on learning theory and behavioural treatments. The other three are as follows: the psychoanalytic theorists whose adherents have attempted the expansion of classical psychoanalytic thinking into the family; the integrative or eclectic theorists whose dual focus gives equal attention to intrapsychic and interpersonal theories, attempting to interdigitate the two into an organised whole; and the communicative-interactive theorists who use general systems theory and interpersonal concepts as their sole model.

Beels and Ferber[7] classified therapists along an activity dimension, viewing therapists as either conductors, reactors, or systems purists. Conductors were defined as charismatic figures who openly confront and challenge the family with their own value systems. Reactors allow themselves to be engulfed by the family and work in pairs so that their partners can rescue them before they are overwhelmed. Systems purists control the family through analysis and mastery of the established family rules. An analogy would be the alteration of the chess board so as to contain only white squares. The established rules would no longer apply. Through droll instruction and modelling, the systems purist dodges, shifts and feints his way through the family rules altering them as he goes.

Crowe's radical-conservative dimension corresponds roughly to the A to Z scale developed by the GAP report in 1970.[8] Both classify therapists based on whether their conceptual focus is narrow or broad. On one end of this continuum are the conservatives (A) who use family techniques to help with their individual therapy with patients. At the radical end (Z) of the scale the therapists evaluate all emotional problems in family terms, including the extended family.

The fourth dimension ranges from a focus on the present family words and actions solely as opposed to focusing on the past in order to gain insight into the present. A transgenerational approach would be located midway on this dimension, for it attempts to understand the present through the use of the past so as to plan and catalyse a new future.

The Family as a Four or Five-Generation System

The fourth dimension mentioned adds a unique perspective too often ignored in family therapy. Family systems are not only integrated and interactive in cross-section; they are equally connected longitudinally along the time axis as is illustrated in the following example.

Mrs G. and her husband were referred to me because of sexual problems. Mrs G. could enjoy sex and have orgasms only through external stimulation. On entry she became unfeeling. Masters and Johnson's treatment had failed. The couple were seen initially and a detailed history revealed that Mrs G.'s sexual attitudes could be traced through her mother to her grandmother. Her mother had married an impotent man who left to fight in the war. She then had an affair with a Polish airman who abandoned her when he learned that she was pregnant with Mrs G. Her husband returned from the war, allowed his name to be given to Mrs G., and then disappeared.

Mrs G. was raised by her mother who had only negative experiences with men. Mrs G.'s grandmother had initially rejected her mother because of her 'promiscuity' and throughout the sexual treatment contact had been maintained between daughter, mother, and grandmother. Any changes that might have occurred in the sexual therapy sessions were constantly sabotaged by the slightest comment by her mother or grandmother about 'nasty men and their filthy habits'. An understanding of this situation led me to request that mother and grandmother be included in the sessions. Many excuses by Mrs G. and her mother and grandmother led to the structuring of tasks at home in which her husband and she were to talk about sex in front of the older generation. They were also asked to talk about and imagine these older family members in their bedrooms while they were sexually active. Their sexual relations rapidly improved as did their relations with their own children. Although Mrs G. was temporarily estranged from her mother and grandmother a newly forged relationship was soon established in which men were no longer a subject of disgust and ridicule.

The sexual sessions were not enough to counteract three lifetimes of learned attitudes which continued to be reinforced through contact. The feedback from one generation to the next, rooted in years of experience, had to be actively altered rather than dwelling solely on the immediate interactions between the marital couple.

The family is a sequence of generations stretching backward into the past whose links in the present make up the extended family. But those present links are also parts of a chain of family cultural transmission which were active and formative in the past. I altered the family relationships of Mr and Mrs G. by changing the nature of the links which had been established and were still operating.

Transgenerational theory also includes a natural extension into the future. A family quandary may relate more to the inevitability of a future event such as the death of a parent, grandparent or other relative, an approaching marriage or a birth. Future family plans are actively mapped out so that the frustration of a future goal rather than a present circumstance or past troubled history may be the cause of the existing crisis. Berne[9] calls this transmission process 'the family parade' and through an extension of transactional theory has attempted to show how a 'family script' which was written in the Napoleonic Wars was being projected forward to the year 2000.

Although individual family members may die, the family provides relative group immortality through its links between past and future generations. Within this perpetuating group the death of individuals does not end their ability to effect an influence on the families' decisions, feelings, thoughts and directions. I can recall at the simplest level several family quandaries generated by the last will and testament of an individual family member. But also, through their influence on the generations which they have helped to create and raise, through incorporation of their values which are then passed on to the next generation, the individual passes an individual uniqueness to be incorporated in the collective family culture.

I have attempted to define and limit transgenerational theory in practice to the family as a four or five-generation system. The limiting number of generations is based on the impact of direct and indirect influences which can commonly reach into the third, fourth and fifth generations. Most children have direct experience of their grandparents. Their parents have had personal experience of their own grandparents. The fifth generation is remote but I have seen occasional families in which the fifth generation has been of profound significance in their influence and importance on the nuclear family being treated. This influence may very well be profound *because* of their longevity and the increased effect that longevity has had on the multiple feedback relationships established between subsequent generations. My own family has had this experience of a long-lived relative being increasingly powerful in their influence.

One of the social revolutions to which modern societies have had to adjust is the increased longevity of individuals and hence their increased influence. Most nuclear families recently established have had the experience of knowing septuagenarian and octogenarian extended family relatives. They may well have relatives in their ninth or tenth decade of life. For this reason the four or five-generation family system is of increasing relevance to family life and society.

Notes

1. M. Bowen, 'Family Therapy after 20 Years' in J. Dyrud and D. Freeman (eds.), *American Handbook of Psychiatry,* vol. 5 (Basic Books, New York, 1975).

2. R.D. Scott and P.L. Ashworth, 'The Axis Value and the Transfer of Psychosis', *British Journal of Medical Psychology,* vol. 38 (1965), p.97. Scott began his work with the families of schizophrenics but since then he has developed a unique crisis intervention family approach based on a catchment area mental hospital.

3. J.G. Howells, *Family Psychiatry* (Oliver and Boyd, London, 1963). Howells began his work in 1949 and developed a system of family psychiatry based on the concepts of 'vector therapy'. He has remained outside of the mainstream of family therapy in Britain.

4. A.R.C. Skynner, *One Flesh, Separate Persons* (Constable, London, 1976).

5. J.W. Stein, *The Family as a Unit of Study and Treatment* (Regional Rehabilitation Research Institute, University of Washington School of Social Work, Seattle, 1969).

6. M.J. Crowe, 'Evaluation of Conjoint Marital Therapy', unpublished MD thesis, Oxford University, 1976.

7. C.C. Beels and A. Ferber, 'Family Therapy: A View', *Family Process,* vol. 9 (1969), p. 280.

8. Group for the Advancement of Psychiatry, *The Field of Family Therapy,* Report No. 78 (New York, 1970).

9. E. Berne, *What Do You Say After You Say Hello?* (Andre Deutsch, London, 1974).

2 ANTECEDENTS OF TRANSGENERATIONAL THEORY

Men from whom my ways begin, here
I know you by your ground

Edward Blunden, 'Forefathers'

And since time never pauses but
Change must ensue
Let us wish that old things may
Fit well with the new

Tennyson, 'Queen of the Isles'

In this chapter I hope to weave together threads of previous social and dynamic theories so as to provide a substrate out of which transgenerational concepts naturally grow. Large areas of important and interesting psychological, social, and biological thinking will necessarily be omitted. Other texts on family therapy have been written which include and integrate some of the omitted material.[1]

Alfred Adler

It is not often realised that the field of family therapy owes an immense debt to the original contributions made by Alfred Adler to psychological theory and practice. He has been credited by Ellenberger[2] with the launching of modern psychosomatic medicine, group psychotherapy, and the first unified system of concrete psychology. More important to the family therapy movement were his seminal contributions to social psychology and the social approach to mental hygiene.

Adler's pragmatic psychology attempted to develop axioms and methods by which a working knowledge could be obtained of one's inner self or the inner selves and behaviour of others without resorting to an abstract and complicated theory. His basic principles are worth recounting and seem surprisingly avante-garde considering that they were systematised in 1927.[3]

First is the principle of unity which states that a human being is indivisible and must be treated as such; such a stance would be agreeable to the most radical of family therapy systems purists. Second, the principle of movement states that life without goals and movement is incomprehensible, a position taken by most behaviour therapists, as well as goal-orientated psychotherapists. The third principle is that of cosmic

21

influence. Sounding very much like a family therapists' credo it states than an individual does not and cannot exist isolated from his family, community, and environment. Community was defined as the structure of familial and social ties. His fourth principle asserts that the parts are spontaneously organised into a structural whole; a very similar statement was posited ten years later by von Bertalanffy in his general systems theory. The fifth principle, that of action and reaction, says that every individual action brings on a reaction from society and vice versa. Baldly summarised these five principles claim that no individual can be considered except in his context, both social and environmental. The relationships of the indivisible individual with his family and community are crucial areas for therapeutic work. His sixth and last principle sets out a standard of normality, adjustment, and mental hygiene for the individual which is defined as the ideal balance between individual needs and community needs. Pathology is then measured by the amount of deviation from this ideal balance. Mental disturbance was not seen as illness, but as a faulty life style. The neurotic life style and life plan were held to originate in one of three aggravated conditions; organ inferiorities (which was Adler's term for congenital and genetic influences), a neurotic family tradition, or existing family pressures.

The step from these Adlerian principles to the treatment of families seems a small one with hindsight. Adler may even unknowingly have developed a rudimentary form of family treatment. Unlike Freud who enjoined analysts from involving themselves with family members, Adler stated 'I always find the hostile reaction of the patient's relatives to the physician of advantage and I sometimes have carefully attempted to stir it up. Since generally the tradition of the entire family of the sick person is neurotic it is possible by uncovering and explaining it to greatly benefit the patient.'[4]

His therapeutic model of child psychotherapy was more directly related to the family therapy model. He never treated a child without requiring the parent's presence in at least some of the therapeutic sessions. He often did home visits and treated the child at home in the parent's presence.

Adler's interest in the family environment led him to investigate the importance of sibling position in the family as a determinant in producing personality traits. He found that each child in a family acquires a certain personality based on his sibling position. The oldest brother for example is raised with the conviction that he is the stronger and more responsible of his siblings. He tends to be more bourgeois, traditional and conservative. In contrast, the youngest brother is likely to be over-protected and spoiled by virtue of his position as the defenceless child surrounded by older siblings and parents. The second child attempts to compete with the older brother while looking over his shoulder in fear of being over-taken by the younger one. In a similar way and in more detail Adler described the personality traits which tended to accrue to only children, only boys in a family of girls and other combinations. The importance of this work has not gone unrecognised. Toman[5] expanded this concept into a two-generational model and detailed the personality traits within various family constellations of spouses, parents and children. This Adlerian contribution to family therapy is incorporated into the process of transgenerational analysis.

Despite his social and pragmatic theoretical positions, Adler did not fully develop his concepts to include the basic tenet of family therapy which distinguishes it as a new and different approach. He continued to treat the individual as the patient in need of treatment, however strongly he stressed the importance of social and familial influences. He may have viewed the family as an organism but he did not take that further crucial step towards treating the family as a patient. But his influence on suc-ceeding generations of doctors, psychiatrists, social workers and thera-pists directed them towards the social and familial factors which he emphasised.

Sigmund Freud

In contrast to Adler's pragmatic social psychology, Freud conceived of the individual as a seething conflictual system locked within itself. He was occupied with the puzzle of the structure and organisation of the human mind rather than the interactions between one mind and another.

His attitude towards the relatives of his patients was one of strict abstention from contact. 'The most urgent warning I have to express is against any attempt to engage the confidence or support of parents and relatives.' Freud felt that 'the interference of relatives in psychoanalytic treatment is a very great danger', and cautioned his fellow analysts from getting involved with them.[6] His only foray into the field of family involvement was the case of Little Hans.

Little Hans was the eldest son of a close psychoanalyst colleague who developed a phobia to horses at the age of five. His father reported the child's material to Freud who interpreted its meaning. The father then returned to his son to explain the meanings. Freud actually saw the child once. But Freud, far from pursuing an interest in family relationships, had reluctantly broken his rule of non-involvement in order to acquire direct evidence for his theory of infantile sexuality.[7] His interest lay only in the direction of the intrapsychic functioning.

However valuable Freud's theories are in explaining intrapsychic phenomena, it is a one-sided view when attempting to translate his theoretical position into interpersonal relationships. Although personality is seen as being rooted in the interplay between parents and children in infancy and childhood, the possibility of developing an interpersonal and family relational theory was sidestepped for the postulation of a codified developmental theory which concentrates on intrapsychic development within the well defined oral, anal, and genital stages. Relationships with other human beings are viewed as internally crystallised 'objects', discounting the subtlety of relationship interactions. The oedipal complex is a wholly intrapsychic development although it grows more naturally from the real interactions between parents and children. The living father in real conflict with the mother for the re-establishment of a previously existing relationship which was actually disrupted by the needs of rearing the child have been encapsulated by way of theory and explanation as an internalised conflict within the developing psyche of the child.

The effect of this emphasis on internalising the external has been to place the Freudian analyst in an awkward position when attempting to elucidate family and interpersonal relationships. His language requires that everything be understood starting from the point of view of the analyst examining the internal workings of the psyche of the patient. Relationship rules are first seen as internalised objects which then must be externalised, rather than simply examining the relationship itself. The double reflection which results has exercised the most brilliant minds in the psychoanalytic movement to develop the field of ego psychology in order to deal with the inevitable distortions. The interaction between transference and counter-transference has also required further theoretical models to be developed.

If the preceding few paragraphs seem unjust they are not meant to be. Freudian psychology has laid the foundation of the intrapsychic working of the mind, which was its main purpose. The usefulness of these concepts lies in the area of the individual as an encapsulated entity, but falls short when trying to develop interactional theories. Just as the elucidation of atomic structure has been of immense help to the understanding of chemistry, Freudian psychology has helped establish a part of the ground rules regarding the limits imposed on relationships between people. But chemistry is interested in the relationships between atoms and the compounds they form. The study of subatomic structure in finer and finer detail is of little value to the chemist who is concerned with the subtleties of the interactions between atoms, mixtures and compounds and their stability under differing noxious stimuli. This metaphor applies as well to the focus of interest in a detailed psychoanalysis of the individual being which is irrelevant to the understanding of the present, past and future relationship rules between family members.

Although the confusion of using the terminology of an intrapsychic theory to describe relationship concepts has led me to discard them, the concepts are an important historical antecedent. Freud did develop certain ideas from dealing with intrapsychic phenomena which have been expanded into the relationship between individuals.

The first of these concepts is that of transference. Transference is defined as the phenomenon occurring when the patient transfers on to the figure of the analyst a repetition of a relationship towards an important figure in the patient's past.[8] More generally it is used as the passing of an attitude or reaction from any person in the past to any person in the present. For example, the feeling that a stranger passing in the street would be friendly is based on the connection of past emotional contacts, some aspect of which is unconsciously stimulated by the sight of the stranger. 'Love at first sight' can also be explained as a generalisation of the term transference. Freud used the term increasingly to indicate that the analysis of the 'transference neurosis' in psychoanalysis was the most necessary of tasks in psychoanalysis.

Transference should be an interpersonal and relationship concept by definition. Although originally employed as a means of understanding the intrapsychic structure of the individual it necessitates a concentration upon the relationship between the analyst and his patient. This concentration led to the realisation that the analyst may also transfer attitudes, reactions and feelings on to the patient (counter-transference). From the resulting complex interactions between the transferred feelings coupled with the true relationship between two individuals, a dyadic phenomenon develops which is much more than is meant by the original terminology.

It is a short conceptual step to postulate a family transference. Walrond-Skinner[9] has summarised the concept of family transference, but the summary points out the difficulty of adapting individually based nomenclature in order to describe relationship rules. Family transference should describe the transference of affect by one family member about another family member on to a third family member. But it is used to describe the entire network created by interlocking transferences as well as the projections which develop between family members. Projections refer to the attribution of one's unconscious thoughts, attitudes or feelings directly to another. For example, Mrs Jones disliked her youngest daughter intensely. She was transferring on to her daughter her intense dislike for her own mother. If Mrs Jones disliked her own daughter rather than face her own self-dislike, she would be projecting. Since the interlocking network implies the presence of both projection and transference, the use of these terms has become almost interchangeable, doing a disservice to the original concepts and sowing the seeds of confusion.

Figure 2.1 Transference in a Family

Another thread running through Freudian psychology is the link between mourning and psychopathology.[10] Freud noted the correlation between the clinical presentation of his cases of melancholia and the normal process of mourning. His attention to the way in which the dead or lost person (object) became incorporated within the psychological structure of the bereaved was of particular interest. He related pathological mourning to 'the shadow of the object' which continued to influence the bereaved in distorted ways. It was as if a person, rather than mourn the loss of a loved one, incorporates aspects of that loved one within themselves and continues to be influenced by them. The effect of this mechanism has immediate implications for those around them.

The importance of mourning and its pathological effects have been taken up by other analytically trained workers. Bowlby has devoted his life to the synthesis of psychoanalytic and ethologic theories and in the process has moved attachment, separation and loss into a central position within his theory of individual psychopathology.[11] His thesis is to a large extent an interpersonal one.

Figure 2.2   Projection in a Family

The presumed presence of an intrapsychic 'object' (defined as the representation of a dead relative) which might operate on the bereaved so as to alter his relationships was a concept which was later adapted by therapists in the family therapy field. Since losses occur in families, each family member would share the loss and the internalised representation. Paul developed this concept through his allusion to 'ghosts from the past'. He defined them as dead family members pathologically surviving as living systems within several members of the same family.[12] A major non-specific effect in pathological families was postulated as a 'fixed family equilibrium'. Any loss was collectively denied as an important affective event. Other therapists have also incorporated the importance of mourning and its links with individual depression and family quandaries into their concepts of the family.[13]

Freud's concentration on the formative nature of the first six to eight years of life is another important strand in the transgenerational tapestry. Although the details of the moulding of characterologic traits are not accepted, the premises that there is a qualitative difference between the type of learning which occurs during those early years and that which occurs in later years is acknowledged. Early learning and experience imply other influences than the internal stages of libidinal development. Behavioural concepts such as conditioning, imprinting and modelling as well as social concepts such as the effects of early socialisation are also important influences on the psychological development of an individual.[14]

Melanie Klein

This is an opportune place to introduce the work of Melanie Klein, whose conceptual theories grew out of her work with very young children. There is no reason to attempt to summarise her theory since in most parts it is of little relevance to the elucidation of relatedness.[15] Skynner[16] has attempted to integrate some of her concepts with more behaviourally and ethologically based concepts in his model of family therapy.

I wish to concentrate on the development of a new defensive process and mechanism postulated by Klein, projective identification. In projective identification, parts of the self and internal objects are split off and projected into an external object. This concept was originally postulated as having taken place in the very earliest stage of developmental psychological life when the infant is less than four months old. It was then felt to exist throughout childhood and adulthood. The infant's mind introjects (takes in or models on) persons or parts of persons or behaviours of persons outside themselves. These external objects become owned or incorporated into the infant and are hereafter termed internal objects. Having acquired an internal object it is combined with pre-existing bits of the infant's psychological structure and this combination can then be projected into an external object (person or bit of a person) as an unconscious defensive manoeuvre in order to ward of psychological distress.[17]

For example, an infant may experience a painful hunger when mother's breast (or bottle) is emptied without satisfaction. The experience is part self and part relationship with mother, the combined whole being introjected. This total experience is then projected into the mother who is experienced as a person who causes the internal hunger pains rather than recognising that the pain comes wholly from within.

This concept has been used by family therapists in an attempt to understand and label the subtle interactions between living, existing relatives and experiences which occurred with those relatives in the early years of life and which continue to influence the current interactions. In a similar manner dead relatives can be seen to continue their influence on interactions between living relatives through the process of projecting the internally absorbed object (relative) on to an outside relation such as a wife or child. The operative conscious statement would be, 'My son is just like my father in his laziness.' The unconscious defensiveness is, 'I am lazy having acquired this trait from my father as a model, but I cannot acknowledge this trait as it is too disturbing; I will project it into my son.' This differs qualitatively from the previously encountered 'family transference', where the operative conscious statement would be, 'I can't stand my lazy son.' The unconscious statement would be, 'I can't stand my lazy father.' In neither case do the actual traits of the perceived individual intrude upon the fantasies.

This Kleinian concept, which is so dense and rich in its meaning when applied to the intrapsychic life, still does not adequately describe the complexities of relatedness which we see in families. A physicist trying to define the configuration of electron clouds within a compound in terms of the complex language of nucleonics would come to a similar impasse. Projective identification is a valuable concept to the family therapist only in that it is descriptive of the mirroring of perturbations in the relationship field externally as represented within intrapsychic life.

Figure 2.3 Projective Identification in a Family

General Systems Theory

The contributions of the analytic schools of thought have provided valuable insights into the intrapsychic life of individuals. But a larger structural framework has been developed by another Viennese scientist, the biologist Ludwig von Bertalanffy. Whereas previously described concepts were a product of the nineteenth century preoccupation with analysis, causality and reductionism as a means of explaining the mind and the observed real world, von Bertalanffy developed a general system theory which sought to bring under scientific scrutiny the exploration of 'wholes' and 'wholeness' which were previously the province of metaphysics. The real world and the mind observing it are no longer clockwork mechanisms whose components are the total explanation of the way in which things work. Its basic postulate is that for an understanding of the world and the mind which observes it, not only the elements which make up a system, but the interrelationships between them are essential for understanding.[18]

Before proceeding into an explanation of systems theory as it applies to families the following models will be used to define some general concepts.

My dessert last night was a bowl of strawberry flavoured jelly. It was composed of various molecules of sugar, protein, colouring, flavouring, and water. These *species* of *elements* were present in a finite but large *number*. Their relationships with each other are such as to assume the shape of the bowl in which they are placed and to exist as a wobbly red mass. When separated the species of elements exhibit the same *summative* properties as when combined, such as weight, mass, and volume. But only when combined will they form a tasty, wobbly red gel, the *constitutive* characteristic of the jelly. Questions may be asked of the jelly.

These questions are based on the terminology of systems theory. What is the *boundary* of the jelly, the interface between it and its external environments? In this case it is the ceramic of the bowl although on a molecular level it might penetrate into the ceramic by one or two molecules. What is its *hierarchical structure*? A hierarchy of structure would involve delineation of the jelly's subatomic elements and their interrelationship, atomic elements and their relationship, molecular elements and their relationships, and larger aggregates and their relationships. Besides structural hierarchy there also exists *geographic* and *temporal hierarchy*. Does the jelly possess the characteristic of *wholeness*, in which changes in every element depend on all the other elements changing? Wholeness implies constitutive properties. For example the jelly can be mashed or diced yet still retains its recognisable identity, but when it is eaten, as it slithers into the stomach its wholeness is destroyed and it can no longer wobble, taste pleasant or retain its colour. What *equilibrium* does it maintain with its environment? Jelly being organic but not living is a *closed system* which by definition is not involved in a dynamic interchange with its environment. Jelly therefore exhibits positive entropy, slowly but predictably and steadily decaying away into its elements. It may also be attacked by *open systems* such as bacteria or man. In order to deal with the *open system* concept our bowl of jelly must be abandoned for a living jelly, the amoeba. The amoeba is an open system in that it maintains a steady state within its environment through a constant interchange with it, maintaining its structure despite a continuous changeover in the elements. It possesses negative entropy as well as the property of equifinality, the characteristic of being able to reach the same final state starting from different initial conditions. The amoeba is actually a *hierarchical order of open systems,* each apparently solid structure at one level being maintained by a continuous exchange of elements at the next lower one, giving the appearance of a long-lived structure. This *active steady state* differs fundamentally from the *homeostasis* of closed systems.

But general systems theory is a theory about order and the rules of order in relationship to time as well as space. For example, the fertilised ovum begins as a unitary whole. It passes through progressive states of *differentiation* until tissues, organs and a much greater complex whole develops. There occurs a *progressive centralisation,* which is the time-dependent evolution of a *decider* or leading part, such as the development of the central nervous system as a control center. Progressive segregation occurs in which the tendency of a system is to pass from a state of wholeness where each of the elements exhibits similar summative and constitutive properties to a state of independence of the elements or *differentiation. Progressive mechanisation* occurs with every step in differentiation since every step in evolution of the parts of a whole prevent others from occurring.

General system theory has been cited as an authoritative theory upon which a more circumscribed interactional or psychological model can be based or with which other models in family therapy may be integrated. In a similar way general system theory provides a basic conceptual framework upon which transgenerational theory draws. The important difference is the emphasis which will be placed on those aspects related to the dimension of time.

Mathematically a system is defined as a set of elements standing in

relation; the elements may consist of points, lines, people, houses or
planets. Complexes of elements are distinguished by

    (a)   their number;
    (b)   their species;
    (c)   their relations.

In a family, the Randolph family, the system is described as follows.
The Randolph family is a complex of elements (individuals). The family
is defined by its numbers, as a family of six individuals; by its species,
three male and three female; and by its relations, parental-child bonding,
emotional bonding. Number and species are summative characteristics.
They are the same characteristics whether the family member exists within

a. Numbers   b. Species

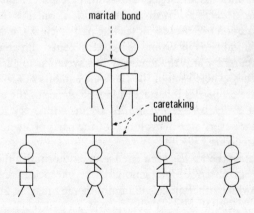

c. Relations

Figure 2.4 The Randolph Family: a Nuclear Family System

or outside of the family. Such characteristics include sex, age, race and so on. Relational characteristics are termed constitutive. They are dependent upon the relations within the family. Molecular bonding, crystalline structure and subatomic bonding are all examples of constitutive properties. Oxygen combined with two hydrogens produces water, whose properties differ from the constituents. These properties are a function of the elements *and* their relationships. Similarly, a family complex cannot be explained on the basis of the individual characteristics of each element. The relations between elements must be elucidated.

A system is defined so as to include not only spatial conditions (three dimensions within a frozen instant of time); it defines a system based on the previous history. The system under consideration should be not only a spatial but a temporal whole. Much of the conceptual and terminological borrowing done in family therapy from system theory derives from the special circumstances of a family frozen in time. The family thus frozen is assumed to be a whole rather than a conglomerate of disparate individuals. The phenomenon of wholeness in a family is illustrated by the following case. Mrs Galway was treated individually for three years in psychoanalytic sessions and lost her cloying dependence upon her husband. This relative independence from her husband seemed to lead directly into symptoms occurring in her son of overactivity, while her husband began drinking excessively. There was no visible change in any of the other children, although this may have been due to my inability to detect such change in a few short interviews. Nevertheless, a change in one element (Mrs Galway) led to change in the other elements in the family system. One cautionary note must be sounded. The assumption that the family members under treatment comprise a system exhibiting wholeness is a fundamental starting point for many family therapists. This dogmatic assumption is best reserved until the family is observed and understood, which leads directly to a discussion of the concept of boundaries.

A boundary defines the limit of a system or the interface between suprasystems or subsystems. The family described was treated as a nuclear family whole. Difficulties arise when a wrong assumption is made about boundaries in determining the limits of the system and its quandary. The death of Mr Galway's aunt directly preceded his drinking by a matter of months and may have been a more important factor in his symptoms. The family boundary arbitrarily set by me may have been too limited. It may just as well have been too wide, for Mr and Mrs Galway were so closely tied in a mutually interdependent relationship that they may have more effectively been treated as a subsystem. Leaving aside the question of wholeness and boundaries, a family would seem to fall logically into the open system category.

An open system possesses the property of equifinality. In a closed system, the final state of the system is determined by the initial conditions. An adequate example in family terms is difficult to imagine. Perhaps the closest one can come to a family as a closed system would be that of a sterile couple living in absolute isolation with enough pre-packaged food and water to maintain them at subsistence level for the rest of their lives. The point is that families are by definition open systems in that they interact and interchange with their physical and social environment, growing and/or declining in relationship to that environment. The same final state in the family may be reached from different initial conditions and in many different ways. Mrs Galway's independence, Mr Galway's bereavement or many other factors may have resulted in the final state in which the family were first referred. In a similar vein it is prudent to note that the family therapist and his intervention are only one of many alternate or simultaneous influences on the outcome of the sessions.

Since transgenerational theory encompasses a model of the family as a spatiotemporal whole, the interesting aspect of general system theory lies not in its description of closed systems but in its usefulness in predicting certain properties of open systems in the time continuum. For example Mrs Galway was once a child in her own family of origin. She progressively grew and eventually *differentiated* from her parents and siblings. When she married she merged herself into her husband but as time passed she moved from her state of relative wholeness with her husband to one of increased segregation and differentiation. This progressive segregation in their marital relationship altered the family system. The concepts of progressive segregation, centralisation and individualisation can all be translated into patterns of development in families over time.

General system theory with its concentration on the properties of relatedness, order and hierarchy provides an epistemology for the belief that families act as if they are whole. But it has also added a scientific explanation for the teleology of families through its exposition of the spatiotemporal rules governing systems.

Murray Bowen

Murray Bowen is one of the original small group of researchers into the families of schizophrenics in the early 1950s. Working at Bethesda

originally and now active as Professor of Psychiatry at Georgetown
University he has been a most original contributor to the theory of
family therapy. He has attempted to develop a family systems theory
based on his own research and has devoted three decades to this effort.
Much of his thinking may parallel and intertwine with transgenerational
theory. But as he states, 'I have never been happy about my efforts to
present my own theory. I can be perfectly clear in my own mind, but
there is always the problem of restating it so others can hear.'[19]

His theory at present consists of eight interlocking concepts. He de-
claims any influence from general system theory although he admits
having read extensively in the biological field of science when these concepts were being vigorously and thoroughly debated in the literature.
One can interpret much of his theory as an attempt to delineate constitutive and summative properties within human relationships.

He postulates that there are two main variables in all human relationships; the degree of anxiety and the degree of integration of self. *Integration of self* refers to the level of fusion as opposed to differentiation of
the emotional versus intellectual functioning. *Differentiation of self* is
defined in such a way that it is a summative property of the individual
rather than a constitutive one. Because of the fixed nature of this concept within the individual, profiles of various levels of differentiation of
self have been developed. The profiles describe individuals with a low
degree of *fusion* (highly integrated emotional and intellectual functioning), whose emotion and intellect are balanced so that while the intellect is in touch with the emotional part of his being the individual
nevertheless maintains an intellectual control, as well as those with a
high degree of fusion, and individuals on levels between.

The development of these concepts leads to the distinguishing of the
solid self, which is the summative property of the individual, and the
pseudo-self which is the constitutive element of self that enters into
relationships and is modified by them. The summative or unnegotiable
solid self is the core of the individual which in effect states: 'This is who
I am, what I believe in, and what I will or won't do no matter what
relationship I am in.' The constitutive property of pseudo-self implies a
relationship fusion which is linked with the fusion property of the
individual, so that those people who are poorly differentiated would
have a greater pseudo-self and lesser solid self. A husband and wife each
possessing large amounts of pseudo-self would fuse with each other
readily. Therapeutic goals based on this property would attempt to
increase the amount of differentiation and strengthen the solid self.

The level of anxiety is a variable which illuminates an individual's level of differentiation. The longer and more intense the level of anxiety for an individual, the easier it is for an observer to distinguish the pseudo-self from the solid self of an individual.

A second postulate states that the triangle, a three-person emotional configuration, is the smallest stable relationship system. It consists of two persons in reasonably close emotional contact and one person who is more of an outsider. In emotionally tense situations the outside position is the most comfortable position. Two persons isolated together will tend to 'triangle in' a third person whenever the tension is increased. This process is illustrated by the common phenomenon of two people trying to establish that there is a common third person of mutual acquaintance about whom they can gossip.

Families are seen to consist of an interlocking series of triangles whose composition is dependent on the amount of anxiety and tension present at any given moment. The concept of triangles in human relationships seems to be an attempt to develop a constitutive characteristic similar to that of valence in chemistry which predicts the combination properties of differing atoms one with another.

Therapeutically this postulate would predict the following method of treatment. The therapist could exclude the most vulnerable member of the triangle and meet with the other two. By persistently preventing the remaining twosome, usually the parents, from triangling in the therapist, while the therapist remains in emotional contact with them, a new situation would be forced upon the twosome. Their triangling moves could be revealed and they would be forced into an alteration with the hope that it would increase their level of differentiation.

The *nuclear family emotional system* is a postulate describing the patterns of emotional functioning in the parental generation of a nuclear family. It refers to the interactions between sexual partners who have established a current long-lasting relationship. The patterns within family culture are thought to be due to the fact that partners will pick each other based on the level of differentiation. A presumption is made that spouses automatically choose their mates from those individuals with the same level of differentiation. Since assortative mating is assumed, it is stated that the lower the level of collective differentiation the more intense and problematic is the fusion of pseudo-selves in the marriage. The fusion can result in family quandaries of three different sorts or in combinations of more than one of them. First, it can be expressed in overt conflict between the marital partners. Second, it can be expressed as an individual problem within one of the partners. The third possibility is the impairment of one or more of the following generation. These three mechanisms are proposed as the manner in which the undifferentiation of the parents, passed on to them from the experiences they underwent in their families of origin, are expressed in their own family relationship. This concept begins to define specific open system characteristics of the family organism.

The *family projection process* is a postulate that elaborates the way in which parental undifferentiation impairs one or more of their children. This impairment is felt to begin with the birth of the child and is initiated through maternal anxiety. Mother-child fusion occurs which is instrumental in causing impairment of the child and the whole process, if followed over succeeding generations, may produce impaired individuals with symptomatic schizophrenia through the production of individuals in each succeeding generation with lower and lower levels of differentiation. The use of this postulate as an explanation for the cause of schizophrenia seems to weaken its value as a concept, since it ignores much of the evidence which suggests that schizophrenia is a multi-factorially-determined syndrome which includes a strong genetic influence. The concept is of more value in its attempt to delineate the development of the family organism over time. A similarity to progressive segregation in system theory can be seen.

Emotional cutoff is a postulate which refers to certain rules governing the attachment between members of different generations in the same family. If children cannot resolve their fusion with their parents the unresolved emotional attachment is mirrored in the undifferentiation to be dealt with in present (marital) relationships and is passed on to future generations. If the attachment is handled by an emotional cutoff either through an internal operation or through geographic distance, the attachment remains unresolved and no orderly process of differentiation occurs through the life of the individual. The result is the passage of a lower level of differentiation to the children, coupled with a repetition of the emotional cutoff between children and parents in the next generation. Emotional cutoff can be seen as a pathological method of separating from the past in order to live a life in the present generation.

This concept implies that a therapeutic technique can be developed to prevent emotional cutoff from occurring, or to modify the process if it has already occurred. Such a technique was devised by Bowen in which he coached family members to re-establish links with their families of origin in order to reverse the emotional cutoff and proceed with a proper differentiation from their parents.

The *multigenerational transmission process* postulates the passage of the family projection process from generation to generation. The family time scale it refers to is measured in three or more generations. It refers to a very specific type of transmission rather than applying to the whole of family culture. The multigenerational transmission process specifically applies to the transmission of levels of differentiation. Those children triangled into a lower level of differentiation than their parents as part of the family projection process tend to marry a spouse at the lower level of differentiation which they occupy. One or more of their children may become the triangled child and the same process will repeat itself until one of the triangled children becomes so grossly impaired as to develop symptoms of a mental illness. The process describes a downward trend in the level of differentiation over many generations. The same process may occur in reverse to produce descendents with higher and higher levels of differentiation. The process also implies a lack of homogeneity in the siblings' level of differentiation.

The *sibling position* postulate is one which had already been described by Adler and elaborated by Toman.[20] The concept as Bowen applies it is that important personality characteristics are due to the sibling position in which one is born and raised. Detailed personality profiles have been constructed of these sibling positions such as the eldest or youngest brother or sister, the only child and twins. These profiles will be described in greater detail in Chapter Five. Bowen uses these profiles in an attempt to predict the personality traits of family members in previous generations about whom details are lacking. He also uses the profiles to determine levels of differentiation in various family members by comparing the ideal profile with the actual personality characteristics of the individual.

The last of Bowen's postulates is the first to expand into the realm of social science, the next level of social organisation. His postulate of *societal regression* states that chronic anxiety in a society causes that society to resort to more and more emotionally determined decisions and eventually results in regression to a lower level of functioning, just as it does in the family. He bases this extension of his family-based theory on the supposition that societal unrest has been steadily increasing due to the chronic anxiety resulting from unique modern stresses including increasing population, decreasing resources and increasing pollution of those resources.

Bowen's theoretical concepts seem to include statements of a confusing and contradictory nature. He implies that his concepts are highly specific yet uses the same word to describe different processes. For example he uses the word 'fusion' to signify an intrapsychic process and an intergenerational process between parents and children. Perhaps his unhappiness with the clarity of his explanation of his theory lies in its written contradictions. The importance of his family systems theory lies in the summative and constitutive relationship rules which are postulated between the different hierarchical levels of family structure. The postulates of sibling profiles, differentiation, solid self and pseudo-self refer in great part to summative properties of individuals. His postulates then proceed to elaborate constitutive rules within the nuclear family such as the nuclear family emotional system, triangles, emotional cutoff and the family projection process. The multigenerational transmission process is a postulate which narrowly defines an element of the transgenerational transmission of levels of differentiation. It encompasses the idea that patterns develop over long periods of time in families and can be followed in retrospect. The relationship rule is one between succeeding generations leading from the past to the present to the future.

There are two further criticisms which I would make of the Bowen theory. The first is that it is an attempt to provide a basic systems theory of family organisation, relationship and structure without an acknowledgement of the principles of general system theory. If general system theory has any scientific validity (and it would appear to have, due to its wide successful applications in the fields of communication theory, cybernetics, biology and many other fields), than it must also apply to human aggregates including families. The second criticism is that his concepts are applied to human relationships with little exposition of clinical or experimental detail or examples of the source of these concepts. Nevertheless, the Bowen theory remains valuable as one of the first attempts to provide a cohesive theory of family organisation, relationships and structure.

Norman Paul

Transgenerational analysis as a phrase originated with Norman Paul. He defines it as the decoding of influences such as patterns of behaviour, patterns of communication, memories, habits, and learned emotional responses to sexuality, death and other life experiences. The goal of the analysis is the attainment of self-knowledge needed for mature and satisfying relationships with other family members. His thesis is that the quality of the relationship between an individual and the members of his family of origin form a crucial and often unrecognised influence upon the success or failure of that individual's subsequent marriage, including the functioning of the children produced by that marriage.

Although his training is rooted in the psychoanalysis of individuals,

Paul realised that patterns of response in his patients could be traced to patterns present in their families of origin. In a study of seventy-five families he was able to connect the identified patient's inability to cope with small losses to patterns of inflexible interaction extant in the family of origin, in some cases long before the birth of the patient.[21] He expanded this observation when writing about the effect that secrets can have in families. He held the view that secrets can be especially damaging when the older generation mould the younger one based on their experience of secret events or emotions without sharing the event or emotion with the children. In a book written jointly with his wife[22] he described in detail a seven-session marital therapy based on transgenerational analysis. The analysis includes most areas of common human emotional experience, although he continues to emphasise reactions to loss.

No systematic theory has been constructed by Paul. But his clinical work provided a model in which he dealt with the untangling of the influences of the families of origin through the use of family charts, conjoint marital and family interviews, task assignments outside of the sessions including visits to the important members of the family of origin, audio-and video-feedback, and the stimulation of emotional expression through cross-confrontation. Cross-confrontation refers to a technique pioneered by Paul in which emotionally charged material from interviews with one family are used to stimulate the expression of emotions in other client families.[23]

Great emphasis was placed on the transmission of family culture from generation to generation to generation. Unlike Bowen he did not restrict his view of this process to levels of differentiation. He includes a host of other influences as each generation in turn married and the spouses were required to deal with the complex, often unconscious, and subtle collisions of two differing family life styles. The clients he faced originally were at the end of a long history of these collisions and the marital problems could often be traced back to the conflict in two disparate transmitted family life styles. Because of his lack of an organised theory it is difficult to provide full details of the innovative concepts and techniques which are encountered in his clinical work. He was the first to develop a clinical transgenerational approach and my attempt to develop a transgenerational theory owes much to his influence.

Other Influences

Attachment theory has been elaborated by Bowlby into a major psychological theory. His emphasis on the nature of the emotional bonds between individuals is of particular interest. He has defined three different forms of bonding; attachment, caretaking and heterosexual. The first two are thought to be the more important and stronger of the three. These bonds will be defined in the next chapter. The description of attachment as a major goal-directed behaviour in itself rather than as the result of other drives is an abandonment of the Freudian concept that all motivational behaviour has its roots in either sexual or aggressive drives. Briefly, attachment bonds are those emotional bonds which are established and maintained by proximity-seeking behaviour, such as clinging, crying out, following or any other such behaviour meant to keep two or more individuals close to each other.

In a recent paper[24] the family and family therapy have been described in the language of attachment theory. Families are classified by the degree and quality of their attachment and caretaking bonds and the manoeuvres developed in order to enable family members to deal with these bonds.

In the historical development of family therapy many of the concepts such as family homeostasis,[25] double bind,[26] marital schism and skew[27] and pseudomutuality[28] were developed during the search for etiological causes in the families of schizophrenics. These concepts in fact apply to all families as universal rules of communication between family members. Their originators have gone on to become distinguished family therapists whose contributions to family therapy have been primarily in the communicative school.

It is difficult to detail all of the other influences which have entered into the crystallisation of my thinking. Many of the concepts prevailing in the literature of family therapy have been studied and absorbed. Behavioural principles[29] are particularly influential on the way in which the task setting and other techniques of treatment are used and have not been fully acknowledged in this historical review.

Finally the whole of biological science has had an influence on the development of a transgenerational theory with special emphasis on the science of genetics. Genetics has the distinction of being the first attempt of science to understand the way in which characteristics are passed from one generation to the next.[30] The geneogram is a direct descendent of the family chart already so familiar to geneticists.

Summary

Throughout this historical review an attempt was made to plait together those theories and concepts which have influenced my thinking in the development of a transgenerational theory. From Adler and his early emphasis on social context as a major factor in the production of mental illness, a historical thread was picked which led through the Freudian elucidation of intrapsychic phenomena and the interpersonal rules governing psychoanalysis. Interwoven with these influences are those of Melanie Klein and her highly internalised models of external relationships, and the elegant and universally applied general system theory of von Bertalanffy. His theoretical treatise on the importance of properties of relatedness combined with the characteristics of the individual elements determining the properties of the resulting wholes, whether they be atoms, planets or people, prepared the way for a revolutionary way of viewing social aggregates.

All of these prior influences set the stage for the concept of the family unit as a whole organism, especially when viewed on a short time scale. Much of family therapy takes its therapeutic time scale as the one or two hours during which the family are seen functioning together as an unhealthy unit in the therapy session. But system theory defines most living systems as open systems both in time and space.

Bowen attempted to define postulates which would explain the open nature of family systems. His attempt to develop a coherent theory has led me to think about my own practice of family therapy, much of which was learned from the innovative and intuitive clinical work of Norman Paul. Many other ideas have entered into the development of a transgenerational theory which seeks to explain family quandaries as a product of the multiple and repetitive collisions of family subculture which occur in families viewed over several generations.

An attempt has been made to weave a tapestry of past and present influences on my thinking in preparation for the task of organising and developing the concepts which I apply to a transgenerational model of the family.

Notes

1. A.R.C. Skynner, *One Flesh, Separate Persons* (Constable, London, 1976); S. Walrond-Skinner, *Family Therapy: The Treatment of Natural Systems* (Routledge & Kegan Paul, London, 1976).

2. H.F. Ellenberger, *The Discovery of the Unconscious* (Basic Books, New York, 1970), Chap. 8.

3. A. Adler, 'Individual Psychology Therapy' in W.S. Sahakian (ed.), *Psychotherapy and Counseling* (Rand McNally, Chicago, 1969), Chap. 2.

4. Ibid., p.71.

5. W. Toman, *Family Constellation* (Springer Publishing Company, New York, 1961), pp. 2-15.

6. S. Freud, 'Recommendations for Physicians on the Psychoanalytic Method of Treatment', *Collected Papers,* vol. 2 (Hogarth Press, London, 1966-74).

7. D. Stafford-Clark, *What Freud Really Said* (Penguin Books, Harmondsworth,

1965), p.141.

8. J. Sandler, C. Dare, and A. Holder, 'Basic Psychoanalytic Concepts, III, Transference', *British Journal of Psychiatry,* vol. 116 (1970), pp. 667-72.

9. Walrond-Skinner, *Family Therapy,* pp. 29-31.

10. S. Freud, 'Mourning and Melancholia', *Standard Edition of the Complete Psychological Works of Sigmund Freud,* vol. 14 (Hogarth Press, London, 1966-74), pp. 243-8.

11. J. Bowlby, *Attachment and Loss,* vols. 1 and 2 (Penguin Books, Harmondsworth, 1971). These first two of three volumes comprehensively put the case for a synthesis of psychoanalytic and ethologic theories into a theory of attachment.

12. N.L. Paul and G.H. Grosser, 'Operational Mourning and its role in Conjoint Family Therapy', *Community Mental Health Journal,* vol. 1 (Winter, 1965), pp. 339-45.

13. R.D. Scott and P.L. Ashworth, 'The Shadow of the Ancestor', *British Journal of Medical Psychology,* vol. 42 (1969), pp. 13-32; J. Byng-Hall, 'Family Myths in Family Therapy', *British Journal of Medical Psychology,* vol. 46 (1973), p. 239.

14. W. Sluckin (ed.), *Early Learning and Early Experience* (Penguin Books, Harmondsworth, 1971). An excellent collection of original research papers devoted to this controversial area. Seminal papers on imprinting, conditioning, maternal deprivation, environmental enrichment and socialisation are included.

15. H. Segal, *Introduction to the Work of Melanie Klein* (Hogarth Press, London, 1975). A comprehensive summary of Kleinian theory including a useful glossary of terms.

16. Skynner, *One Flesh, Separate Persons.*

17. Segal, *Melanie Klein.*

18. L. von Bertalanffy, *General System Theory* (Penguin Books, Harmondsworth, 1973). It is well worth reading this book in order to recognize the true scope of the applications of general system theory to family therapy, psychology and many of the related sciences.

19. M. Bowen, 'Theory in the Practice of Psychotherapy', in P.J. Guerin (ed.), *Family Therapy* (Gardner Press, New York, 1976), pp. 42-91.

20. W. Toman, 'Family Constellation as a Basic Personality Determinant', *Journal of Individual Psychology,* vol. 15 (1959), pp. 199-211.

21. Paul and Grosser, 'Operational Mourning', p. 340.

22. N. Paul and B. Paul, *A Marital Puzzle* (W.W. Norton, New York, 1975).

23. N. Paul, 'Cross-Confrontation', in P.J. Guerin (ed.), *Family Therapy* (Gardner Press, New York, 1976), pp. 520-30.

24. D.H. Heard, 'From Object Relations to Attachment Theory: A Basis for Family Therapy', *British Journal of Medical Psychology,* vol. 51 (1978), pp. 67-76.

25. G. Bateson, D. Jackson, J. Haley, and J. Weakland, 'Towards a Theory of Schizophrenia', *Behavioural Science,* vol. 1 (1956), pp. 251-64. A concept which refers to the family as a feedback system which is designed to maintain itself in a relatively stable state, so that when the whole family or any part of it is upset the system will attempt to operate to restore the pre-existing balance.

26. Ibid. Double-bind refers to pairs of communications, closely related but on different levels. In order for a double-bind to exist two or more people must be involved with (a) a primary negative injunction at one level which includes a threat of punishment; (b) a conflicting secondary injunction; and (c) a third injunction preventing escape from the field of interaction.

27. T. Lidz, S. Fleck, and Cornelison, *Schizophrenia and the Family* (International Universities Press, New York, 1965). Dysfunctional families were divided into those with marital schism in which each spouse competed for their children's support and marital skew in which one parent allied with a child against

the other parent who maintained a dependent position.

28. L. Wynne, I. Ryckoff, J. Day, and S. Hersch, 'Pseudo-mutuality in the Family Relations of Schizophrenics', *Psychiatry,* vol. 21 (1958), pp. 205-20. A surface alliance that obscures underlying conflicts and differences.

29. V. Meyer and E.S. Chesser, *Behaviour Therapy in Clinical Psychiatry,* (Penguin Books, Harmondworth, 1970).

30. A.M. Srb, R.D. Owen, and R.S. Edgar, *General Genetics* (W.H. Freeman, San Francisco, 1965).

3 TRANSGENERATIONAL THEORY

And visit the sins of the fathers upon the children unto the
third and fourth generation.

From the Bible, Old Testament, Ecclesiastes 1:8

The thing that hath been, it is that which shall be.

Ecclesiastes 1:2

Introduction

How does a family maintain and pass on its unique identity and cuture?
What goes into the passage of family tradition from one generation to
the next?

It took many years for biologists to tease out the rules which govern
the biological communication between generations. Genetics is the
science built from those rules. It deals with the method by which biological information is passed from parent to offspring. Information from
previous generations is now known to be communicated via amino acid
codes contained in a complex **DNA** molecule which is physically dupli-
cated in the new organism.

But biological forms of communication are only one method of passing on characteristics to the succeeding generations. Another form of
communication exists. Animals with sufficiently organised nervous
systems can pass on learned behaviour to their offspring as well as to
other members of their species. The rapid spread throughout Great
Britain of the behaviour of blue tits serves to illustrate the phenomenon.
From a small area in the north of England where blue tits had learned
that they could peck open the top of milk bottles left on the doorsteps,
the practice spread throughout the country within a few years. This
spread was effected behaviourally, not biologically, with birds learning
by example from others of their species.

The cultural and traditional environment of a family is established
through the same sort of Lamarckian evolution in that acquired practices,
behaviours and beliefs are passed on to succeeding generations. The
acquisition of these practices, behaviours and beliefs may have been planned, incidental, or accidental. They may have been adaptive and enhanced
survival such as the acquired dietary taste of certain Arab populations
for grasshoppers; they may have been incidental, having no influence on
the survival of the family group, such as a family tradition to knock on

wood to prevent bad luck; or they may have been acquisitions which are poorly adaptive so that although the family may survive for a long time it will eventually perish, such as those families which restrict their diet to a small number of foods.

Transgenerational theory attempts to highlight areas involved in the communication of acquired practices, behaviours and beliefs between generations. There is no developed science at present in this area which details rigorous laws governing the passage of family culture and tradition. Transgenerational theory is a limited first step in the exposition of rules and laws which determine this passage.

Inherited, Moulded, and Constitutive Features

Human beings are born into the world with very little more than their inherited (genetic) tendencies, traits, and physical makeup. Among these inherited features are characteristics such as height, sex, eye colour, hair colour, physical appearance, potential intelligence, and basic emotional reactivity. Some of these features are strictly determined genetically such as eye and hair colour; other features are inherited as ranges of possibility dependent on the environment such as height, general intelligence, or emotional reactivity.[1] Acquired features are passed on in two different ways. The first is the acquisition of features which are moulded into an individual by parents, extended family and immediate cultural and social milieu in the formative years. An illustrative analogy would be the custom of binding feet in China. The feet can only be bound and remain small if the binding is done during the critical period of physical growth of the child. Attempts to bind an adult's foot in the hope that it would become smaller would be manifestly absurd. Once the foot is bound throughout the entire growth period, it can never again reach its full potential growth. Similarly, acquired characteristics which are moulded into the child at an early age during the critical periods of emotional and psychological development are relatively fixed and characterologic in nature. The moulding process occurs primarily in the first eight years of life in human beings.

Evidence for the existence of the moulding of individuals in their early life is abundant. In the developmental theories of analytical psychologies,[2] many of them postulate periods of psychological developmental stages which begin at birth and last until the ages between six and eight. These periods or stages must be traversed successfully by all human beings and leave certain fixed characteristics within the individual. Most of the theories, whether based on Freudian libidinal stages such as the oral, anal, and genital, or other developmental stages, agree that childhood learning and experience somehow moulds or fixes certain acquired characteristics in the child which are subsequently difficult or impossible to change. Pathology within the individual is often described in terms of the failure of the individual, when young, to have successfully acquired the skills, organisation or characteristics required at that particular critical period of growth and development.

The rapidly developing science of ethology, the science of the study of natural animal behaviour, has provided a parallel concept to that of the analytic psychologies. Imprinting is a phenomenon that imposes certain behaviour patterns on individuals by very early exposure to a given stimulus. It was first described by Lorenz[3] to explain the way in which species recognition was moulded into the nervous system of young geese. In imprinting, learning occurs in a qualitatively different way than in that of normal adult associational learning. First, there is a critical period during which the imprinting must occur and beyond which sensitivity to the specific area of learning is drastically curtailed. Second, the effort expended by the individual in acquiring the imprinting is directly related to the effectiveness of the learning. In imprinting the first thing learned is the one that is retained after the critical period has passed. An animal who is fooled into recognising another species as its own is unable to change that imprinting (a fact which zoo-keepers feel explains the difficulty in breeding animals raised in isolation by human beings). Finally, in imprinting, negative or punishing stimulation actually enhances learning to the same extent as positive stimulation.

But although analytical psychologies discovered the existence and importance of developmental stages and ethologists have delineated more clearly the rules governing this imprinting process, neurobiology has provided some physical evidence for this qualitative difference in learning.

In human beings the brain is known to reach its maximum physical weight at about fourteen years of age. The main weight and volume increases occur during the first two years of life with growth slowing down markedly thereafter. But the maturation of the brain follows definite cycles of myelination as well as other characteristics of cellular maturity. Most of the development of the various areas of the brain are finished by the age of ten except for the reticular formation and the intra-cortical neuropil of the association areas which continue throughout life.[4] Without going into fine detail, the developmental stages in our psychological life correspond roughly with developmental stages in the maturation of the brain at a time when a very special type of learning is evident.

An integration of this information leads me to the hypothesis that critical periods of learning exist in infancy and childhood during which acquired behaviours, beliefs, and practices are moulded into the child. This moulding process is qualitatively different from adult associational learning. It appears to be incorporated into the wiring diagram of the brain; that is, into the structural connections between various areas in the maturing brain. These connections are fixed and can be modified but not directly changed after the period of maturation of that particular area has been passed. This moulding process follows rules similar to those of imprinting. Moulding is one of the major ways in which acquired communications are incorporated from one generation to the next in the transgenerational passage of family culture. Between the age of ten and fourteen the ability to mould into an individual various acquired traits and patterns of behaviour ceases as the brain matures. Moulded characteristics are not ordinarily open to change by the relationship system within which the individual happens to be placed although they do determine the choice of relationship system which is optimal for the individual. Both inherited and moulded characteristics are summative by the definition given in general system theory.

The second category of acquired features are those which are acquired in later life through associational learning. Associational learning occurs throughout the remaining life of the individual and includes emotional, experiential and cognitive learning. Associational learning probably occurs through the forging of new connection networks between the major established pathways which were laid down during the moulding process. Modifications are possible in the output effect of the architecture of the connections even though the connections are permanent. Human complexity owes much to our capacity to continue modifying our responses through associational learning.

It is important to distinguish these different forms of acquisition of individual human features from the constitutive characteristics which we possess. Acquired individual beliefs, behaviours and practices include those which significantly depend on the relationship field within which the individual exists. My reactions at home depend on who is present as well as what I am like and what I wish to do. A person reacts to those others around him and they to him. The interaction is determined by the individual acquired and inherited features of all the individuals present. Constitutive features only *seem* to dwell within individuals. In fact they are activated when an individual is in contact with others. The strength, quality and direction of the constitutive feature is determined by the relationship field. There is no direct connection between constitutive features and associational learning except that in therapy these two areas are most open to change. Features which are learned associationally are much easier to modify than those moulded into oneself.

Acquired features or characteristics of the individual can be passed on through several different and simultaneous means of communication. These can be thought of as languages. The first language which we are able to understand is the emotional language with which we make contact with those caring for us in our infancy. This language is primarily one of facial and bodily position with some non-specific sounds. The second of the early languages is that of behaviour. We learn to do by watching others. We teach our children by example before they can be taught by words. The spoken language is the third language by which we are instructed and acquire our characteristics. Each of these three languages as they become operative are used simultaneously and in conjunction. When these means of communication are integrated and convey the same message they are highly effective in presenting a whole communication to the individual. Conflicts between these communications convey both mixed meanings and a model of mixed communication. The final form of language is the written language. It is the last language learned and is capable of teaching concepts of great complexity as well as maintaining a more objective continuity between generations. Written language has enabled cultural concepts to continue for over five millennia.

Transgenerational Passage

Within the family all forms of learning affect the developing child. A child may have moulded into him the relationship influences within the family which are constitutive for the rest of the family, as well as moulded characteristics which are passed down from previous generations. These influences may be directly handed down as original to the family of origin or they may be indirectly received through those nuclear family members. Direct influence also occurs between the developing child and the extended family. Direct moulding occurs when a developing child is brought into contact with any of the existing personalities in the nuclear and extended family constellation. For example, consider the way in which a child may be taught to control his anger. He may be spanked, isolated in his room, frostily ignored, silently condemned, or even encouraged openly or subtly to continue his tantrum by any family member. Any of these reactions carries with it a model upon which the child will base his own future reactions as well as a model of the way in which adults train children to control their anger. Both the parenting behaviour, the beliefs and the control are simultaneously handed down to the next generation directly.

Indirect influences are more subtle in that they are handed down after having been passed through the previous generation, without the conscious awareness of that generation. An illustration of this indirect process follows in which the husband and wife mould their children's character by passage through them of the influence of their own parents. Let's say the husband has a strong affinity for certain characteristics which his father possessed such as his father's stubbornness. This affinity encourages him to react in a particular way with his son. From birth his son is endowed with a potential to fit into his father's personality (after all, he does have his grandfather's nose). If the infant is stubborn he is indulged at first and the development of stubbornness is encouraged. As the child grows, he is imprinted through the modelling of stubbornness and the encouragement of that trait until it is moulded into him. All things being equal, the child will develop along those lines until as an adult, he will possess the same quality of stubbornness that his grandfather possessed without any direct contact with him.

Complications set in when each of the family members pass conflicting reaction patterns on to the same child. His father may expect stubbornness while his mother expects flexibility. A child whose genetic inheritance conflicts with both of his parent's expectations is triply in conflict. As an example, the daughter of a man whose father was a professional accountant and a woman whose mother was a tennis professional is herself both clumsy and intellectually dull by nature. The child is encouraged by her father to be studious by giving her a desk, many books, spending time with her doing mathematics problems and entering her in a private school. The mother takes her daughter to Wimbledon for the Lawn Tennis Tournament every year from birth and plays tennis with her from the age of three. Mother sabotages her studies through tennis lessons and subtle derision of intellectual pursuits. The father fights back by emphasising his daughter's obvious clumsiness and lack of native ability in physical sports. If only she would concentrate more on her studies ... His wife fights back by pointing to the daughter's poor academic record. If only she would concentrate more on her athletics ... Both husband and wife are forced to agree that their daughter is a failure at being what she should be. The daughter blames herself for her failure to fulfil either of her parents' expectations. The parents become angry that their daughter could not become what they expect her to be (what their own parents were). And none of the three participants in this process are aware of the long process they have lived through, its origin or its ongoing effect.

The recognition of the process of transgenerational passage in reverse order requires a knowledge of the relationships, personalities and histories of each of the three or more generations involved. In order to bring about a change in this process it may be necessary to involve, directly or indirectly, the entire extended family.

The Passage of Behaviour, Belief, and Tradition

Transgenerational passage is a concept that incorporates the transmission of the entire gamut of family-related traditions, beliefs, and behaviours.

By tradition, I include the passage of such things as racial and ethnic values and customs, religious and national tradition, class distinction and all other areas which are closely linked with the broader environmental culture.

The passage of family beliefs incorporates attitudes towards life, death and sexuality. Choice of occupation and educational aspirations, attitudes towards money, politics, and attitudes towards other families and cultures are also passed on. The hopes of the older generation may be passed on to become the accomplishments of the following generations. A father whose father wished him to become a doctor, lawyer, concert pianist or banker may pass this hope on to his children. The grandchildren may successfully achieve a goal set three or more generations previously, much to the delight of those surviving members of the older generation. Many of these shared family values or beliefs are intimately connected to family behaviour patterns.

Family roles, such as what fathers do as opposed to what mothers do, how close or distant grandmothers or grandfathers are to their grandchildren, whether extended family ties are close or distant, are passed on as beliefs as well as practices or behaviours. Even the determination of who constitutes an extended family member is passed on as a behaviour. Family conflicts are also passed from one generation to the next. At times the conflict is already moulded into an individual family member such as father, mother, uncle or grandparent and passed on as a model of conflicting and contradictory behaviour within the relative. It is observed as a contradiction between what is done by that particular relative and what is said. Family conflict may also be passed on as a result of existing clashes between two or more older generation members (mother versus father, father versus grandfather, uncle versus father and so on). Finally, the learning of the expression of emotions is passed on including positive feelings such as love, trust, and happiness and negative feelings such as anger, despair and sadness.

In order to understand a particular family's quandary, the specific traditions, beliefs, and behaviours of that family must be ascertained through the exploration of that particular family's history.

Bonds and Bonding

Bonds are defined as the emotional attachment between two or more individuals. Bonds are what distinguish family members from 'outsiders'. Bonded individuals remain close to each other emotionally despite geographic distance. They attempt to maintain contact through visits, letters, and phone calls, but even if permanently separated physically, bonded individuals can remain attached to each other. Because bonds are forged emotionally, most of our strongest emotions arise during the formation, maintainence, renewal and disruption of bonds.[5] Because family quandaries are often emotional problems, an understanding of bonds and bonding within the particular family is necessary.

Bonding begins at birth when an infant and mother become attached to each other. The pattern of bonding between mother and infant is set in the pattern of bonding moulded into the mother when she was developing. Bond formation is a process which is learned through the experience of forming bonds both in the family of origin and the extended family as well as observing those bonds which already exist. The quality of those bonds which already exist serve as a model for future bond formation. Observation of the bonds between my parents served as a model for the bonding between myself and my wife; observation and exposure to the bond between my parents and their siblings provides a model for the bonding between myself and my siblings as well as affecting the bonds that I form with my uncles and aunts.

Bonding has been subdivided by Bowlby[6] into attachment bonds, and two specialised bonds; caretaking and heterosexual. Attachment bonds are the general class of emotional bonds already described. Caretaking bonds are those formed between persons who care for their young and the young themselves, that is, parents and children. Heterosexual bonding refers to the marital bond. These three classes of bonding, one general and two specific, are moulded into the infant from the earliest exposure to bonds and define some of the basic differences in relationships in families.

The assessment of a family quandary must take into account the various types of bond and explore their quality, strength, and durability, and the recurrent patterns in bonding which are apparent in the family history and the existing family members.

Families in Collision: The Choice of a Spouse

When Mrs Webb was asked why she had married her husband she replied that it was love at first sight. Mr Webb emphatically agreed; theirs was a whirlwind courtship. She had sensed that he was quiet, patient, kind and looked as if he needed someone to care for him. She later described her father as quiet, patient, kind, and the sort of man her mother could and would pamper and indulge. After several months of marriage her husband had begun to shout at her. She grew bewildered and anxious at this incongruous behaviour. She had chosen her husband as a person who seemed to fit naturally into her life. They seemed to fit together like hand and glove; it was as if they possessed matching and complementary personalities which immediately interlocked to form a strong heterosexual bond. Mrs Webb's choice of her husband was based on the unconscious recognition of similarities between him and her father. But she had failed to recognise that Mr Webb was not a perfect match of her father's personality. Although her husband had been argumentative throughout his life she had ignored the mismatch because so much of the rest of his characteristics fitted. When the reality of the difference between her husband and her own expectations of her husband, based on her experience of her father, became apparent she was unable to reconcile them.

The choice of a spouse is a seminal life event since it heralds the birth of a new nuclear family whose evolutionary potential is to grow into a large extended family in its own right. Most family therapists acknowledge the critical role that the marital coalition plays in determining the viability of a family. The emotional, sociological, and interpersonal forces in marital choice are of vital interest in the investigation of any family quandary.

In many Eastern civilisations, marital choice is largely a matter to be arranged between the two nuclear and extended families of the prospective bride and groom. This tradition takes far more care to ensure the compatibility of the two families. But Western societies favour giving a great deal of personal freedom of choice to their children. This freedom of choice is, to a great extent, illusory.

Marital choice is first limited by the field of eligibility. Geographical location, social class, age, race, religion, incest taboos and physical parameters such as appearance, height and weight all serve to narrow the field of eligibility of marital choice. The remaining field may be quite small, as obtains in rural areas, or numerous as in urban areas. The tendency to make a marital choice based on similarities in the mutual possession of many of the above-named parameters is well documented.[7]

But within the field of eligibility the final marital choice is based on other factors.

The influence of the parental image in the conscious determination of the choice of a spouse has been confirmed in several studies.[8] Patterns of choice have been uncovered in which the spouse is chosen based on the image of the parent of the opposite sex, the parent of the same sex, or a combination of traits possessed by both parents. Another important pattern has been reported in which the choice of a spouse is based on the complete opposite of a parental figure. A parental image is defined not in terms of facial features, but in terms of parental personality, opinions and temperament. In general, a person tends to fall in love with someone who resembles the parent with whom he was most closely bonded as a child. Secondarily, a person is attracted to a choice of a partner possessing opposing characteristics to a parent with whom an unsatisfactory relationship existed as a child.

Marital choice has also been investigated with regard to the concepts of assortative versus complementary mating. Assortative mating is the tendency for men and women to choose their partners by seeking in them the features of personality that they possess themselves. A man who is happy and carefree and slightly irresponsible would seek a woman with a similar characteristics. Complementary mating occurs when people marry because they see in each other features which they do not possess and feel would complement themselves in a marriage. A happy, carefree and somewhat irresponsible man would seek a woman who was sober, careful and responsible.

Much of the preceding work refers to the conscious awareness of each of the marital couple as to the reasons for their choice. 'But love is blind, and lovers cannot see the pretty follies that themselves commit.' *(Merchant of Venice, Act 2, vi.36)*. Marital choice is often grounded in unconscious factors.

In a simple example, such as Mrs Webb, she felt an immediate pull of attraction to her husband. Similarly, her husband felt that she was like his mother and in some important aspects she was. Neither husband nor wife were aware that these compelling similarities to their parents formed the basis for the sudden emotional attachment and choice. They were equally unaware of the stark differences between their unconscious expectations of their partner and the reality. At the end of the honeymoon period both partners found their illusions continually jolted by reality until they were shattered. Much of the work of forming and maintaining a strong marital bond involves learning to accept the spouse as the person they are rather than the person they were imagined to be.

But if the difference between image and reality prove to be too great then the marital bond is sure to suffer. A man may have unknowingly taken his close feelings for his father as the basis for his choice of a woman with a masculine appearance. The wife's close relationship to her father moulded her character and was the foundation for her choice. While the wife's image of her husband corresponded to a large extent with the reality of his personality, she was quite unlike his expectations of her. The give and take adjustments become too one-sided and the marital relationship becomes a troubled one.

Matters are complicated further when the choice of a spouse is based on moulded expectations of relationships derived from any of the family members extant during childhood. Influences incorporated from grandparents, uncles, aunts, cousins or close friends of the family may be relevant to the marital choice. The marital partner may be felt to possess characteristics which reawaken the intimate relationship which a person had with their grandmother or even through the transmission of the expectations that the child (now grown) would have liked to have in an intimate relationship with his grandmother. It is not easy to correlate the tendency of two persons to combine in a marital bond when they exercise their free will.

The reaction between one person and another is the integration of a very large number of unions of moulded and constitutive character-istics. The forces involved for each of the characteristic areas such as sexual experience, aggressiveness, interest in sports and empathic aware-ness, to name a few, are variable and the intensity of the bond formation depends on the combined forces of attraction in all areas of each individual. These combined forces of attraction may be termed the valence, after the term used in immunochemistry to denote the chemical forces holding two complex organic molecules together. Since no two people could ever make a perfect fit an element of reversibility in the relationship always remains. In general, two people who can bring large portions of their character configurations into a close fitting juxta-position will show much stronger and more lasting mutual attraction than two persons with less extensive juxtaposition. If you can imagine these personality features and characteristics which have been acquired through transgenerational passage as invisible but tangible areas which combine to envelop a person in a specific reactive configuration, then the combination of two of these valency envelopes can be seen as the marital bond.

So far I have been dealing with two individuals in isolation without considering their surrounding family environments. Anyone who has had to sit down and thrash out the invitation list to a wedding must realise that the joining of two people is also a marriage of two large extended families. In Western societies the children bring together their extended families whereas in Eastern societies the extended families bring together their children. In either case there is a collision of family culture and tradition, beliefs and behaviours. The effect of the collision is an ongoing one. Extended family ties are maintained and may be strengthened after marriage. The ambivalent but ubiquitous jokes about mother-in-law and her interference are testimony to the awareness of the ongoing effects of family collisions in the general population.

Marital bonds can be maintained through external pressure by the extended family even when the strength of the valence is relatively small. One common example of this phenomenon is the 'shotgun' wedding. This forced union of a couple by family pressure occurs when a sexual relationship has resulted in pregnancy. Shame and guilt in the couple related to their upbringing is reinforced by their respective families. The couple may have already decided to marry but the forced marriage shatters their illusions of free will and may create pressure from family members which is unbearable. The threat of the death of an infirm relative upon hearing of the shame may be used to force the marriage to occur. Here the extended families unite momentarily as pressure is exerted to force a union which otherwise would have been a matter of free choice. The child, when it is born, is in a particularly vulnerable position since it bears the responsibility for the union even before birth. The child is frequently unaware of the cause of this burden since it is a shameful secret kept hidden by the parents and their respective families.

Family pressure does not only exert itself towards seeking a particular match. Pressure may be exerted from one or both families of origin to prevent a match. Here the outcome depends on the strength of valency of the couple and the way in which the family pressure is reacted to by each of the partners. If they react by resenting any attempt of their family to limit their independence the pressure may actually increase the likelihood of a match.

The family collision becomes more open when children are produced from a marriage. Each of the parents have been moulded in a unique family culture and there are bound to be large numbers of differences in parenting practices and beliefs. These differences begin to show in the newly created nuclear family and through the contact which is maintained with the respective families of origin. Which family culture gains ascendency depends on many factors.

The geographic availability of family members in the extended family

is a major factor in the influence that they bring to bear on the development of a child. There is a tendency in Western societies for couples to
settle in the geographic area in which the wife's mother lives, known as
the matrilocal tendency. Another major factor involves the parenting
responsibilities of the couple. Usually the mother is most responsible for
the early acculturation of the child so that it is her family traditions and
culture which are most strongly represented in the moulding of the child.
Where family cultures collide, both within the couple and through exposure to the extended family members, potential conflicts may be
moulded into the growing child. These conflicts are continued after the
moulding process has ceased through the conflicting family cultures in
the family as they have been passed down from their respective origins.

Family Losses, Family Replacements

Life events research[9] confirms that exits or losses from the social field
precede the development of stress in individuals which can lead to
psychiatric symptomatology. The death of a family member is ranked
as the most stressful of life events that families and their individual
members must face. It is an immediate and irrevocable disruption in the
continuity of family life and often sends a shock wave travelling through
the entire extended family network. A family culture must be able to
survive beyond the death of its individual members in order to maintain
its integrity as an organic whole. Such survival must take into account
the natural reaction of its members to loss.

Grieving the loss (through death) of a spouse, child, or other immediate family member such as a parent or grandparent seems to be an
inherited reaction. The mourning process is nature's way of healing the
wound created by the loss of a familiar and strongly bonded family
member, as evidenced by its presence in all primates, most mammals and
some birds. Descriptions of such grief reactions among animals abound
in ethological literature, such as the especially poignant account given of
the effects of family loss on a wild chimpanzee colony.[10]

The reaction of an individual human being to the loss of a loved one
has been described in detail both in its normal and morbid aspects.[11]
Normal grief is recognised when an evident loss has occurred which is
followed by the three stages of grief; numbness, disorganisation, and
resolution. During the second (disorganisation) stage there are recognised
symptoms including physical, psychological and behavioural disturb-
ances. The physical symptoms include palpitations, digestive complaints,
sighing, sleep and appetite disturbance, 'heartache', and a hollow empty
feeling inside. Emotional symptoms include increased guilt, hostility,

anger, sorrow, and episodic weeping spells. Behavioural symptoms include pining, searching, aimless wandering, loss of normal conduct patterns and a preoccupation with the deceased. Morbid grief delays or distorts the onset and progress of the normal grief process.

The following family study illustrates some salient features of the morbid grief process.

This 42-year-old woman was an only child whose father died when she was nine months old. She was named after her mother who never remarried after her husband's death. At the age of forty-two her mother died and the loss threatened to overwhelm her. She was seized by uncontrollable weeping and was unable to function in any of her extensive business or social interests and duties. She isolated herself from her family and friends while ruminating over the intense adolescent conflicts she had had with her mother. She was filled with guilt at the way she had mistreated her mother. Much of this behaviour was part of a normal mourning process, but it meant that her husband had to shoulder all of the family, social, and business interests as well as dealing with his mother-in-law's extensive estate as executor. During this trying period, their eldest son became a serious behaviour problem and her husband was required to deal with the eldest son on his own. On a trip to the boarding school where his son was enrolled her husband became ill. Nine months after the death of her mother, her husband died from that illness.

For two days after his death she remained unusually calm with rare outbursts of weeping. She refused to see her children. She blamed her eldest son (who was named after her own father) for the death of her husband. She took photographs of her husband's office so that it could be maintained exactly as he had left it. She began to act like him, taking on some of his mannerisms. For four years she refused to go out in public. At first she refused to allow her husband's name to be mentioned in her presence. She often felt her husband was present. She felt her husband spoke to her and through her to others. She never fully forgave her son and refused to allow him to take part in any aspect of the family business until she died forty years later. She never remarried and remained in mourning for the remainder of her life. She was Alexendrina Victoria, Queen of England.[12]

The disruption in both the individual and the family were profound and lasting. No one individual can isolate the effects of a grief reaction, either normal or morbid, wholly within themselves. The pattern of the reaction to loss is one which reverberates throughout the family for generations.

The delays and distortions in morbid grief have been studied with the help of a morbid grief scale[13] which lists the most frequently observed reactions including absence of expected grief, delayed reaction, avoidance, panic attacks, anniversary reactions, over-idealisation, identification symptoms, recurrent nightmares, extreme anger, extreme guilt, prolonged persistent grief and physical illness. Correlation of these items reveals three patterns. First, a pattern of avoidance in which there is an avoidance of persons, places or things related to the deceased, combined with extreme guilt and anger and related to a delay in the onset of the grief process. The second pattern of over-idealisation of the deceased combines an absence of expected grief, over-idealisation, and extreme anger directed towards others. Such was the pattern of Queen Victoria's grief. A third pattern is the combination of prolonged grieving with recurrent nightmares and the development of a psychosomatic illness.

These individual reaction patterns are mirrored in the way they affect the entire family, producing a more general family reaction to loss. Often more than one person in a household is bereft by a loss and the individual reactions intertwine. For example the pattern of individual avoidance became a family style in a family of four after the death of a child. The death of the child, his pictures, his name and his very existence were never mentioned by any of the existing nuclear family members. The patterns of response to loss by families have been explored in greater depth.[14] Pincus details the extent to which previous family relationships determine the response to loss. Particular interest is shown in the effect of delayed or absent grief which can surface later in the form of a family quandary.

If the family members are unable to mourn separately or collectively a family pattern develops which is then perpetuated through transgenerational passage. Morbid grieving or lack of grieving becomes a family reaction pattern which has been handed down from one generation to another whose reaction patterns are similar. Inability to mourn a loss indicates a difficulty in relinquishing the emotional bonds forged with the deceased. Unrelinquished bonds can affect current relationships in two ways. The inevitable life events such as marriage, maturity of the younger generation (which normally leads to separation and independence), and other deaths are dealt with in a resistant way. Changes in family structure become less fluid and there is an attempt to freeze the generational hierarchy of the family against the passage of time and the family's normal evolution. This attempt at a family stasis is accomplished through the shifting of the bond from the deceased to another member of the family who acts as a replacement for the deceased. The second way in which the unrelinquished bond can affect current relationships is by remaining attached to the deceased rather than altering through the normal resolution of grief. Queen Victoria's reaction was one of remaining attachment to her husband (and mother) with devastating effects on the family.

Conversely, if the family can deal with the death of one of its members through acceptance, toleration and encouragement of the expression of those mixed thoughts and feelings about the deceased which are present, then the family evolutionary process will be a smoother one. The pattern set with major losses will teach family members to face less severe losses such as geographic separations, the maturity and independence of the younger generation, and their subsequent marriages. Acceptance of grieving as a normal activity leads to a family style of acceptance of these less traumatic life events which contain similar mixed negative and positive feelings.

Replacements occur in families when marriages or births coincide with the loss of previously bonded family members. Replacement of bonds is distinguished from a grieving experience which allows the development of new bonds. For the person entering a family as a replacement there are far-reaching implications due to the constant interaction relationships within the family which attempt to mould into the new member those features and characteristics possessed by the absent family member.

For an infant born into a family as a replacement, the moulding process has only the child's innate tendencies to prevent an implantation of many of the characteristics of the deceased. The replacement of a deceased family member by the choice of a spouse incurs the added problem arising from the spouse's moulded characteristics, constitutive relationships with his or her family and innate characteristics, many of which will differ markedly from those of the deceased family member. If the marital valency is weak then the marital bond will be poorly formed.

A replacement may be made in a conscious choice shared by all participants including the extended family and the individual involved as the replacement, or it may be a process which has occurred on an emotional level, neither understood or acknowledged by any of the family. When family members reattach a bond from a lost family member to a new replacement the conscious awareness of each of them will heavily influence the course of the development of the new family member and his or her integration into the family. For example, Charles may have been consciously named after his recently deceased uncle and consciously guided to become a lawyer as his uncle was. He may have been openly encouraged to develop his uncle's habits and mannerisms and been sent to the same school as his uncle. This process which began at his birth would have moulded into him many of his uncle's acquired features until they were natural parts of himself. He would be aware and accepting of much of the role. But if Charles has been so treated and yet has never been told of his uncle — who he was, what he did, and on what emotional basis Charles has become a replacement — he will grow up in a family reacting to him as if he were someone else, with no explanation. This would be especially difficult if his innate characteristics included musical tendencies, mild dyslexia and a natural shyness, and not all of his immediate family or extended family shared the same replacement bonding with him. The summative characteristics of the child (or spouse) are the most serious obstacle in the path of moulding a replacement. If the characteristics fit and match those of the person who was lost, little readjustment is necessary. If not, family quandaries are inevitable as a square peg is forcibly hammered into a round hole.

The strength of the need for a family replacement is determined by the number of family members who generate the need and their ability through geographic closeness to influence the developmental properties of the person who is newly arrived in the family. An aunt living three thousand miles away from her nephew may dearly wish a replacement bond with that nephew but cannot heavily influence her nephew's wife even if a baby has been conceived at the correct moment. The nephew's need for a replacement of his favourite uncle will be much more important in determining to what extent the child replaces the former relationship.

The following clinical study illustrates the way in which a daughter was moulded into a replacement of her father's mother. Sarah was referred for depression and was seen with her parents. She had been born ten months after the death of her paternal grandmother. Her father, an only child, had been very close to his mother. Their only separation had been enforced by the Korean conflict. After he returned from the armed forces he continued to live in the family home even after his marriage. In desperation, his wife planned her first pregnancy with the sole purpose of forcing her husband to move from the home of her in-laws. Her husband never forgave her for this manoeuvre. Shortly after the birth of their eldest daughter, his mother became ill and died of that same illness two years later. Their daughter Sarah was born the year following her paternal grandmother's death. When she was born he felt she looked exactly like his mother. She grew up with him treating her as if she were his mother; he fostered the same over-close relationship with her. Sarah's mother was jealous of the over-close relationship which had developed between her daughter and husband. During adolescence the family tension mounted as Sarah began to develop as a woman. When her body began to develop it became clear that she would take after her mother's earthy form rather than her paternal grandmother's slim figure. The growing tension at home was obvious to Sarah but there seemed no apparent reasons for it. Her father began to withdraw from her as her development as a woman strained his ability to treat her as a replacement for his mother. Sarah became depressed.

Another example of a replacement is that of Mr Barclay and his wife. Mr Barclay was referred for marital therapy following the onset of acute anxiety and continuous nagging questioning of his wife. She believed that the difficulties began when she started training as a social worker. The marital quandary was the spiralling lack of trust between them. She had been a housewife whose warmth at home was matched by a fear of new relationships outside of the home. He had been a dependable but unemotional man who had seemed a pillar of strength to her. When she started her course on his insistence and encouragement, she became much less dependent on him for her practical needs while his emotional needs remained. Further investigation revealed that he had been strongly attached to his father's mother who was described as a warm, caring, giving but lonely woman whose husband died prematurely. She had a peculiar name of American Indian origin; she had lived in Mr Barclay's family home until her death when he was eighteen. Two weeks later he met his wife. The qualities which most attracted him to her were her loneliness and her warm and giving qualities. She had an unusual name and her father was Canadian.

He realised at once the parallel between his grandmother and his wife although he had failed to connect them previously. He had replaced his grandmother with his wife. When she began to become more independent his feelings of loss were reawakened.

Family Secrets

Family secrets are those behaviours, beliefs, traditions, or feelings which cannot be openly communicated between family members. Not only does each particular secret bit of information exist in itself, but there is continuum of family secrecy which pervades a family culture. A particular secret may be trivial but there are secrets in families which have a profound effect on the entire family network.

One of the most important ways to maintain an intangible boundary between one culture and another is by restricting the information flow between them by taboo, secrecy, or shared practices which remain the property of the small group. But secrecy, as well as maintaining a boundary between a family and its surroundings, can create boundaries and barriers within the family.

Secrets can develop out of a sense of fear, guilt, or shame as well as out of a sense of belonging to an exclusive group. The fear is related to the presumed consequences of the revelation of the secret; this revelation might prove the destruction of the organisation and structure of the family unit. The expulsion of the member who dared to start the communication process might occur. Let us consider the development of a secret.

Harry, a fifteen-year-old boy, was given a job for the summer on a yacht. His family culture held a rigid secrecy about sexual matters. The family were even more secretive about sexual matters than other families in the surrounding culture. Harry, while sleeping aboard the yacht awoke to find the first mate fondling his penis, now erect. Upon awakening he shouted out, frightening the first mate away. Isolated and alone, he can talk to no one nor can he report the incident (one doesn't talk about sex). In his anger, he began to stay up late at night, roaming the ship and stealing money. He was caught, accused and finally referred to a child guidance clinic. He attended with his parents who implored him to tell them why he was stealing, yet refused the least hint of a discussion about sexual matters. Finally Harry invented a plausible excuse about the pressure on him from his schoolwork. The secret had now solidified within him, tied in with the family secrecy about sex. When he married his sexual performance was poor; his wife was frustrated but he wouldn't talk about it. The area was closed, not open to change. Through the existence of an encapsulated secret, changes which otherwise might have been possible were frozen and immobilised.

Secrets within the family setting may be of several different varieties. There are secrets made of events in which all family members either take part, witness, or have knowledge, yet are bound not to discuss. Such a shared secret may become a shared family group preoccupation[15] in which the secret is maintained and its import strengthened within each family member while avoidance of communication about the secret material is a shared activity. Such a preoccupation removes from the family large areas of interactional possibilities. Deaths and the circumstances surrounding them are often the focus of this sort of shared secret. For example, the death of the younger sister of Mrs Berry in a car accident deeply affected her, her husband, and her two children for whom Mrs Berry's sister would often babysit. Each of the family members admitted that they often thought of her but they were never able to share their thoughts and feelings together. At times the home would take on the atmosphere of a mausoleum. Eventually one of the children was referred for behaviour problems.

A family must devote a great deal of its energy and talent to maintain avoidance of formative experiences in its life. This effort is not only lost to other ventures, it creates and elaborates a style of response which is subject to transgenerational passage of the pattern of response without the simultaneous passage of the content.

There are secrets which are shared between the senior generation and kept from the children. The children, who are ignorant of the content of the secret, suffer the consequences without knowing why. John a sixteen-year-old boy, was the eldest boy of parents who married as a result of a premarital pregnancy. The secrets which the parents kept from the children included that of the premarital pregnancy as well as the existence and death of a firstborn child, Joan, whom John replaced. None of the other children were aware of these facts or the continuing emotional effect on their parents. John was continuously being required to live up to an idealised and perfect image of an 'angel' whose existence was unknown to him.

Secrets can also begin as feelings, fantasies, or actions encapsulated within one family member. These secrets are kept from all other family members. But as in the example of Harry, they can affect future relationships by binding and freezing potential areas of change within a family or an individual. For example, Mr and Mrs Closet and their four children were seen in family sessions due to the frequent marital arguments which had erupted since the termination of Mrs Closet's individual psychotherapy sessions. Since that time she had begun to feel her husband's detachment from the family in a more realistic way than previously. His response was to begin drinking heavily. After several fruitless conjoint family and marital sessions an individual session, arranged at his request, revealed that he was having an affair which was only the last in a long line of extramarital liaisons. This information, imparted in the strictest confidence, explained his lack of involvement. Mrs Closet's increased awareness of his withdrawal from family life led to increased stress. Since the result of the revelation of the secret would have certainly led to the break-up of the family, Mr Closet requested that therapy be terminated. The family left in an uneasy truce.

The previous examples indicate the existence of specific secrets held for various reasons within families, as well as a continuum of secrecy which exists as a major relational property which differs from family to family, and generation to generation. The atmosphere within a family may stimulate the sharing of fantasies, beliefs, and emotions, or the withholding of them. Pressure to share everything can be as damaging as pressure to share nothing.

Family Evolution

Family evolution refers to the change in family culture as it is passed down from generation to generation. Family beliefs, practices and traditions which have been handed down through the generations alter and change. My family ancestors who lived in Poland three centuries ago certainly lived a very different life with many reactions, customs, practices and beliefs different from my own. Some of the family cultural elements may have survived through transgenerational passage, but others have disappeared or changed while new practices, beliefs, and traditions have been acquired.

This family evolutionary process is Lamarckian in nature; it is acquired cultural patterns which are passed on to the next generation. Family evolution occurs much more swiftly than genetic evolution can hope to do. Although it took many millions of years before animals could evolve into birds who could fly, man succeeded through cultural evolution in a period of years.

For family evolution to occur there must be a variation between family cultures, a means of passing on the revised instructions that produce a moulded variant individual, and a difference in the fitness of such variants. The variation in family cultures and in the larger cultural heritage that they share is legion. The development of these variations have occurred as a result of processes similar to those in genetic evolution. In his description of cultural evolution in operant behavioural terms, Skinner[16] used the analogy of a culture corresponding to a species, with the same people transmitting both genetic and cultural endowments. New cultural practices are compared to mutations which spring from idiosyncracies of important leaders within that culture. For example the food allergy of a strong leader may be passed on as a new dietary law. Geographical isolation, taboos, or racial, national or religious rules may lead to the isolation and 'inbreeding' of various practices leading to the establishment of variations in culture. Finally in the case of family cultures, 'hybridisation' can occur in which the marital coupling of partners from two different cultures can produce a new and unique family culture of its own.

The importance of the concept of family evolution to family therapy is its emphasis on the possibilities of change in a family system over time. The process of family evolution can also work so as to produce the quandary which is presented to the therapist. Since family culture is acquired, the surrounding cultural environment can greatly influence the moulding of the younger generation. Immigrants living in alien cultural surroundings find their children assimilating the culture around them whatever the wishes of the older generation. The result is a quandary between the older generation and the younger one, as has begun to happen in the Indian, Pakistani and West Indian communities in England.

In the formation of the marital bond the family collision resulting is one of cultural practices and beliefs as well as people. The marital quandary may be rooted in those differences whose resolution represents an evolutionary step which will then be moulded into succeeding generations.

A family evolves over the generations as a result of change in the physical, social and cultural environment as well as through internal idiosyncracies and hybridisation. New knowledge can be widely disseminated and put to use using modern communication methods. Such knowledge which leads to changes in beliefs and practices can instill new traditions within a family overnight. One need only look at the effect of the exposure of previously isolated primitive tribes (which are usually composed of several large extended families) to Western culture and its beliefs and practices. Within one generation many customs are lost and by three or four generations most of them have ceased to be memories. Family evolution provides a concept in which the differentiation of children from their parents can be seen in a broader perspective.

Notes

1. I.M. Lerner, *Heredity Evolution and Society* (W.H. Freeman and Company, San Francisco, 1968), pp. 150-71.

2. A.M. Freedman and H.I. Kaplan, *Comprehensive Textbook of Psychiatry* (William and Wilkins, Baltimore, 1967). pp. 269-383.

3. K. Lorenz, *On Aggression* (Methuen and Co. Ltd, London, 1967), pp. 56-7.

4. P.I. Yakovlev and A.R. Lecours, 'The Myelogenetic Cycles of Regional Maturation of the Brain', in A. Minkowski (ed.), *Regional Development of the Brain in Early Life* (Blackwell, Oxford, 1967), pp. 3-64.

5. J. Bowlby, 'Affectional Bonds: Their Nature and Origin', in H. Freeman (ed.), *Progress in Mental Health* (J. and A. Churchill, London, 1969).

6. Ibid.

7. J. Dominian, *Marital Breakdown* (Penguin Books, Harmondsworth, 1974), pp. 21-30.

8. Ibid., pp. 32-42.

9. E.S. Paykel, 'Life Events and Acute Depression', in *Separation and Depression* (AAAS, 1973), pp. 215-36.

10. J. Goodall, *In the Shadow of Man* (Houghton Mifflin Co., Boston, 1971, pp. 219-30.

11. C.M. Parkes, *Bereavement. Studies of Grief in Adult Life* (Tavistock Publications, London, 1972) *passim.*

12. C. Woodham-Smith, *Queen Victoria,* vol. 1 (Book Club Associates, London, 1973).

13. S. Lieberman, 'Nineteen Cases of Morbid Grief', *British Journal of Psychiatry,* vol. 132 (February, 1978), pp. 159-63.

14. L. Pincus, *Death and the Family: The Importance of Mourning* (Tavistock Publications, London, 1976).

15. A. Cooklin, 'Family Preoccupation and Role in Conjoint Therapy', unpublished paper read to Royal College of Psychiatrists, 12 June 1974.

16. B.F. Skinner, *Beyond Freedom and Human Dignity* (Penguin Books, Harmondsworth, 1973), p. 126.

4 THE GENEOGRAM: THE FAMILY TREE AS A TOOL

I keep six honest serving-men,
(They taught me all I knew)
Their names are What and Where and When
And How and Why and Who.

R. Kipling, *Just So Stories*

A geneogram is a visual diagram of family relatedness, structure and history. It combines the usual demographic data such as age, sex and marital status with the dates of important life events such as births, marriages, divorces, and deaths. The geneogram also graphically represents the skeletal relationship structure of two or more generations of a family upon which their collisions, patterns, bonds, and the transgenerational passage of their culture may be superimposed.

The geneogram is more than a standard geneologic device or family tree. Although it does contain the usual information about the ancestry of individuals and their families, it also serves to depict the important relationship structures and patterns both past and present. It is the equivalent of a family life chart both as the family now exists, as it existed in the past and through speculation as it will or might exist in the future.

Although the geneogram is fairly widely used by family therapists, few articles have been written giving details of the rationale for its use[1] or the method of its construction. The paucity of articles may relate to the difficulty in describing an ongoing visual and dynamic process in the static medium of printed words.

Gathering information is only one of the many functions of the geneogram. For example, the geneogram functions as an educational tool. It can educate the family into an organic view of itself, provide a rationale for changes in secrecy boundaries between family members, and allow a working blueprint for change to be explained clearly to the family involved. The process of construction within the session can engage all family members in a common task, neutralise destructive conflicts temporarily and bridge intergenerational barriers. The geneogram also allows the therapist a quick and thorough entry into the family's cultural development, tradition, and belief, enabling the therapist to make sense out of the gestalt of those family members present in the therapy session. Finally, the geneogram provides a neutral task which may relieve the anxiety of a new therapist when confronting the unknown, possibly hostile or engulfing family.

Construction of the Geneogram

The geneogram may be constructed on a blackboard in the office in the presence of one or more family members, or it may be drawn by each family member on paper once the symbols used in its construction have been explained. After having been taught the means of construction of a geneogram family members can be asked to construct their own diagrams at home. In this way they can gather information from sources in their family at home to fill in missing data about their family.

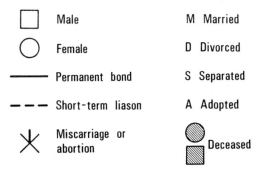

Figure 4.1 Key to Geneograms

The symbols used in the construction of a geneogram are shown in Figure 4.1. These simple symbols can be used to build up a picture of the most complex family structures. A solid line (———) between a circle and a square indicates a long-term union, either a marriage or a longstanding relationship such as common-law marriage. It is a symbol indicating that heterosexual bonding has been established. A broken line (————) between a circle and a square indicates a short-term sexual liason, such as an affair which may be included because of its importance to the development of the family quandary. A line descending from the union between a man and a woman, whether a marriage (solid line) or an affair (broken line) indicates the offspring or issue of that relationship. Children are usually listed in order of birth date from left to right, including miscarriages, and are joined on a solid horizontal line if they are full siblings. Full names may be written above each of the circles and squares and ages may be written within them. Marriage dates are written above the union line while dates of separation and divorce are written immediately below the union line.

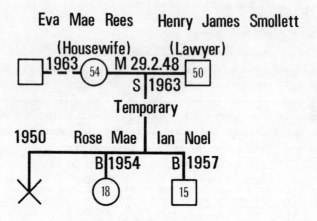

Figure 4.2   Geneogram of a Nuclear Family

Figure 4.2 is a visual representation of a nuclear family. The geneogram at its present stage reveals that Mrs Eva Mae (Rees) Smollett, a 54-year-old housewife, married a lawyer, Henry James Smollett, on the 29 February 1948. Following a miscarriage in 1950, they produced a daughter in 1954 named Rose Mae, and a son, Ian Noel, in 1957. Seven years later, in 1963, Eva had an affair with an unnamed man and separated from her husband. The separation was temporary. So far the geneogram depicts a two-generational family structure whose fourth-dimensional origin occured with the marital bond in 1948. That bond was stressed by an affair and temporary separation in 1963.

Figure 4.3 continues the geneogram construction further back in time and into the extended family including grandparents, uncles, aunts, and cousins. Arthur Michael Rees, a farmer, and Rose Mae married in 1922. They had three children, Kevin, Neal, and Eva Mae. Their respective ages at the time of the interview were sixty, fifty-eight and fifty-four. Neither Kevin nor Neal married. Arther Rees died in 1963 while Rose Mae died in 1967. George Smollett, a lawyer, married his wife, Rose, in 1919. They had two children, George Andrew, fifty-eight, and Henry James. For convenience the convention of listing offspring by date of birth from left to right has been ignored in order to show the combination of the two families of origin at the time of marriage. The ages within the circles or squares and the dates of birth give enough

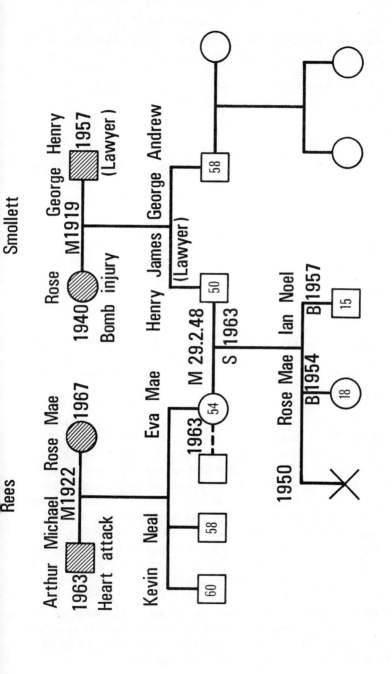

Figure 4.3 A Geneogram of an Extended Family

information to keep the birth order straight. Alternatively, separate diagrams for each side of the family may be done before combining them. To continue the description of the family shown in Figure 4.3, George Andrew married and had two daughters whose names and ages were unavailable. Rose Smollett died in 1940 while Rose Mae Rees died in 1967 from unnamed causes. Arthur Michael Rees died in 1963 from a heart attack, and George Smollet died in 1957 from unnamed causes.

A comparison of the foregoing diagrams with their written explanations should clarify the usefulness of drawing out the family structure rather than writing it down. The organised visual display depicts relationships with an overview lacking in the verbal description.

Up to this point the family diagrammed has been a relatively simple one. There are families whose complexities can tax the imagination in attempting to record their geneogram. Three of the most common complexities are reconstituted families, multiple births, and adoption. The geneogram can be of special use in recording reconstituted families. The therapist can clearly delineate the origin of each of the various children in the family to himself as well as to the family members who may never have encountered such a factual display of the structural anomalies in their family.

Figure 4.4 shows all of the previously mentioned complexities in one geneogram. The family is actually a composite of several families. June and David Rudge were married in 1950 and produced three children, Joan, and twins Simon and Justin. The twins are represented on a separate vertical line branching into two further vertical lines. That they are twins should be clear from their single date of birth as well as their equal ages. David Rudge died in 1955 in a car accident. June remarried in 1960 to Barry Hamblin. Barry had been previously married from 1958 to Heather who was pregnant with Margaret prior to marriage. On his divorce in 1960, in which June was 'the other woman', he remarried to June. Heather remarried in 1965 to Mark Sutcliffe who was fifteen years older than she. Heather had again been pregnant prior to marriage. She gave birth to John in 1966 and three years later gave birth to Josie, now a ten-year-old mentally subnormal child. June and Barry found that they couldn't have children so they adopted Dora in 1970. Mark Sutcliffe adopted his stepdaughter, Margaret, in 1970. Margaret married in 1978. In this composite family it would be possible to imagine that Margaret and her husband were referred for marital problems and that Margaret still maintained relationships with all of her relatives. It should be clear from the geneogram that there are solutions to drawing the most tangled of family relationships.

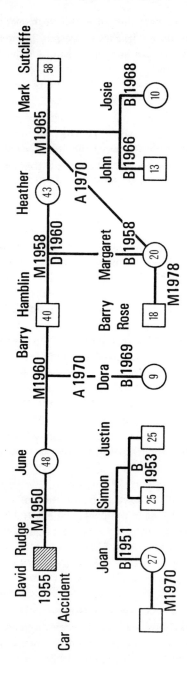

Figure **4.4** A Complex Reconstituted Family

So far my description has been limited to the mechanics of constructing a geneogram. This description has been necessary in order to convey to the reader the methods of recording, but has not yet dealt with the dynamic construction process.

The Process of Geneogram Construction

The production of the geneogram is a process in which the family members and the therapist must co-operate. The process is complex and may involve a lengthy interaction between the family members, the therapist and the diagram being constructed. It is within that process that the geneogram ceases to be a sterile shorthand of history and relatedness. It becomes instead a tool used to explore the family quandary, its origins and its possible solutions.

Here I feel it is necessary to insert a detailed clinical example of the process of geneogram construction in order to illustrate its complexities. In the following transcript I have eliminated extraneous material but have kept the temporal order of all of the interactions between the family members, the diagram and myself. This was the first family therapy session of the Slater family. They were referred to me after the identified patient had been discharged from an in-patient unit following her refusal to co-operate with the treatment offered to her. The geneogram was used to build the family structure in front of the family on a blackboard, involving all of them in the process. The initial tone of the session was one of anger and frustration. The family members felt that the psychiatric services had rejected them and that their referral to me was one of measured desperation.

Diagrams of the geneogram being constructed have been placed at appropriate intervals within the transcript in order to show its buildup throughout the session.

Therapist I know that you have been admitted to hospital with a diagnosis of anorexia nervosa but you were unable to keep to the regimen and your discharge caused a great deal of discomfort among your family. I look at things from a family point of view so you might find things strange at first. I'd like you each to tell me how this illness is a problem for you.

(Angry silence.)

Brother (George) Someone has to say something!

Father (Richard) Our problems don't necessarily arise out of Doreen's illness. There were problems simmering beneath the surface before that surfaced, erupted and then went back again.

Therapist Sometimes problems get buried and come back in different ways.

Father That's right. It was unfortunate that when Doreen first developed this I had trouble at work and the frustration was taken home. There were lots of changes. I coped with them but I snapped their heads off at home.

Therapist Can I interrupt for a second. I like to draw diagrams of the families I see on the blackboard. How old are you Doreen? (See Figure 4.5)

Sister (Doreen) Twenty-two.

Therapist How old are you? What's your name?

Brother George.

Therapist Who were you named after?

Father He was named something else but we found they didn't like it in Ireland.

Therapist What was that?

Father Named Patrick but apparently that's a Catholic name so we changed it.

Therapist Your name is?

Mother Jillian Victoria.

Therapist And your age?

Mother Fifty-eight.

Therapist And you are ...?

Father Richard Arthur and I'm fifty-two.

Therapist So you are six years older than your husband. George, did you know you were named Patrick?

Brother Yes. But I've never been called it. I have two birth certificates.

Therapist Different years?

Father No. You can change the name within three months.

Therapist I didn't know that. And when were you two born?

Brother 2 October 1955.

Sister 8 May 1952.

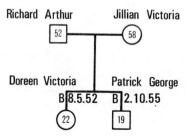

Figure 4.5 The Process of Geneogram Construction, I

Therapist Now we were talking about ...

Father How I brought short-temperedness home with me. It's always been a family trait, but the three of us have it in a different form than Mick.

Therapist Which three? Mick? Who's Mick?

(Laughter.)

Father That's the name she's called. That's the Irish part of her.

Mother Don't you write that down.

Therapist And you are not Irish?

Father No. I'm English. I flare and forget. She flares and then she sulks for days.

Sister If there's a feud she will go away to her bedroom and sulk. But we'll sit and fume in the sitting room.

Father But we tend to forget afterwards. Mick at times will bring things back that have happened in the past the next time she flares.

Brother I'm surprised she can remember them.

Therapist I've suddenly realised looking at you in the office and looking at your family geneogram on the board how isolated it looks. There are just the four of you. Is that actually true? (See Figure 4.6).

Father Well, I mean, let's face it, I have a sister, one sister.

Mother Oh dear. You want to put all that down. There won't be room on the board for my side.

Father I have one sister and one nephew.

Therapist One sister who is married and has a son.

Father My nephew is married and has two daughters. The only other relatives I have are two cousins, one in Canada and one who lives in Hastings.

Mother And you never see any of them.

Therapist Your parents are dead?

Father Yes. My family were never close unlike Mick's side which is close knit.

Therapist Are your family in Ireland or over here? (See Figure 4.7)

Mother They are all over the world but mostly in Ireland.

Therapist So you are cut off.

Father Yes, she's the odd one out. That of course has a bearing on our problems, must have.

Mother Yes, and more so now because until these last few years I used to go regularly every year but since The Troubles over there I can't bear to go there. It's awful. I know I ought to go because my father is elderly and I want to see him.

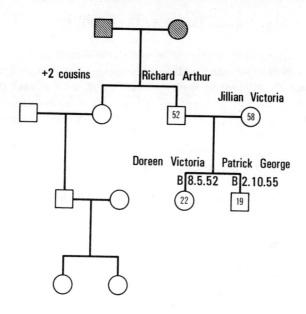

Figure 4.6 The Process of Geneogram Construction, II

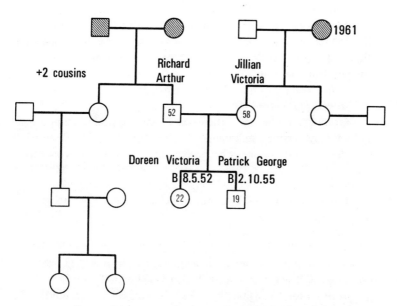

Figure 4.7 The Process of Geneogram Construction, III

Therapist How about your mother? Is she still alive?

Mother No. She died thirteen years ago. But the way things are over there, I look at The Troubles in a different way than them and it causes friction. I've lived in England most of my life since the war so I look at it from an English point of view. My sister came over with me to join up but she got married instead.

Therapist Is that when the two of you met?

Mother Yes. We met at a dance. He was passing through on the way to Africa.

Father It became a competition. All the blokes were after her and they were on permanent staff and I was in a transient unit. She was very popular.

Therapist Why was that?

Father She was good looking, a good figure and all.

Mother Compliments are flying aren't they?

Father She was a good dancer. She was good fun, and very sociable in those days.

Mother See what you have done to me. Look at me now!

Therapist You tend to do it to each other, don't you? That's the trouble with marriage; it ruins great romances.

Mother It does. It should be abolished.

Therapist We're kind of talking about and around sex really. How has that side of your relationship gone? Its not the kind of thing you like to talk about in front of children. I don't want you to spread out the lurid details but I'm wondering if you two were ever content with the physical side of it.

Mother You mean since we were married?

Therapist Or before.

Mother Oh not before — there wasn't any physical relationship before, only petting and kissing.

Therapist But you never had sexual intercourse before you were married?

(Silence.)

Mother Oh come on. You may as well be honest, if we are going to bring that up at all. I wouldn't let him.

Therapist You mean he tried.

Mother Definitely. You might as well be honest.

Father Well if we're going to be honest let's be honest. I was pretty pushy back then and I got what I wanted.

Brother I can't imagine him ever feeling that way. I accept that he probably did but I can't imagine it.

Therapist So you don't come across that way to George.

Father No. I think I come across on the cold side to them. I'm emotional inside but I strain to control it. It comes out most when I'm angry.

Therapist But it doesn't come out in other ways like sadness, love or those soft feelings?

Father They can answer that better than I can. Doreen can twist me around her little finger.

Brother He's tougher with me.

Mother You get everything you want, too.

Therapist How about you?

Mother Oh I don't get anything. I don't. I've stopped asking. (Laughter all around.)

Therapist Does that include sexual relations?

Father We stopped it. She didn't want it so we stopped. Three years ago around the time of Doreen's illness. Since Mick had the change of life.

Therapist So your periods stopped three years ago and Doreen's never started?

Sister Mine started and then they stopped when my mother stopped.

Therapist So you are going through the menopause with your mother?

(Roars of laughter.)

Doreen I don't get hot flushes or anything.

Therapist So your relationship must have changed in some way three years ago. Before that did you enjoy your relationship?

Mother Its not something you want to discuss before your family is it?

Therapist No. I'm not saying you should. But what I would like to do is get the two of you on your own so we can explore the effects of this change away from the children.

Brother I object to being called a child.

Therapist Well you are a child to them aren't you?

Father No.

Sister Of course he is.

Mother Oh, he is.

Brother Because they are used to treating me as a child they still treat me as a child in many respects, but when I go away to university I'm treated as an adult.

Mother You ask to be treated like a child sometimes. All children do until they get married and go away.

Therapist Is that what it was like with you? (See Figure 4.8)

Mother Yes. The Paisleys were like that. My parents never interfered after I married.

Therapist And who is the dominant one of you two?

Father She has to be dominant.

Therapist Yes, I should have guessed that because that's the way the sexual side has gone as well.

Father She comes from a matriarchal family and has continued to exercise that.

Therapist Did you know that when you married?

Mother No, well he didn't know it until it was too late.

Therapist So there are two big areas of conflict between you two with the kids trapped in between. First is the sexual conflict and the second is who controls the family. If you both come from different families, brought up in different ways ...

Mother Yes, his father was just like him. My sister is the only one who lets her husband run the family.

Therapist Does being like his father turn you off of him? I mean is that one of the reasons you're not able to be close together?

Mother No.

Therapist Does he turn you off?

Mother Completely!

Therapist Is it that you don't like him any more or are not in love with him any more.

Mother Yes, I'm afraid that is it. It's no use beating about the bush saying I do if I don't, is there? I suppose my feelings have just gradually worked off over the years.

Therapist You have just fallen out of love with him?

Mother I don't even like him, I hate him — no, I don't wish him harm, I don't hate him.

Father She has hated me for thirteen years!

Therapist That would be back in 1961. What happened back then other than your mother dying?

Father Ah yes, but something happened before her mother died that caused it. She had an affair with another man and I turned to someone else myself.

Mother Richard had another woman and he wanted to divorce me and take the children as well.

Therapist I see. Did you know about this?

Brother Yes, but it is only recently that we've been told.

Sister I felt before that there had been something like that. I wasn't surprised. I didn't worry, and I don't think George thought about it, he was out of the house.

Therapist But you two stayed together.

Mother Well, he wanted a divorce and he wanted the children and I knew that he couldn't have the children so I took them and went to Ireland for a change and I was there for four weeks when my mother died from a heart attack. And then Richard came over for the funeral and he asked me to come back and promised that things would be different.

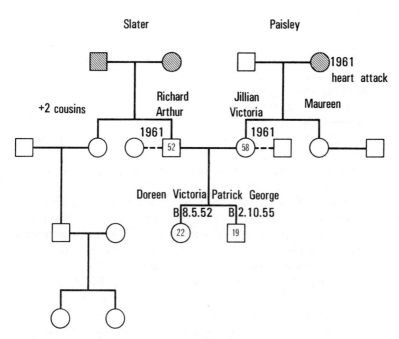

Figure 4.8 The Process of Geneogram Construction, IV

Therapist So here is one of the fundamental arguments.

Father I feel that I fulfilled my part of the bargain, that I have but she has not. She has never forgiven me and never will.

Therapist You two don't have a very good model for marriage do you?

Sister But I have to live with it. No wonder I've been depressed almost all my life.

Brother But we don't have to follow that model do we?

Sister But I can't get out. I mean I'm stuck, I've got nowhere to go. He's alright. He's at university so he's well out of it but if I leave I don't know what will happen to them.

Therapist Even if you leave you won't stop your way of thinking about them.

Mother What can we do about it?

Father She'll have to learn to live with it until she conquers this emotional bond she has to live with.

Therapist Which bond? (See Figure 4.9)

Father The bond which makes you worry even if you weren't there. I've been through it with my parents. My sister opted out. She was at nursing school and she got married and opted out completely. And I was stuck at home.

Mother Well, of course we lived with them for five years after we were married and they were always fighting and ...

Father I was always there and even when we were on our own I still had this worry, this emotional conflict over the fight that went on at home between my mother and my father and my sister ...

Therapist Are you the younger brother?

Father Yes. My sister is the same age as my wife. And when my mother died, my father lived for some years afterwards. You would never know that they argued because as far as he was concerned the only things that existed were the happy times and I wondered then why I fought and battled with them both to keep them together.

Therapist Its terrible what parents do to their children, isn't it?

Mother It is. I don't think people should have any more.

Sister No children, no world.

Therapist If you didn't have Doreen or if she starves herself to death then you could split.

Father You are assuming that we want to split. She might want to split but I don't.

Mother That's what we're trying to avoid. Doreen starving to death. As for me leaving where would I go?

Doreen They can't agree on anything.

Therapist It seems to me that families are composed of different units and it sounds as if your marital, your parent unit is the major problem and that you are both reacting in different ways, opposing ways to the quandary you're in.

Mother You're right. That's exactly it.

Therapist And Doreen and George are doing the same thing that you and your sister did with your parents.

Father You see, even when my mother died there was conflict between me and my father and my sister over the will and the possessions.

Therapist When did she die, your Mom?

Mother Twenty-three years ago wasn't it?

Brother 1951.

Therapist So Doreen wasn't born then.

Father Doreen was conceived after my mother died because my wife wanted to start a family then.

Mother I don't remember that.

Father Well, its true. It was your choice.

Therapist Rather than his?

Mother I wouldn't say rather than his. It was one of the few joint things we made.

Therapist See that. No wonder you're stuck. No wonder you can't opt out. How about George? Was he planned?

Mother He was planned. He didn't just happen.

Brother I'm surprised.

Father Ten years after we were married she had him planned. We lost one between Doreen and George, at three months.

Therapist I didn't know that. How did that affect you?

Mother Well, don't forget that the first six years of our married life we lived in two rooms in his father's house and that was a very unhappy time for me.

Therapist How did you get on with his father?

Mother Very, very badly. In fact, for years he never spoke to me and I used to take pills for my stomach all the years we stayed in that house. I felt that Richard was happy there with his father and mother and he didn't want to move. He had everything and even though it was affecting my health he wouldn't do anything about it.

Therapist When were you married?

Father 1945, in August.

Mother So in fact we have a very bad start right from the beginning.

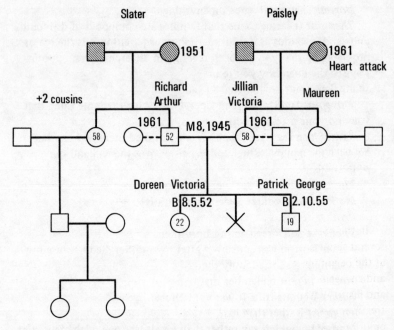

Figure 4.9   The Process of Geneogram Construction, V

Therapist Well, time is moving on and I think we'll have to stop there. I want to see the two of you alone next time. I don't know if you have learned anything new today about your parents but if you can ...

Father They must have. They said they didn't know she was good looking.

Therapist ... if you can go away at least remembering that the family quandary has to do with them and not with you I think you'll have gained something.

Brother I think we dimly realised that before we came.

Therapist Yes, well maybe none of the other doctors spelled it out. As I see it Doreen has to learn to be able to opt out more while you two have to come to some sort of resolution, and you need someone else to do it because you've been at it for several decades without doing it on your own.

Mother What will happen to your lovely little picture now. You'll have to rub it out, won't you?

Therapist No, I'm going to copy it down on to paper. I'm afraid we haven't spent any time on anorexia. But it didn't seem as important.

Mother No, we haven't, have we?

Sister Thank God.

In the process of building the geneogram in front of the Slater family several simultaneous aims were achieved. The anger and tension present at the beginning of the session were replaced by a feeling of involvement and engagement. I was able to concentrate on the family's development and history instead of being drawn into a sterile discussion about the treatment of anorexia nervosa. There was a stimulation of shared emotional closeness between all the family members and in that sharing some of the secrecy in the family between the two generations was breached. Most importantly the family quandary was separated from the individual illness. The family quandary involved fundamental and long-lasting conflicts between Mr and Mrs Slater which were themselves based in the influences from previous generations. Their marriage incorporated the socio-cultural differences between the Irish and the English. The individual family cultures added a matriarchal versus patriarchal conflict to the family collision when they were married. The death of Mr Slater's mother was followed by her replacement through the conception and birth of their daughter. The death of Mrs Slater's mother occurred in the midst of the dissolution of their marriage. Mr Slater ended his affair and rushed back to his family but the damage was done. Mrs Slater blamed her husband for her mother's death and she lost all feeling for him gradually over the remaining years. Yet her loss of feeling was only part of the picture since she needed her husband as a person whom she could continuously hold responsible for her mother's death. She continued sexual relations with her husband until her menopause. Her daughter was unhappy but trapped at home. She was very sensitive to the tension at home but unlike her brother she could not leave. The illness she developed was an individual response to the tension. By the end of the session the illness was placed in a proper perspective. Mr and Mrs Slater were later seen in joint marital sessions and their daughter returned for several conjoint sessions. She gained weight although remaining below her target weight and became much less sensitive to her parents' arguments. She eventually moved away from home in pursuit of her own career as a dress designer.

I have attempted to describe the way in which the geneogram construction process combined history-taking with the interactions between family members and therapist throughout the session. It is this process and its exploitation as a tool which opens the way to the analysis of a family quandary and the planning of therapeutic tasks and techniques which aim at the resolution of the quandary.

The Need for Detail

There are requirements for enquiring into fine details in a geneogram which arise from four major therapeutic purposes. The first of these purposes is to distinguish fact from fantasy accurately and clearly in order to establish the life history of a family. The structural skeleton of the family provided by the geneogram must be combined with a chronological skeleton, a 'life chart' of the important events in family life.

One of the short-comings of the human memory is its inability to record dates infallibly and order events in their correct time sequence. Full names, ages, dates of birth, adoption, separation, divorce, marriage, and death are all chronological landmarks to a family whose members each argue the case for the accuracy of their recall of detail. The exact dates can be determined through the use of corroborative accounts from the various family members interviewed together or separately. Written corroboration is often available from documents such as birth certificates which families store but to which they seldom refer. Chronological landmarks can settle fractious and divisive arguments about fact. These arguments are used by family members in the family sessions to avoid painful emotional issues. Comparison of previously-held but erroneous beliefs about the chronology of family life events gives access to painfully felt emotion and conflicts between family members which seemed to originate in arguments over fact. The establishment of chronological framework provides the skeleton upon which the muscle of powerful fantasies may be successfully explored.

The second purpose for detailed enquiry relates to the natural avoidance of emotional displays by family members. By encouraging families to bring to the surface their painful feelings, such as anger, sorrow, jealousy, mistrust or hatred, and unload them in the family therapy session without first having established a framework of events to which these feelings have been attached, a therapist may feel stranded in an unknown swamp and may sink in the resulting quagmire of emotions as a result. But if the therapist sinks, so too does the family. Most families, if given the chance, will avoid the expression of painful or unpleasant feelings. This avoidance can also engulf the therapist. A detailed enquiry into the family's developmental history will allow a controlled exploration of those events which arouse strong feelings. The empathic therapist will already be alerted to those areas of avoidance before the emotions crest like a tsunami to pour into the session in an uncontrolled and destructive form.

There is an example of this ability to control and direct the display of emotions in the Slater transcript. The death of Mrs Slater's mother was an area which I sensed would be emotionally explosive. I postponed exploration but later returned to it. It was at that point in the interview that the pent-up feelings of anger and sadness which were present in much of the session were finally connected with the course of events which seemed to have precipitated them. The family members were by then aware that I would continue drawing the geneogram and that there was no point in 'beating about the bush'. The controlled result of this detailed enquiry eventually provided the entire family with an understanding that the marital subsystem required help and was the major cause of the family quandary.

The third purpose of detailed enquiry comes in dealing with the continuum of secrecy within a family. I have often encountered the truth about premarital pregnancies, affairs, abortions, adoptions, and other, more terrible secret material during the process of neutral but direct enquiry about exact dates, numbers of pregnancies, medical histories or legal involvements. Since these secrets are not known by all family members present in conjoint sessions, unresolved conflicting statements, professed ignorance, or embarrassed silence may be the first indication that there is a secret present. Geneograms may actually have to be done separately with suspect family members if it is clear that certain detailed information has been deliberately withheld in a conjoint session. It is important to note the vague feelings of disquiet or reluctant eye contact that occur when detailed enquiry is poised on the threshold of an area of secrecy. One family which I visited at home chose such moments to bring out the tea and biscuits.

Finally, a detailed enquiry serves the purpose of thorough exploration of the family culture and the connection of collision of family cultures to the family quandary. The family usually appears in the session presenting a quandary which is unconnected to the manner in which the family's culture has conveyed the family to their present dilemma. Often, no illness in the family surfaced directly from their quandary; instead it appeared like Athena, born full-grown from the head of Zeus (that Zeus swallowed his mother whole who then delivered her within him carries this metaphor to its logical conclusion).

The connection of the quandary to the family culture is illustrated in the family which was referred with a ten-year-old boy with a travel phobia. His father seemed puzzlingly over-protective and treated his robust son as a delicate and precious specimen. Father's first statement that he himself was an only child had been accepted until in a later geneogram session he revealed that his mother lost four previous children by miscarriage or stillbirth. He was very precious to his parents and was treated as such. This pattern of child-rearing was brought by him into his marriage and conveyed to his child despite the very altered circumstances of his new family.

The Geneogram as a Tool

The geneogram is a tool which provides both overt and covert uses. Any tool requires knowledge, skill and practice before it can be used to its best potential. Knowledge and skill can come with practice but as any amateur do-it-yourself craftsman can testify, the initial results may not seem worth the effort. The geneogram is a tool whose uses increase with practice. The therapist who has gained skill in its use may find it a therapeutic method in itself.

The first open use of the geneogram is to enable a therapist to systematically take a history in a thorough and neutral (non-partisan) manner within the family session. Traditionally doctors have relied heavily on history-taking as providing 75 percent of the necessary information required for diagnostic purposes. There is no reason to suppose that this contribution should be any less in exploring and diagnosing a family quandary. In this history-taking process the therapist questions the family members about their names, siblings, parents, dates of birth and so on, all of which are recorded. The information gathered builds a family tree while nodal points of family additions and losses are noted, and any areas of conflict or missing information are explored further. As a history-taking tool the geneogram is as useful as the therapist employing it is skillful.

The history-taking process logically extends to use of the geneogram as an educational aid. The family must be apprised of the basic premiss of family therapy; that the family is an organism. To family members labelled with an individual illness such as depression, agoraphobia or frigidity, this concept is an alien one which must be taught. The inter-linked structure of a geneogram provides a lucid illustration of the family organism. The family educational process can then proceed to the transgenerational model of the family organism possessing the fourth dimension of time. Repetitive patterns which are visible in the geneo-gram structure from generation to generation can illustrate this point. In fact, most of the concepts applying to family therapy can be usefully taught to families using the geneogram which has been drawn on a black-board in front of the family during the session.

One further overt use of the geneogram as a tool is seen in its ability to pick out solutions to the family quandary based on similar solutions which have come to light through the exploration of extended family patterns. Many of the quandaries which have brought a particular family to therapy have been encountered and mastered in parts of the extended family without professional guidance. The geneogram is used to explore the diversity of extended family repertoires. A client family will see the solution to their quandary as much more natural if it has been planned on the model existing within their own family's experience. Blueprints for change in the client family are planned with them and gain their acceptance more readily if the change required is one which they already experienced vicariously in their uncle's nuclear family or in the nuclear family of one of their cousins.

The uses of the geneogram already mentioned can combine to provide a self-contained therapeutic method in and of itself. The following example illustrates this use on an individual patient.

Mrs Lewis was referred suffering from unremitting bouts of depression following a second marriage. Crying spells, sleep disturbance and loss of appetite were accompanied by suicidal feelings and a lack of trust in her second husband. Sexual relations with her husband had be-come totally unsatisfactory. The marital couple were in a spiralling cycle of mutual rejection.

The first session proceeded from a quick review of the present symptoms into the drawing of a geneogram (Figure 4.10). For three generations in Mrs Lewis's family most of her female relations had been unable to maintain stable marriages. Her mother had been divorced no less than five times. Mrs Lewis had been especially unhappy while dis-cussing her mother's many marriages and divorces. She felt that her mother was an incompetent woman who needed men to help structure her life, yet couldn't live with them once she had them. Her maternal grandmother, in contrast, had divorced her husband and never remarried,

preferring to remain independent. Her grandmother had proved her
resourcefulness. Mrs Lewis had been raised by her grandmother at times
and by her mother at other times during her childhood. She was
presented with two conflicting models of motherhood and relationships
between men and women. Mrs Lewis was able to realise that she had
made a poor marital choice in her first marriage and had developed her
symptoms because of her worry about having made another bad match,
confirming her fears of being like her mother rather than her grandmother.

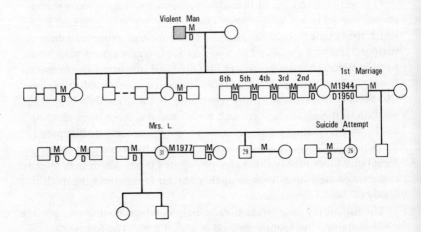

Figure 4.10 Geneogram of Mrs Lewis

The awareness of her transgenerational input was catalysed by the
process of creating a geneogram. She realised that she was the product
of familial patterns of poor marital choice and relationships. She further
realised that her symptoms grew out of the conflict of her early moulding: whether to emulate grandmother, independent and resourceful without a need for men, or whether to follow her mother's path, inadequate
and dependently bonded to men in short unhappy conflictual relationships. Her own desire was to fulfil a woman's role of sexual and family
life. This desire conflicted with her craving for independence. At this
point in the interview she suddenly recalled that her symptoms had
begun when, after two months of marriage, her husband had reneged on

their agreement to have children soon after marriage. The development of her symptoms made sense to her in that her anger at her husband was caught up in her own conflict about her need for a man upon whom to be dependent as opposed to her need to be independent. Her lack of trust in her new husband was translated by her into a lack of trust in her own abilities, her self-esteem was greatly lowered and her symptoms developed. The session concluded with her own conscious decision to attempt to merge the best of her mother and grandmother as models. She became more independent from her husband and he reacted by feeling less threatened by her and drawing closer. Their marital and sexual life improved during the following month so that by her return appointment her symptoms had disappeared. At her one-year follow-up appointment she remained happily married without further difficulties.

In this example the geneogram served as a treatment method on its own. History-taking is not ordinarily a substitute for treatment. But when awareness and insight gained from the exploration of the past leads directly to family members changing their behaviour towards their family, the exploration is the treatment. The geneogram is an excellent way of systematically providing increased awareness of family influences upon family members. The meanings which are inherent in the family patterns are readily perceived by family members without the need to provide extensive theoretical explanation. If in each of three or four generations marital disharmony has been the rule then, as in the case of Mr and Mrs Lewis, it is not surprising to find the same quandary developing in the present relationship. Mrs Lewis was fortunate in having been moulded in two differing ways so that her insight could lead to a spontaneous and conscious process of integrating her two models, changing her behaviour and relieving the family quandary.

This overt use of the geneogram is a limited one. There are those families whose members understand the meaning of their family background, realise the transgenerational patterns that influence their interactions, yet cannot alter their relationship rules. In fact, the knowledge of repetitive and destructive family patterns can lead families to fatalistically accept the unchanging nature of their quandary. The therapist is then placed in the position of providing cassandraic insights which further entrench the family in their pathology. In these families the use of the geneogram must be to change the present through the understanding the therapist gains of the family. The geneogram enables the therapist to plan tasks and changes in relationship in order to alter previously inflexible family positions.

So far the uses of the geneogram have been described as those which are open and straightforward. But there are covert experiential elements in the use of the geneogram. The first and most obvious is the introduction of the geneogram as a task which involves the entire family. The family members are provided with their first experience of task-setting as well as being required to work together and involve themselves in a common enterprise. This experience may be the first time in many weeks, months or years that a fragmented family share a common task. While briefly working together they may prove the feasibility (if only temporarily) of a new way of relating.

Engaging the family in a common task is less traumatic when the sensible and legitimate task is that of helping inform a stranger about the intricacies of the family's origins and structure. The family work together in order to give an account of their quandary and its historical background and in so doing become engaged in the therapeutic process.

While using the geneogram I became aware of another covert use to which it can be applied. The geneogram eases family members unknowingly into the discussion and experiencing of deeply felt emotions. Some of these emotions were being consciously withheld while others were not known to be present until memories were stimulated by the systematic geneogram construction. For example when the Dudley family were being seen in a session, Mr Dudley was describing the death of his first-born daughter with little emotion. Mrs Dudley reacted angrily and chastised him for his lack of reaction. Neither of them had shared their feelings in relation to the tragic death of their daughter and Mr Dudley in turn became angry. In his anger he disclosed to the family the fact that he had been attending a spiritualist in attempts to contact their daughter. He began to sob uncontrollably as the memory returned to him. The emotions which are stimulated are shared amongst other family members present in a context that makes sense to them because of the manner in which the feelings are linked to the original events which stimulated them.

The neutralisation of destructive conflicts is another feature of the covert use of geneograms, for it is temporarily able to concentrate the attention of antagonists on to common ground. This use was put into play several times in the Slater interview, when the parents were combining in their hostility towards their daughter and when their anger towards each other was threatening to break through in a destructive way.

Neutralisation of conflict and the stimulation of emotion which is then shared have led to the covert use of the geneogram as a method of bridging the intergenerational gap between family members. The construction of the geneogram allows the family members of the older generation to expose their lives in a new way to the scrutiny of the younger generation and vice versa. Through relating the experiences, anxieties and fantasies which were present in their own youth, the older generation create new conditions of relating to their children and grandchildren. Empathy is increased and a bridge of understanding can be established which will hopefully widen into a highway of mutually-shared emotional links. For example, when Mrs Burgoyne had finally managed to cajole her mother into a therapy session she was apprehensive about her mother's hostility. Mrs Burgoyne had suffered from years of bitterness between herself and her mother in reaction to her pre-marital pregnancy. When her mother told of her own premarital pregnancy and subsequent forced marriage the years of bitterness were temporarily forgotten in a wave of mutually felt and shared emotion. These intergenerational bridges can become key elements in the planning of further therapeutic moves towards change.

Since the geneogram can be used to provide a breathing space for the family members and the therapist, it can be used by the therapist as a way of distancing the immediate engulfing emotional climate before it becomes too great a burden. For the therapist who works alone there are times when it is essential to have a method of easing his own anxiety. A geneogram used in this way must be judiciously applied. Searching for past causes in order to avoid present emotions, and with no prospect of future changes, is history-taking for the therapist, not the family. Similarly an interminable analysis of the information obtained can help conceptualise the quandary of the family without making the solution less painful or less difficult. If survival in a particular family requires history-taking too often the therapist must look to his awareness of his problems with his own family in order to continue successful treatment of that family.

For example, a husband and wife were continually in conflict over their middle son who was caught stealing. I returned to the geneogram session after session until the family were obviously disconcerted with my obsession. I was aware of an emotional block in myself, while the sessions had taken on the indefinite quality of a Pinter play. At that point I carefully and consciously considered my own family structure and conflicts. The awareness of my similar position as a middle son whose adolescent thieving was a source of conflict for his parents at one time enabled me to feel and express my own emotions in the following session, and use my family's successful handling of the crisis in a constructive way rather than continue unnecessary history-taking.

Summary

The geneogram is a formidable tool for use in the practice of family therapy. Its mechanical construction can be readily assimilated by professionals and family members alike. Its uses are broadly characterised as overt and covert. Overt uses include history-taking of both matters of fact and of feeling. The family can be educated into the basic premises of family therapy, transgenerational theory or other theories related to the family approach. The information acquired can be used by the therapist as a blueprint for change, and in some instances the geneogram construction can become a therapeutic technique in itself. Covert uses of the geneogram are experiential and include uses of benefit to the therapist and the family. The geneogram introduces family members to the task-setting process, engages family members in a common task, neutralises conflicts and stimulates emotional sharing. It allows the building of new bridges between family members.

Finally it can be used as a means of keeping the therapist from being engulfed by the emotions of the family. Care must be exercised so that the geneogram is not employed by the therapist to avoid facing the issues of change in therapy, rather than aiding these issues.

Note

1. S. Lieberman, 'Transgenerational Analysis: The Geneogram as a Technique in Family Therapy', *Journal of Family Therapy*, vol. 1 (February, 1979); P.J. Guerin and E.G. Pendagast, 'Evaluation of Family System and Geneogram', in P.J. Guerin (ed.), *Family Therapy* (Gardner Press, New York, 1976), pp. 450-64.

5 TRANSGENERATIONAL ANALYSIS

Boy, the quarrel was before your time,
the aggressor no one you know
You've got their names to live up to
and questions won't help,
You've a very full programme ...

> W.H. Auden, 'Which Side Am I Supposed to Be on?',
> 1932

For in the background figures vague and vast
Of patriarchs and of prophets rose sublime
And all the great traditions of the past
They saw reflected in the coming time.

> H.W. Longfellow, 'The Jewish Cemetery at Newport'

Those who cannot remember the past are condemned to
repeat it.

> George Santayana

Transgenerational analysis is the analysis of the passage of family culture
in its broadest sense from one generation to the next. Within the boundaries of analysis are those beliefs, conflicts, customs, myths, patterns,
practices and styles which determine the uniqueness of a family.

In a family session the geneogram is used to obtain as much information as possible about the client family and their quandary. The chapter
on transgenerational theory developed various areas of emphasis: the
passage of behaviour, belief and tradition from one generation to the
next, the meaning and importance of emotional bonds formed between
family members, family collisions during and after marital choice, the
role of family losses and their replacements, the family secrecy continuum and the developmental process of family evolution. But these sup-
positions must be translated into a practical approach to the family
members presenting themselves for help.

I wish to deal in this chapter with the practical analysis of the
material obtained from family sessions. Since material from family
sessions assaults the therapist's senses visually, verbally, and emotionally
from many different family members simultaneously, some sort of
analysis is required in order to simplify the complexity of communica-

tion and sieve out extraneous material. It is in the correct choice of significant material that the therapist's skill and judgement is proven when constructing meaningful hypotheses about a particular family and its quandary. There are six areas of family life upon which I have concentrated my attention in family sessions. They have provided me with a workable shorthand for understanding a family and its transgenerational influences.

Sibling Positions and Family Constellation

The theory of family constellation and its importance as a basic personality and marital determinant was developed to its greatest level of sophistication by Toman.[1] He first defined the family constellation as the parents and siblings of a particular individual and later expanded it to include an individual's parents, siblings and also his parents' parents and siblings. An individual's sibling position in his family of origin was held to determine his or her character in so far as oldest siblings have much in common with each other, as do youngest siblings, only children and so on.

There are at least seven areas of interpersonal learning and moulded behaviour which can be defined and considered in terms of the amount of experience a particular sibling position will convey. These areas include learning within relationships with adult family members (parents), opposite sex siblings, older (dominant) siblings, and younger (submissive) siblings. There is also a continuum of relationship skills determined by the total number of siblings present in the family. In this continuum larger numbers of siblings in a family tend to produce a greater versatility of range of skills. Self-reliance and leadership skills are also subject to influences of sibling position.

Not only do sibling positions determine certain personality characteristics, they may also determine the outcome of a subsequent marital choice and the satisfactory experience of the marital partners within the marriage. Finally sibling position influences the children produced from a marriage, depending on all of the respective sibling positions of the child, mother and father.

There are twelve major types of sibling position. A brief description of each is provided in order to illustrate the differences in their moulded characteristics. *The descriptions are by no means comprehensive nor can they be accepted rigidly.* The descriptions are broadly applicable, all other influences being equal. For example, a sibling whose only other sibling was six or more years older would have had relatively little contact with that older sibling and might be more likely considered similar in character to an only child due to the wide age gap. Neighbourhood and extended family influences can strongly affect these profiles as well.

The Oldest Brother of Brothers

The oldest brother of brothers is the stronger, wiser and most responsible of siblings in that he grows up as the first-born and is literally stronger, wiser and more responsible than the brothers which come afterwards for much of their early years. His initial relationships are with adults so that he has solitary experiences of the adult world in his early formative life before his brothers appear on the scene. But he also learns to relate to his younger brothers when they appear. It is no cultural accident that the first-born son has had a special role as keeper of tradition and authority in many societies. Being the older brother of brothers means that he will have little experience of women while growing up. His mother will be the sole feminine influence of any close nature. This inexperience with an intimate female sibling relationship will limit his ability to identify the feminine side of himself and limit his skill in relating to members of the opposite sex as he grows older. Since he has no experience of dominant siblings, he will tend to feel the natural leader of any peer group or marriage relationship. His lack of siblings as an infant and toddler will have thrown him more on his own resources, leading him to play more on his own and establish a pattern of self-reliance which will be emphasised when his next youngest sibling appears and his mother's time is taken up by the new baby.

The Youngest Brother of Brothers

The youngest brother of brothers is the baby of the family. He is usually more spoiled, more dependent and in danger of remaining so. He is often over-protected by both parents and older siblings and his path in life is eased by the experience of his brother before him. Never having had his parents solely to himself, his relationship skills in dealing with them are less sure than those of the oldest brother. He can never dominate the siblings in his own family in his early years. This places him in the frustrating position of striving to outdo his older brother(s) who have sheltered and broken ground for him, without being able to better them until later in life. Leadership skills do not come naturally to him, there being no one younger to lead, and playing alone would have been a difficult occupation when older siblings were available and often willing, so that self-reliance would have been stifled. Because of a lack of sisters the youngest brother's ability to relate to members of the opposite sex would be curtailed, and would have to be learned when grown up. The position as baby of the family may lead to resignation and acceptance of this role or over-compensation into vaulting ambition in order to escape from the earlier position.

The Oldest Brother of Sisters

The oldest brother of sisters remains the self-reliant, strong, responsible and dominant sibling who tends towards an assumption of the role of leadership in all situations but has a lack of general relationship skills to the one-sided nature of his position as oldest. His experience with his sisters gives him the added ability to relate to peers of the opposite sex more readily, although his relationships will tend to remain ones in which he is dominant. His lack of brothers will cause him to find relationships with male peers to be more difficult and less rewarding since he would never have experienced the rough and tumble life that comes in childhood with brothers. If he were the oldest brother of mixed siblings his ability to relate with both sexes would be enhanced.

The Youngest Brother of Sisters

The youngest brother of sisters will have difficulty in relating to the older generation since his sisters will most probably have taken over some of mother's role. His relationship with his sisters will be a sub-missive one although his natural male aggressiveness will increase conflict. He will at least have experience with the opposite sex and will have gained some expertise in living with women which will make him more familiar with the situation when he marries. His relationship with same-sex peers will suffer through his inexperience at home. The masculine side of his nature will be less freely expressed and his tolerance of his non-dominant position will be greater. Leadership skills and self-reliance will be lacking since they will not have had the natural opportunity to develop. He is in danger of being spoiled, dependent and somewhat effeminate while remaining as the baby of the family.

The Oldest Sister of Sisters

The oldest sister of sisters has developed along similar lines to the oldest brother of brothers. She will have had an early experience of being on her own with her parents, forging relationship skills which will serve her in later years. Having been used to playing on her own she will be able to rely on her own resources. When her sisters are born she will be able to dominate them and lead them, providing strong experience of leader-ship skills, but she will not have the experience of flexibly being able to submit to other older siblings while dominating younger ones. Since the family will consist of sisters, mother and father, no experience can be gained in relating to the opposite sex on a day-to-day basis. The oldest sister of sisters is in a good position to stand on her own feet when she grows up and will be more likely to seek satisfaction in a career or as the dominant partner in a marriage.

The Youngest Sister of Sisters

The youngest sister of sisters will have little experience of being on her own and will always have had to share her parents with her sisters. She will have had no relationship with brothers so that her ability to relate to men will have to be learned in later life except for her relationship with her father. Because of her position as the baby in the family she will tend to be spoiled, pampered and dominated. She is more likely to become daddy's little girl and remain so. None of her intimate family relationships will naturally equip her with experience of leadership, self-reliance or dominance. Her ability to manage on her own will be much less than that of her oldest sister. She will have had little opportunity to learn from her own mistakes as there will have always been those around her to teach her the tasks with which they struggled and she is faced.

The Oldest Sister of Brothers

The oldest sister of brothers will have her position of leadership and authority challenged by her naturally more aggressive brothers. Nevertheless, the self-reliant qualities developed while she was the sole child in the family will remain and may even be enhanced through her conflicts with her younger brothers. Her relationships with her brothers will be competitive. Her relationships with other women will be limited in experience to those with her mother in her early years so that she might become a most competitive peer with others of her own age and sex. If she has gained the upper hand in her sibling rivalry with her brothers she may remain in a comfortable position of dominance to which she will have become accustomed. Loss of her leadership role as the oldest and first-born would increase her insecurity about her natural dominant position and make later relationships more ambivalent.

The Youngest Sister of Brothers

The youngest sister of brothers occupies the most submissive of postures in the sibling position catalogue. She is the baby of the family, dominated by men, over-indulged, spoiled and allowed little space to develop along the lines of self-reliance. Her ability to relate to her brothers will be limited by her submissiveness and she will have few opportunities to develop leadership skills since her relationship with other women will be based on that of being the youngest and weakest in the family. Her relationship skills developed within the family atmosphere will be strictly limited and would have to be developed in later life. Relationships with the older generation will be diluted by her relationships with her brothers.

The Middle Children

Families consisting of more than two children provide middle positions which allow for a greater development of relationship skills. The middle sibling experiences both dominance and submissiveness in his or her sibling relationships. The leadership skills are developed in relation to younger siblings while relations with the older sibling teach a follower role. Middle siblings tend to be able to compromise, take the middle road and generally assume a moderate stance as a result of the middle position in the family in which compromises tend to become necessary. The eldest is seen by the middle child as having been given more responsibility, authority and privilege while the youngest is seen as having been indulged and allowed to behave in ways unacceptable for himself.

While taking these skills of greater flexibility into later life, the ability to take a definite stand when required does not come naturally to the middle child. Relationships with peers of the opposite sex are determined by the position of the middle child in relation to siblings of the opposite sex and their positions.

The Only Child

The only child occupies the peculiar position of having grown up solely in adult company for the most formative years of life. The only child is more subject to the idiosyncratic influence of parents' strengths and conflicts. The only child cannot gain from his or her brothers and sisters the relationship experiences lacking from being with parents. The only child also misses out on learning the art of raising children by objectively watching the treatment of siblings by his or her parents. The only child is also deficient in experience of relating to other children in an intimate way through lack of that experience with brothers and sisters. Since their sole early childhood involves child-parent relationships they tend to seek a similar relationship when they have matured, picking a spouse who tends to be more of a parent to them or a child to them than a peer. The only child is deficient in dominant and submissive relationships as well as relationships with the opposite sex. Having had parents as their sole model of behaviour they are raised from an early age to be self-reliant and adult-like, or paradoxically extremely dependent and childish.

The only child position is a deficient one unless mitigating circumstances such as the presence of intimate relations with extended family or neighbours prevail.

These sibling position profiles are only idealised representations. Their significance lies more in the revelation of expected tendencies than specific details about each and every family member. Variations from these tendencies in the particular family member being seen or discussed provide some insight into his or her development. For example, deaths of siblings can alter the expected character effects. The number of years between siblings also has an effect in that the closer together chronologically the more attached and rivalrous two siblings will tend to become.

In analysing a family the parent's sibling position in their own family of origin is as important as that of the children. If father was the oldest brother of brothers he will form a special bond with his oldest son, both of whom share unique experiences conveyed by the sibling position. It may be that if he has no eldest son he will attempt to mould his daughter into one, or expect more from a son, the youngest brother of sisters, than the son is able to achieve. Sibling positions can therefore provide important signposts towards the type and quality of bond formed between the older and younger generations as well as providing information about character. Sibling position can also explain why one child has been singled out for carrying certain symptoms. If, in each generation, the youngest daughter is expected never to marry and to care for the parents in their old age then the youngest daughter may very well be treated for rebellious behaviour in adolescence, especially in this era when greater cultural freedoms are clashing with family expectations and culture.

Finally, sibling position can give important data on the likely problems to be encountered in a marriage. Broadly speaking, the suitability of a marital bond will be based on the compatibility of the husband's and wife's sibling position. By compatible sibling positions I mean complementary positions occupied respectively by each party. For example, if the oldest brother of sisters marries the youngest sister of brothers then each partner has recreated a living-together situation similar to that which existed in their own family of origin. The couple at least starts off having set up a relationship which repeats one that is familiar to them in many aspects. But if the youngest brother of brothers marries the youngest sister of sisters both would be entering into a marriage which recreates none of the sibling relationships which were familiar. Each would be awaiting the other partner's dominance while neither would have experience of living with a member of the opposite sex.

Since marital choice is not determined by sibling position but by other factors already discussed, there is much scope for erroneous choice and subsequent conflict. For this reason it is important to know the sibling position of parents or members of marital couples. Several studies of marital couples have confirmed the validity of these claims[2] although one failed to confirm that marriages are less successful if the sibling positions conflict.[3]

I have tried to describe sibling profiles and build a case for their importance in analysing family quandaries. The transgenerational analysis is based on each family member's sibling position and the inter-relationship between these positions from generation to generation. Awareness of the broad sibling position profiles is tempered by attention to the more parochial attributes of various sibling positions within the family in question.

The Importance and Timing of Entries and Exits

A history of all the major life events, the entries and exits from the family system, is vital information in the understanding of the family's culture and evolution. The chronological timing of these events provides an insight into the designation of family members who may be replacements for dead relatives. I believe that the forming and sustaining of bonds and the family reaction to disruption of those bonds are occurrences which figure prominently in the precipitation of family quandaries. The detailed information obtained in a geneogram which includes dates, ages and timing of life events while providing the chronology of the life of the family is sought as a preliminary to the more thorough exploration of losses from the family and their subsequent replacements.

Seeking information about the effect of deaths can be a trying and painful emotional experience for the family who resist the expression of long-buried feelings, as well as for the therapist who must be able to tolerate the feelings being stimulated, remain empathic, and continue to question the family members despite their distress or avoidance. Inexorable and pitiless but empathic questioning is necessary in order to break through the barriers and family relationship rules which are defensively produced. The investigation of losses should begin with the factual account of those losses as they occurred during the nuclear family's existence, often proceeding from the present into the past. When did your father die? What was the cause of his death? How did he die? How did you (each family member) react when he died? How did

your mother (aunt, sister, brother, etc.) react? The questions should
seek to re-establish a vivid memory of the loss and its effect while seeking out the current feelings welling up beneath the surface of the family
as the investigation proceeds. Since the dates, causes and reactions to the
losses are so crucial to the understanding of the family quandary the
investigation may need to continue back through all of the losses
sustained in the family's total life experience.

For example, John Patton was a sixteen-year-old lad who was
referred with his family for therapy following dreadful rows at home
with his parents during which he had slapped his mother. The family
were seen together and consisted of John, Marsha (aged twelve), Albert
(aged nine), and their mother and father. John's behaviour during the
beginning of the session was exemplary, yet he was criticised harshly by
his parents. Their geneogram construction revealed a hesitancy and
secrecy on the part of the parents. We were side-tracked and unable to
continue due to a lengthy argument about John by his parents in which
the children were all eventually included and which led to John walking
out. It was two sessions later that a detailed history of losses in the
family revealed the birth and death of a fourth child named Joan. She
had been born out of a premarital pregnancy and the pregnancy had
precipitated the final decision of the parents to marry. Joan was born
but lived only three months. She was remembered by her parents as
perfect in every way. After her death the parents quickly tried for a replacement child and John was conceived. He could never live up to their
image of Joan's perfection, so that his normal behaviour was perceived
from the start as extremely disruptive. The parents couldn't relinquish
the image of the child which had forcibly cemented their relationship.
Only by probing into the area of losses from the family was the information about Joan obtained and related to the present quandary. The
question in the third interview which had started the parents talking was,
'Had there been any other deaths in the immediate family that you
haven't mentioned?' This question was met by a pregnant silence which
was broken by my statement that there was something important to
them that they were not sharing with me.

The quandary in the Patton family became clear as did its solution
through the analysis of the family history. A family which began its
life through a forced marriage and pregnancy had continued to exist as
a monument to the dead child who had been idealised and replaced by
her brother. After thorough explanation of the circumstances, the
parents became more realistic in their expectations of John and he was
freed from attending the sessions in which a forced mourning procedure

was adopted with the parents.

Deaths are the most memorable and easily documented of losses from a family but there are other losses which can be equally upsetting. The effect of divorce has many repercussions for children as well as the extended family and is a major loss from the family system. Although divorce has been increasing both in frequency and rate during the past century in Western society; the effects of divorce have been a subject little explored in the family therapy literature. Divorce is a major disruption of the nuclear family. It can stimulate the same feelings of loss which death does while the divorced spouse remains available without requiring a permanent readjustment.

Exploration of divorce in the family history can arouse all of the old hurts and pain which were present during the destruction of the original bond. The circumstances surrounding the divorce and its aftermath may contain within them the seeds of the new family quandary. For example, a family in which the husband had been married for the third time had as its presenting complaint the marital strife between the couple. The wife had been cited in the husband's second divorce as co-respondent and the role she had played in the ending of that second marriage was remembered with bitterness by the husband. His family background revealed a history of marital strife and divorce in previous generations.

Permanent losses of family members through adoption out of the family or through estrangement or immigration are also important to establish in the chronology of the family. These losses may either have precipitated the family quandary or become the irrevocable result of the quandary. The injudicious placing of an infant for adoption haunted one family for many years during which the parents were unable to share their feelings of loss and grief. They each blamed the other and their marriage became one of constant bickering.

I am equally interested in the entries into families and their timing. Family members come into a family either through birth, adoption or marriage. The circumstances surrounding the entry of a family member through marriage are as important to ascertain as any detail in family life. Each new marriage is a nodal point in family life. The presence of children in a session is no barrier to a full exploration of the courtship. The children may have already heard of some of the details but are entitled to hear the rest of the story except for those intimate sexual details which remain between the married couple. In my experience, many of the families referred to me arrive with their present quandary rooted in those early crucial months or years of courtship and marriage.

Investigation of the marital bond involves a thorough exploration of the timing of its establishment from the first meeting through to the honeymoon period. How had they met? Was there a wide or narrow field of choice? Had it been love at first sight? Were either of the choices made consciously or unconsciously on the basis of parental images? Had there been a death or other family loss prior to courtship? Was another sibling married about the same time? Was the marriage made on the rebound? Was there a forced choice through pregnancy or imagined pregnancy? Was it an arranged marriage? The answers to these questions and many more tell how and on what basis the marital bond was forged. The subsequent adjustment of the marital partners is dependent on those initial circumstances.

Similar detailed information obtained about each birth and adoption into the family in question may be necessary. I use details such as whether a child was planned or unplanned, which sex was wanted, and what circumstances occurred during the pregnancy and birth of the child to explore the parents' preconceptions about each child before it was born.

The whole of the data on family entries and exits is analysed for the patterns of response to loss which have run through the generations of the family, as well as the patterns of accomodation which have been present as each new member of the family appears on the family scene.

Clues to Replacements in Families: Names and Resemblances

There are broad sociocultural determinants which coexist with more narrow familial tendencies in the naming of children. In Jewish families, it is a religio-cultural tradition to name children after family members who have died. Greek families name the first son and daughter after the paternal grandfather and grandmother respectively. Some English families name children after living relatives or friends while others choose names for their aesthetic appeal, making certain that the names are not family names. In a seminar when I raised this subject I was informed of a Scottish family in which tradition dictated that each of the first three sons bore a name reserved for that sibling position over the generations, so that, if one knew the code, the sibling position of each male member of the family could be ascertained.

The naming of a child after a living or dead relative may be done openly by using the same name and spelling, or it may be done more subtly by using a variation of that name. Names are significant when they indicate the occurrence of a replacement in a family. This is heralded at an early stage by the awareness that both parents show towards the significance of the name. The parents often begin to react to the infant in such a way as to mould in some of the characteristics of the relative whose name is used. Their expectations of the development of the infant are coloured by their expectations of a relationship similar to that with the original relative. This process can be casual or intense depending on the underlying strength of the bonds between the parents and the person after whom the infant is named, and is further compli-cated if this person is aware of the significance of the name and takes an active role in influencing the growth and development of the child.

Ann Carter was named after her aunt, her mother's sister. Her aunt was a constant influence in her life, living on the same street and taking care of her own ageing mother. Her maiden aunt's devotion to Ann's grandmother was a model which Ann was expected to follow by both mother, aunt and grandmother. Ann was endowed with a warm, affec-tionate and caring disposition but unlike her aunt also grew into a sexually attractive young woman. Her family brought her to treatment because of their fears that she might become sexually promiscuous. The clue to the transgenerational influence initially was her name. She was herself fearful of her own sexuality with no awareness of the basis for that fear.

The significance of a name can be more obscure. An Indian family explained that the name of their son could not possibly have any signif-icance since the name was chosen because it was the name of a particular subdeity in the Hindu pantheon. This fact was important in itself since personality characteristics of a child are matched with those same characteristics assigned to the various subdeities. For example, Rama is a name given to children because of its association with righteousness and nobility. The name of the Indian lad proved to be more significant, since it was revealed through intensive questioning that both his father and grandfather had been named after different attributes of the same deity.

The point I am trying to raise is that the name one receives from one's parents is the first transgenerational transmission to the newborn child. It is a form of self-fulfilling prophecy in which the parents declare their feelings and expectations towards an infant whose character is not yet moulded. These feelings are usually a combination of the intrinsic feelings of the parents and the influences of other relatives on the parents. Through names, continuity with one or the other of the married couple's families can be ensured or denied. Family names can be continued or tradition scrapped, but either choice is a statement of transgenerational influences.

The choice of a particular name may determine the attitude of the extended family toward the child. Myrtle Greer's grandmother had a schizophrenic sister named Myrtle who was alive but remained unvisited and shunned in a mental hospital. Her grandmother shunned Myrtle from her infancy. An antipathy developed between them which strained relations between her grandmother and her entire family of origin. Myrtle developed genuine feelings of distaste and dislike towards her grandmother in reaction to the rejection. When her grandmother died she was filled with remorse and guilt which affected her children and husband, leading to her referral.

I have observed that names can also designate to which of the two extended families a child is assigned. One son may be named from the maternal side of the family, another from the paternal side and a third may have a combination of the two in separate names. The first son would be the mother's to mould in her family tradition; the second child is the father's to mould in his family tradition; and the third child may either symbolise the merging of traditions or the conflict of traditions between the two parents.

I have not dwelled on the symbolic meaning of the name itself, such as Faith, Charity, or Jesus, although I am aware of their significance and potential importance in family quandaries. I seek out a person's full name because I have found its symbolic meaning to be a shorthand in the family for making their children recipients of particular transgenerational influences. For this reason transgenerational analysis uses a person's full name as a possible clue to these influences — a marker in order to trace personality similarities, replacements, and other patterns which were passed from one generation to the next.

Physical resemblance of family members from one generation to the next can also provide evidence for the decoding of transgenerational influences. The resemblance may be genetic, as in children born with prominent features (such as red hair or a large nose) which are similar to those of a relative, or they may be chosen, as happens during marital choice. The resemblance may be actual and obvious to all; or it may be either subtle or fantasied with no objective physical resemblance at all. The process with children begins often at birth with statements like 'He's got your father's eyes', or 'He looks just like your Aunt Hazel'.

The family photo album is a valuable resource in the decoding of these resemblances for it provides a record of the actual physical details of relatives' appearance. The relatives may have changed or died or become unavailable through distance so that the photos may be the only objective evidence remaining. Family resemblance may be striking between two family members when they are compared photographically in pictures taken when they were the same age. Members of the older generations will be aware of the resemblance. As the child develops they may have commented upon it as well as reacting to the particular child as if he or she is a budding younger version of the older relative.

Mr Merkin noted the resemblance between his youngest daughter and his own mother when his daughter was very young. His daughter was moulded into the personality characteristics which his mother had possessed. She was even given his mother's pet name. In her late teens her struggle to become independent led to severe conflict at home. Her father had, by this time, forgotten about the physical resemblance until it flooded back to him in a therapy session while viewing old photos.

Physical resemblances may actually be purely fantasies — wishes on the part of relatives for a living image of a dead relative. I have been occasionally surprised by the vehemence with which a claimed family resemblance is held despite objective proof to the contrary. The claimed resemblance (presumed to be present from birth) is absent in photographs.

The choice of a marital partner may have been made initially on the basis of physical resemblance to a loved relative. Photos will often reveal this similarity and can provide an objective entry into the entire issue of marital choice and its transgenerational determinants.

Family Collision and Differences in Family Culture

Family collision alludes to the fact that each of the participants in the marital bond have been moulded in their own unique family culture prior to their marriage. Many of the differences in their expectations of each other are clashes of those cultures. Parenting practices, duties of wives or husbands, and relationships to extended family members, are three important areas of disagreement which may become family quandaries, but the conflicts can extend to clashes over religion, politics, sexual practices, reactions to loss and so on.

My concern in the transgenerational analysis of the information gleaned from the geneogram process is to build a picture of the two extended families within my mind. I try to reconstruct the accommodations that the marital couple or parents have made in order to reconcile the differences in their background. I can then predict those areas which remain and which may require work to resolve the problems for which the family is seeking help. Since each of the two family cultures still exist, the current relationships of the extended family with the nuclear family are as important as those which existed in the past. Each of the two family cultures have differences and similarities in their expectations. Analysis of the differences serves to uncover areas of conflict which are seminal to the development of the family quandary. These conflicts may remain buried or papered over for the sake of the marital coalition, while the family have become focused upon superficial problems which they bring into the therapy session.

The investigation needed to analyse these differences begins in the courtship period. Did each of the two families approve of the prospective spouse? What were their objections? Did these objections become modified? Did a family feud develop over the marriage? What happened to extended family relationships after the marriage? How much contact was maintained? Is it still being maintained? What are the current relationships with in-laws, parents, siblings and other relatives like? Do they give advice, interfere, or help? The investigation should follow the path of the various relationships to the present.

Mr and Mrs Bowden were married after a courtship in which both families objected. Mrs Bowden was never certain of her feelings towards her husband but she was certain that she wanted to escape from her parents and that her parents disapproved of her marital choice. When the marriage occurred both sides of the family maintained a distant and cool relationship with the couple and often predicted that the marriage wouldn't last. The couple were referred with a list of problems including marital difficulties, non-consummation of the marriage, depression of the wife, and apathy in the husband. Mrs Bowden came from the North of England and expected a home always open to the neighbours, and a husband full of talk who was active and somewhat explosive. Her husband was Sussex-born and tended to be naturally quiet and reserved, and minded his own business to the exclusion of the neighbours and often his wife. Any conflict led him to maintain a deep silent sulk. It was this north-south conflict which had come to symbolise their marriage for them. They ignored past transgenerational influences which had left them isolated from their families of origin without any family resources to tackle their differences. When a discussion ensued in therapy in which I focused on their respective families of origin, it became clear that the family feud had been acted out in the marriage from the wedding day when both sides of the family met at the wedding but did not mingle with each other afterwards. The non-consummation was real, and it was a symbol of the inability of the two to resolve their transgenerational differences.

In the preceding case, the lack of resolution between the married couple existed because their differences were too great. Other quandaries involving only one or two areas can be more amenable to correction. The Slater family had resolved their Irish-English differences and some of their sexual and marital role expectations during their years of marriage. Their true quandary was related to the reaction to loss which they were unable to fully deal with together and therefore isolated themselves from each other.

The family collision is a concept in transgenerational analysis which can be pictorially observed in the geneogram by following the various two sides of the families as they funnel themselves down the generations to the presenting couple or family. Differences in religion, race, family constellation, nationality, or regional origins, and any difference which is made obvious by a socio-cultural factor like occupation of grandparents, education, or urban versus rural upbringing, are important areas of exploration when faced with an apparently inexplicable difference in the expectations of the marital partners.

Family Patterns

When looking at a geneogram of a family there are certain patterns which immediately stand out. The most prominent is the repetition of family constellations. Perhaps a grandparent may have grown up in a family whose family constellation was exactly the same as the family being treated. Or the parent's family constellation is the same as that of their child's family. Just as the sibling position brings with it certain characteristics, the family constellation also brings certain similarities of experience and identification. If I was raised as an only child, and my mother was raised similarly, then there is an interlocking shared experience between my mother, myself, my parents and my mother's parents. Each repetition of the same family constellation in regard to the position and sex of the children will increase the chances of stronger bonding between those similar units.

Repetitive patterns are also evident in common life experiences. If there are spinsters in each of several succeeding generations then a pattern is established. If there are successions of premarital pregnancies the family shows another pattern. One family may inexplicably reveal that in each of the generations the men have died very young and the women have never remarried. There are patterns of succeeding replacement figures which can be discovered as soon as the dates of birth and death are known. One family pattern may be the presence of a professional in each of the generations, or the tendency for the nuclear families to remain geographically in a 'tribal area'. Alternatively, the pattern established may be one of immigration. In one family previously mentioned, a pattern of divorces had been established through three generations.

The significance of these patterns lies in their tendency to predict the future course of the family in treatment if they are left to their own devices. If the family is unhappy with that prospect then change can be based on the alteration of the pattern. The realisation of these patterns is part of the analysis which can be helpful to the therapist as well as the family members. For Mrs Lewis (see p.89) the family divorce pattern had not been given conscious thought until the therapy session brought it into the open.

There are variations in family pattern which can be of importance. The tendency for an event to occur in one generation and then skip the next generation to occur in the third generation is not unusual. There are families in which the grandparents were divorced, the parents have lived together contentedly, and the children are in the process of divorcing. The same phenomenon can occur with premarital pregnancies, desertions or spinsterhood. The implication of this phenomenon, 'skipping a generation', is that the generation in question has been programmed to react in an opposite way to its immediate predecessor. I have found that members of such families respond well to paradoxical injunctions.

One family pattern that is not unusual to find in psychiatric clinics is that of the psychiatric patient. One family whose sixteen-year-old-son was referred for treatment had a pattern of referral of patients to psychiatric hospitals which was present in three preceding generations. The mother's great-aunt had been sent as a teenage girl to a mental hospital because she was a 'wayward child'. Her own uncle and sister had been referred for psychiatric treatment as well and her son was now being brought for treatment. None of the patients had been diagnosed as having a major psychotic illness. Since admission to hospital in the early part of this century was a stigma and ordeal as well as compulsory, the pattern of the use of psychiatric services seemed to have persisted despite social changes. Perhaps the initial establishment of the tradition of usage of psychiatric facilities plays an important part in the referral of patients to the psychiatric services.

When the pattern was pointed out to the family members in the previous family they were surprised. The problem which was one of disobedience to parents was the same problem which had seen mother's great-aunt into hospital fifty years previously. After explaining that their son's behaviour was not sufficiently unusual for psychiatric treatment they were reassured, and I hoped that a new tradition might be established in which adolescent rebellion would no longer be labelled as 'sick' behaviour.

Family patterns are an important element of the transgenerational analysis. When they are present they reveal transgenerational passage as a working mechanism to the family members. They can provide the family and the therapist with a clearer picture of the true nature of the quandary for which the family presents for help.

Secrecy and Boundaries

I have mentioned previously that secrets are signposts to the boundaries which exist in families. They are like a communication dam behind which the potential energy and power of shared communications are held. Since the release of a boundary is sure to alter the structure of the organism, secrets are of great potential use to the therapist and family.

I look for evidence of secrets among those emotional issues which I know to be culturally sensitive. Any acts, beliefs, thoughts or feelings which are shameful, taboo, or otherwise anathema to the socio-cultural society in which the family exists, are probed for by me. If it is a devout Catholic family I ask about birth control and abortion. If it is a Jewish family I enquire into mixed marriages. The existence of premarital pregnancies is an almost universal act which is secretively guarded in the older generation.

The boundary between the secret-holders and those ignorant of the secrets is an important one to discover. A family which shares little between any of the family members has boundaries quite different than a family in which there is free communication between members of the same generation, with secrets withheld from the generations preceding and succeeding them.

During the process of building the geneogram and its subsequent analysis the secrets within a family are often extracted with little pain. In the Slater's transcript there were several occasions when a well-guarded secret was inadvertantly uncovered. Sharing these secrets with the therapist allows the therapist to enter into the family system. I am convinced that some secrets are released as a 'rite of passage' which allows the therapist entry into the family in a more intimate relationship than that usual for strangers, whatever their helping motivations.

Secrets are power and they are often used in an attempt to bind the therapist or a family member in a common boundary against the other family members. I never agree totally to withhold a secret shared with me from other family members. Some secrets shouldn't be shared, for they might bring about the destruction of a family unit without further-ing the growth and development of the individual family members, but I always insist on the freedom to use my judgement over any information shared with me.

The use of the previous six broad areas of analysis allows me to formulate goals for the treatment and alleviation of the family quandaries presented to me.

Notes

1. W. Toman, *Family Constellation* (Springer Publishing Company, New York, 1961). As well as detailing his theory on the very precise concordance between sibling position (by birth, sex, and rank) and adult personality, this book includes a guide for securing data on family constellations as well as algebraic representations of sibling positions and mathematical formulae for use in research.

2. W. Toman, 'Family Constellation of the Partners in Divorced and Married Couples', *Journal of Individual Psychology,* vol. 18, pp. 48-51.

3. G. Levinger and M. Sonnheim, 'Complementarity in Marital Adjustment: Reconsidering Toman's Family Constellation Hypothesis', *Journal of Individual Psychology,* vol. 21 (1965), pp. 137-45.

6 THE FAMILY THERAPY PROCESS

'Where shall I begin please your Majesty?' he asked.
'Begin at the beginning,' the King said, gravely, 'And go on till
you come to the end: then stop.'

Lewis Carroll, *Alice in Wonderland*

This chapter introduces a section of five chapters which contain the
clinical account of transgenerational practice. My clinical experience has
been obtained primarily in the adult psychiatric services. My clinical
background includes experience in conjoint marital or family therapy
with over one hundred families in a number of settings over the past
eight years. In addition I have treated individual family members using a
transgenerational approach and supervised a number of cases treated by
professional colleagues. Most of the designated patients were late adoles-
cents or adults. The geographic location has included inpatient and outpatient units located in both American and British teaching hospitals. I
have also seen families while working in mental hospital settings. This
range of venues has allowed me to work with a very wide range of
families of differing ethnic and social backgrounds. Most of the families
were treated without a co-therapist. The length of treatment has ranged
from one session to eighteen sessions over a period of as many months.
Sessions were usually spaced on a fortnightly or monthly schedule and
lasted between one and two hours.

The psychiatric diagnoses of designated patients have included the
psychotic disorders, such as schizophrenia and manic-depressive
psychosis; personality disorders; the addictive states such as drug and
alcohol addiction; and the entire range of neuroses. Not uncommonly,
some of the family members who were not designated patients also
presented with diagnosable psychiatric illnesses. Their illnesses included
the same wide range of diagnostic categories. Where drugs were required
for the well-being of any of the family members they were prescribed.

The use of a family approach has had to take into account the constraints of the adult psychiatric services. Each new referral required
evaluation in order to establish that the family transgenerational
approach was suited to the needs of the referred family member(s). The

114

referral procedures are important in a general adult psychiatric unit. Family therapy cannot automatically begin in the first session. Some child psychiatry units have established the routine of seeing the nuclear family conjointly in each referral. This practice serves to emphasise the importance of the family system but increases the danger that those families not yet educated into a family approach will never be seen. Some embarrassment may also occur in sessions in which individual organic diseases are first explored in a family setting as if they were psychological.

I begin family therapy formally after the initial assessment has determined which of the organisational levels of intervention (social, family, whole person, organ, tissue, etc.) would be most economical and effective. Hatfield[1] addresses this issue of hierarchical levels while engaged in a family-oriented general practice. For example, a patient referred with symptoms and signs of acute appendicitis would hardly require a family intervention. The level of intervention would be the diseased organ, a subsystem of the individual, namely the appendix, by removing it surgically. Similarly, the referral note and the initial interview are used to determine which subsystem of the family (or the individual) requires intervention for the resolution of the presenting problem.

More recently most of my referrals have been made by professionals who are aware of my area of expertise and interest. Family and marital problems are now referred to me in such a way that the referral note alone informs me of the nature of the family quandary.

The Referral

Referrals for treatment can be sparse, inaccurate or misleading. I no longer assume that referrals made to a family therapist must necessarily be family quandaries. In order to illustrate the need for caution in forming unwarranted conclusions, I would like to present a pastiche of referral letters which I have received and whose family members have been seen.

> Dear Doctor,
> Can you please see A. Horn re: his sexual problem?
> Yours etc.

The preceding referral note is an example of an impoverished communication and is not atypical of some of the tersely worded letters I have received prior to my initial assessment interview. Mr Horn was seen alone but a short chat convinced me that his wife was directly involved and required in the interview. Luckily she was in the waiting room and she agreed to take part in the remainder of the interview. This referral gave no information as to the true nature of the problem, whether family quandary or individual pathology. He could have been a man seeking help for impotence caused by a spinal tumour, a man seeking help for his wife in an unconsummated marriage, or a man with any number of marital or family problems. The first interview soon fixed the problem within the family. Mr Horn had been having affairs since his marriage twenty-two years previously, at the rate of at least one per year. Three years before referral he began having sexual relations with his thirteen-year-old daughter. Six months before referral he left his home to live with a younger woman who had been a baby-sitter for his children. One month prior to referral he returned home. His daughter, frightened at his return, informed her mother of their sexual relationships. Mrs Horn had put up with her husband's previous affairs with resignation but now she threatened him with divorce and prosecution unless he saw a doctor about his 'problem'. After receiving this information I was able to frame the therapy sessions around the marital subsystem.

Dear Doctor,

Mr Saroyan is a 55 y/o West Indian Porter who has been to the surgery every day during the past two weeks. He has complained of many physical aches and pains, none of which have any basis in fact. Our health visitor has attended your family therapy seminar and would like us to refer him and his family to you for your assistance. Thank you for your help.

Yours etc.

The preceding referral letter illustrates a case in which a patient and his family were incorrectly referred for family therapy. Mr Saroyan and his nuclear family were seen several times. They were interviewed in front of a one-way screen, videotaped, and several home visits were done. But when I eventually untangled the emotional issues from the facts, Mr. Saroyan's physical health remained the one shared concern of the family. His health had deteriorated over a three-year period since his mother died, but no amount of explanation, discussion, revelation of secrets, task setting, or sharing of feelings about loss altered the family's primary concern nor convinced them that Mr Saroyan's physical symptoms were due to emotional causes. In desperation, I assumed my doctor's role, accumulated all of Mr Saroyan's hospital notes, did a thorough physical exam and ordered laboratory studies. I found that the family quandary was a very different one to that which I had been presented. Mr Saroyan had been suffering for years with temporal lobe epilepsy and essential hypertension. A recent heart attack and arterial disease in his legs, which caused him great pain on walking, had prevented him from working. The family, far from being over-concerned, were rightly concerned with his health which was poor. The quandary was at the cultural boundary between their West Indian background and the middle-class English helpers who had not understood his communications. The therapy was a reversed procedure in which I was educated into the family culture until I understood the real nature of their concern. Family therapy for their relationship problems was the wrong level of intervention. This was clear when Mr Saroyan's physical illnesses were treated.

Dear Doctor,

John Harrow is a 17 y/o schoolboy, just about to study for his 'A' levels. His father is a consultant physician. Over the past year or so he has been tearful for no apparent reason. The core of all this is that he feels, in theory, stupid – that everyone is better than he is. He has totally lost confidence in himself and his work. Also he feels that people are always going to reject him so he withdraws. The background is that his parents are very caring although his father tends to be stern, and their expectations of him academically are very high and he feels he cannot cope. About a year ago he was rejected by a girlfriend. This was not a very advanced relationship but it made a big impact on him. In spite of his view of himself, he is a very capable and intelligent boy – no one else shares his views of himself. He is taking low doses of antidepressants, first prescribed by his father, with little or no effect. Could you please see him? Thank you for your help.

Yours etc.

The preceding letter has been included to illustrate the plight of an adolescent who was inaccurately labelled as mentally ill while actually experiencing normal adolescent adjustment problems. The referral was for individual therapy, and the father's profession was a key element in the family quandary. After an individual session with John I could make no individual diagnosis of depression. The individual symptoms had intensified when his father had started to treat him with antidepressants.

The family quandary involved the inability of John's father to separate from his professional role as a doctor and assume his family role as a father. Labelling John as ill escalated his problems for he began to be treated differently at home, at school, and even by himself. His referral to a psychiatrist confirmed his deepest fears about himself.

This referral illustrates the 'self-fulfilling prophecy' phenomenon in which an adolescent or child, not having been ill in the medical sense, is labelled as such through misdiagnosis, and then begins a long career in search of neurotic 'mental illness' or 'personality disorder' as doctors, family members, neighbours and other community helpers reinforce the belief that he is ill. The individual comes to believe in his illness until his identity as a mental patient solidifies. Family therapy was indicated because of father's crucial role in defining John as a mentally ill person, rather than a normal adolescent. When the family was seen, a geneogram was constructed and explained. The transgenerational influences all pointed to a family quandary: father's avoidance of his parental respons-ibility and discipline by incorrectly diagnosing his child rather than interacting with him. One family session was all that was necessary to remove John's label and return his adolescent strife to its proper arena.

Dear Doctor,

Mr and Mrs Sturdy are the Welsh couple about whom we spoke in the corridor. At present their problems are centred on their mutually exclusive academic aims and pursuits, but I feel the conflicts are more fundamental than that, arising partly from their different expecta-tions from the marriage, based on their very different backgrounds, and also from sexual difficulties. They are very interested in the wel-fare of their five-year-old daughter although Mrs Sturdy resents the effects her presence has had on her career. They are both meticulous and ambitious and rather competitive with each other in the academic field, as well as with regard to their daughter. I do hope you will be able to help them.

Yours etc.

The preceding letter illustrates an appropriate referral whose accuracy was tested in the initial interview. The initial interview was also used to begin the therapeutic process. The referral indicates that the quandary is a constitutive one, a relationship problem. The family quandary exists in the marital valency-conflict of the marital bond between husband and wife. There is a hint of the transgenerational influences and family col-lisions in the reference to 'their very different backgrounds'. This family was engaged and treated in family therapy based on the analysis of their transgenerational influences.

The referral letter in an adult psychiatric service brings many types of problems, only one of which is the referral of families for treatment. Family influences must be weighed against other biological, social and cultural influences before a decision is made to treat a problem as a family quandary. A flexible approach helps to avoid the engagement of the wrong subsystem in therapy, while encouraging family members who require prolonged education and explanation to continue in treatment until their relatives can be engaged and involved.

In many referrals to me it would have been inappropriate to use family therapy although family sessions and the exploration of family dynamics have been helpful in clarifying the nature of the problem being presented. Contraindications to family therapy sessions are few, but there are circumstances in which family therapy is not possible. For example, an individual who is isolated through death and distance from all other family members cannot begin family therapy. Families hoping to cure an organic condition by the use of family therapy are unlikely to benefit. The family members must have some motivation for therapy, however strongly the therapist feels that the family is the correct unit of treatment. Unmotivated and unengaged family members may attend sessions but will resist efforts by the therapist to change them.

The following referral is one which recently arrive on my desk. I leave it to your imagination and fantasy to determine the appropriateness of the referral and the need for further information before offering a family-oriented treatment.

> Dear Doctor,
>
> Thank you for seeing this man and his second wife. I have already asked Dr Peters to see them in February. We agree that conventional psychiatry might not help much with their problems and he did suggest a referral to you if matters don't improve. Mr Brennan at least has asked for help. Basically I feel that he is not solely responsible for their quarrelling and has been seeking a way of changing. I do appreciate your help.
>
> Yours etc.

Educating the Family

Family therapy does not yet enjoy instant acceptance and recognition as a valid method of approaching problems amongst the helping professions. The medical model remains as the traditional doctor-patient relationship which assumes that pathology is encapsulated within the individual. Although the helping professions have become more aware of family-based theories and treatment, the traditional treatment still remains individually centred.

It is no surprise that family members often require reorientation and education into the basic concepts of family therapy before treatment can begin. Since most referrals come through the helping professions, the referred patient or patients have already had their pain and unhappiness explained in traditional language several times before reaching my office. They may already have used and exhausted conventional methods of individual somatic and psychological therapy. To such patients, family organisms, transgenerational influences, family collisions and conflictual bonding will cause confusion if introduced without explanation. They must first undergo a basic re-educative process. The following example will serve to illustrate this.

Mrs Rifle had been treated by various psychiatrists for six years before her referral to me. She had originally suffered a severe attack of influenza followed by apathy and depression. She had been admitted to hospital and her subsequent history was a dismal progression of admissions in which the entire range of antidepressant medication and electroconvulsive therapies were used in an attempt to cure her depression. After several serious suicide attempts she was referred to me by a bewildered and uncomfortable junior doctor. The following dialogue is a telescoped version of the re-educative process used to engage her in a family-oriented therapy.

> *Therapist* We've talked quite a bit about your background and your career as a patient. But you've made it clear that you never really accepted that you are ill or were ever ill.
>
> *Mrs Rifle* Yes. But all the doctors I've seen before have told me I'm ill.
>
> *Therapist* I'd like you to think about what your problems are now, not what the doctors said.
>
> *Mrs Rifle* I don't really know ... (long pause) ... I think my husband could be much more helpful than he is.
>
> (There follows a lengthy explanation of the ways in which her husband never makes a decision at home and leaves all the decisions to her.)
>
> *Therapist* Perhaps your husband might join us to talk about these

problems.

Mrs Rifle But I don't see how they are anything to do with my illness. Either you have an illness or you don't.

Therapist Right now you are complaining more about your relationship with your husband. There doesn't seem to be an illness. You seem to be suffering more in your relationship with your husband than an illness.

Mrs Rifle No one has ever told me this before.

Therapist Look, (turns to blackboard) here is you and this is your husband. I'm going to draw a circle around the two of you. That's the boundary line where you two are located. You are both a unit inside there.

Mrs Rifle (still puzzled) Yes?

Therapist Can you see that because you two are isolated from both your families that the relationship between you is very important?

Mrs Rifle (tearful) But he thinks I'm mad. He treats me like a child.

Therapist We must get together and talk with him to see if there is a way in which you both can learn to change the way you think and react towards each other. Families are the place where all our strongest feelings are allowed to be shared and expressed. You don't do that with your husband and you don't have any contact with your parents. You've cut yourself off from them and there's nothing but you two isolated ...

Mrs Rifle I think of my parents often.

Therapist They still exist inside you but you have no relationship. Well, let's ask your husband in first and later we might try and get your parents involved as well. Shall I write to him or phone him?

Mrs Rifle No. He'll come; I'll tell him.

When an individual is referred with a label marked 'illness' the initial session must determine the validity of that label. If it is not valid or only partially so, I redefine the problem, introduce doubt about the 'illness' and connect what is happening within the patient to what is happening outside of them in their interlinking relationships within the family. The geneogram may be used to facilitate explanations of relatedness and transgenerational influences. My redefinition of the problem to myself is insufficient; it must be explained to the patient. This education process is crucial to the success of future work. Once a person understands that their 'illness' is linked to their relationships with others, new solutions based on transgenerational analysis will be more acceptable to them.

The referral of an individual family member makes the educational process more difficult because of the immediate lack of evidence about relationships which exists in a conjoint interview. Use of the geneogram provides the educational focus. The individual family member is first given a professional opinion which refutes their previous diagnosis. The orientation of a family therapist is explained; the family is an organism linked by relationships and the disorder which seemed to be in one person is a reflection of a family quandary. The geneogram shows the relationships, patterns, and bonds which make up the quandary. The family member is encouraged to question this redefinition. Patients treated for many years with drugs and individual therapy may be angered by the shame and guilt which they have had to bear, by the stigma attached to them, by their loss of self-esteem, and by the waste of time in their lives. Conversely, some patients cling to their illness like a well-worn and familiar coat rather than accept a family reorientation. More usually the reformulation of their problem is welcomed and eagerness to involve other family members in their therapy is evident.

When the first session is a conjoint marital session, the educational needs may differ. Marital couples may accept that the difficulty has grown from their relationship, but blame each other as individuals for the responsibility of causing the referred problem. An acrimonious exchange may break out in the initial session. For example, one working-class couple was seen after the husband had had an affair. As soon as they entered the office they began hurling abuse at each other which culminated in the following exchange:

> *Husband* (to therapist) I don't know why she insisted that we come to see anyone for help. The only help she needs is a fat p —— up her bloody c——!
>
> *Wife* That's right. Sex is all you ever want. Well you can take your f——ing p—— and stick it up anyone you f——ing well please, but I'm not having any of it. (To therapist.) He comes to me for sex after what he's done. Can you imagine, Doctor? Why don't you tell him what a bastard he is?

This couple had seen therapy as an opportunity to air their grievances, entrenched in their own positions, filled with anger and resentment. My role was to be that of judge, jury and executioner. The educational focus is on their own responsibility in bringing about the current crisis rather than focusing on their spouse. A blaming session is not a useful way to begin a marital therapy.

The educative process into a transgenerational model starts each of the marital pair at the origin of their relationship. They are asked to explore their reasons for choosing each other. The discussion shifts to that time in the past when the bonding began between the pair. The transgenerational influences brought to bear on them, the moulding of their own personality, and the family collision are all explored. Geneograms may be used as an educational and explanatory tool to bring out the various family influences. The marriage of the couple can be the last detail drawn into the geneogram, graphically depicting the collision of the family cultures involved. In this way, the marital problem is no longer depicted as isolated between two individuals. It is connected to their families of origin, reorienting them in the process to a broader view of their quandary.

For example, a couple who had married after living together for some time had been referred for marital therapy after the wife had been treated for depression which began shortly after marriage.

Therapist Is your position with your wife similar to your position in the past with other people who have been unhappy and in need of affection? Relatives, perhaps?

Wife I think that does apply. He has had a tendency to take up with females that have all been a bit off their rockers.

Therapist That makes me feel that if you improved, he won't feel that you need him as much and your relationship will suffer.

Husband Yes. I visualise a time in ten years or more when she is feeling happy and strong and she won't really need what I give her as much.

Therapist (to husband) How could you have gotten yourself into that position again and again if you didn't get moulded by someone in your family?

Husband Oh, I see. Well, I haven't been in that position. There is no one in my family like that.

At this point in the interview a geneogram was built up in front of the couple of the husband's family of origin. We eventually came to his description of his maternal grandmother.

Husband My grandmother didn't really have anything in her life. She's a lonely old lady, my grandmother, and she had nothing but a hard time all her life. It's a shame.

Therapist Do you still see her?

Husband I used to go and see my grandmother nearly every day.
Now I go whenever I can.

Therapist She sounds as if she is really one of the crucial people in
your life.

Husband Yes. Especially when I was young.

At this point a parallel between the husband's grandmother and his
wife is apparent to me. He continues by revealing that he often amused
his grandmother in an attempt to cheer her up. He used similar descriptions of his relationship with his wife. I called his attention to the
parallel as it became more and more obvious. He was moulded in his
relationship with his grandmother and his wife was replacing aspects of
that relationship.

In the preceding example of engaging and educating the marital
couple, attention was diverted from their present marital strife while the
couple were required to reconnect to their family of origin. Exploring
their marital bond as a collision of family cultures removes the sense of
isolation which occurs in a couple who feel the marital subsystem is the
sole source of the quandary. Their bonds with other family members
become equally important and their awareness is expanded to include a
transgenerational view of the quandary.

In a conjoint family referral the interlinking role of the family
members in creating and maintaining a quandary may be as difficult to
point out as in an individual session. Family quandaries usually exist and
are maintained by all of the members of the family, including the poorly
functioning member, the identified patient. The anxiety and pain of all
other family members will be increased if the therapist removes the
burden from the identified family member through an explanation of
the family approach. Families are tenacious in their need to sustain their
view of their identified family member as ill. For this reason I usually
begin a conjoint interview with the identified problem and work through
it towards a family view.

Mr and Mrs Bloch requested an appointment for their eleven-year-old
son whose behaviour was becoming increasingly disturbed. He was rebellious at home and they believed that he was being victimised at school
and not performing to his capacity. The initial interview was arranged
so that the nuclear family would attend in a conjoint session. It included
Mr and Mrs Bloch, Sandy, the identified patient, and his thirteen-year-
old sister Amelia, who was partially blind with mild congenital heart

disease.

Mrs Bloch explained at the beginning of the interview that they were very concerned about their son. He had been aggressive towards his sister, rebellious towards his parents and disobedient as well. He would not do as he was told, kept his room in a dreadful state and had been banned from playing sports for one school term. Mr Bloch and Amelia concurred in all of these accusations. I wondered why these behaviours were seen as symptoms of some illness which warranted psychiatric treatment. I mentioned to the family that my own children had done similar things but perhaps the situation in their family was different in that they hadn't encountered this type of behaviour before. His parents were irate when I pointed to the essential normality of their son's behaviour (he was rebellious but not ill). They admitted that his behaviour was alien to them and their own upbringing. The re-education process began when I refused to accept that their son was ill and required the family to re-evaluate the entire situation. The vacuum which occurred in the family session became filled with a history of the many problems that had befallen the family in the past few years including family deaths and serious physical illnesses which had caused the parents to withdraw from each other. Mrs Bloch began to weep and Mr Bloch withdrew into himself. These behaviours were identified as they happened and their meanings explored. The entire session became one in which the original symptoms of the family quandary were redefined. By the end of the session the parents accepted their role in the family quandary and had agreed that Sandy needed to be given more responsibility for himself. They had been holding him back because of the deaths which had occurred in their families of origin and their need to strengthen the remaining family bonds. Amelia remained dependent due to her illnesses and had not provided a model for differentiation of the children. The family accepted the view that Sandy was only one element in the family problem and agreed to return to explore their other problems.

To summarise, the process of engaging a family or its members in family therapy must begin with an education process. The family members must understand and accept the family orientation of the treatment. Usually, the first step in this process is a professional pronouncement on the lack of signs and symptoms related to an individual mental illness. This task is easiest for the therapist when no mental illness exists. But in families with schizophrenic family members or any other diagnosable mental illness the redefinition can still be accomplished if the quandary is caused by the relationship difficulties in the family which exacerbate the individual illness. The next step in the education process is the provision of a new model based on the family relationships through the use of explanation using examples from the family life or a geneogram. A new framework is constructed and taught to the family so that they can work with family and transgenerational concepts. The initial educative process ends with a return to the presenting problem which has now been redefined in family relationship terms.

Therapeutic Alliance: The Contract

The willingness of family members to participate in family therapy sessions should not be accepted at face value. I have had the experience in which family members attend out of politeness or loyalty to their general practitioner, with little investment in the therapy sessions. Without an agreement or contract in therapy, family members may nod acceptance while month after month goes by with little work done. An elusive non-verbal shroud will hang over the entire process of therapy. An example was a teenage girl who was referred by her psychiatrist for family sessions. She arrived at the first session with her mother and father. Her medications had relieved the symptoms of schizophrenia for which she had been treated, but she was not working as her parents wished and she spent much of her time alone with no hobbies or other outside interests. The family attended for four sessions, listening politely and answering questions about their background. Tasks of the simplest type were not performed and at last I asked the family why they continued to attend their sessions if they were not going to use them. I was informed that they had only come because the psychiatrist had referred them and they were awaiting my pronouncement of their daughter's cure and discharge. Their daughter revealed that she had a boy-friend who occupied much of her time and whom she was hoping to marry soon. No verbal contract or therapuetic alliance had been forged between myself and this family.

Family therapy requires the active participation of the family members in order to succeed. The doctor cannot merely prescribe while the patient passively accepts. Family members must agree at some level to the active role required in their treatment. I recommend thorough exploration of the initial resistances and motivations regarding family therapy before asking family members to return and work in further sessions.

Although I resist making a formal written agreement because I feel it would hinder a flexible approach, I insist on distinguishing the referral and exploratory sessions from the therapeutic work which requires an undertaking on the part of the family members present to become actively involved. With the receipt of that undertaking the therapy can begin. Thereafter, whenever resistance to the therapy process occurs I can refer back to our original agreement and the undertaking that was made.

Beginning Therapy Sessions

I am aware that I have artificially divided therapy sessions from exploratory ones for purposes of discussion. The effect of redefinition and the education of the family can be therapy in themselves as I have previously indicated. Although some family quandaries may respond to history-taking redefinition as the only necessary therapy, many family quandaries require structured changes in the family relationships in order to achieve resolution of their problems.

My primary goal in family therapy is to achieve a resolution of the family quandary that will generalise outside of the therapy session. When family members return to that bastion of engulfment and defensiveness, the family home, the true test of therapeutic effectiveness begins. Families may understand their dynamics, patterns and transgenerational inputs during therapy sessions; they may change their behaviour in my presence; but upon arrival home where no therapist is present, generalisation of their insight or new behaviour is lacking. The familiar dysfunctional patterns may be reconstituted as soon as the family members take their leave of the therapist at his doorstep. For this reason alone I would de-emphasise the role of the therapy session as the primary location for changing behaviour.

As a general rule I see family members as seldom as is consistent with maintaining continuity, usually once every two to four weeks. I consistently accent the necessity of work which the family members must do outside of the session. Tasks are set which must be accomplished and reported on during the next session. Resistances to task completion are explored and family members are coached within a session so that they will be able to practise a new way of relating during the following weeks at home. Family sessions at home without the therapist are encouraged. In these home sessions, family members are encouraged to talk to each other about painful issues, make their own geneograms, recontact distant relatives or look at family albums. It is hoped that these activities will give the family members a growing sense of change while away from the therapist, and reduce their dependency upon the family therapy session.

Therapy sessions do have definite uses within the constraints outlined above. Once the family members have agreed that the family approach best fits their quandary, the brief time spent in sessions is planned so as to enable family members to make maximum use of them. Sessional time is spent on exploration, introduction of new behaviour, or digestion and reflection of changes which have already occurred.

Exploration in a session involves the family members in detective work. Unexplained present interactions are traced to their origin in past relationships and influences. Where did *that* behaviour come from? Who in your family did that? Who did you do that with when you were young? Exploration of the transgenerational influence raises further questions about the present interactions leading to investigative tasks which can be assigned for completion before the next session. In this way a rationale is provided for family members, enabling them to recontact relatives and ask questions of them which were previously unasked. These sort of tasks not only gather information, they lead to changes in long-standing relationships.

For example, Bertha Hall was a 25-year-old woman suffering from anorexia nervosa. During a family session she was assigned the task of contacting her father. She felt her father would be uninterested, distant and unwilling to supply details about his family. On her return, having completed the task, she enthusiastically chattered about her father's family for most of the next session. She noted a change in her relationship with her father and felt relaxed in his presence.

Exploration in the conjoint family session may also uncover present interactional conflicts.

Therapy sessions may be used to introduce new experiences and teach new behaviours to family members. A comprehensive and continually expanding range of techniques is available for use by the family therapist. These techniques can be used to plan emotional growth experiences for family members. Some are original to family therapy sessions, while others have been borrowed from the armamentarium of behavioural, gestalt and psychodrama techniques. Videotape and audiotape feedback have also provided valuable aids in therapy sessions. These techniques are described in detail in the next chapter. Their general aim is to facilitate change in the session as a first step towards generalising the newly established behaviour in the home. Learning new interpersonal, emotional or sexual skills without experimentation and practice is difficult. For example, the sharing of unexpressed angry feelings can first be facilitated in a session. Once the feelings are started the family members are sent home to continue work on them using specific tasks.

Sessional time is also used to digest the changes which have occurred. During the course of therapy the presenting problem may have melted away. If the initial problem has long since disappeared, the way in which this has happened may be obscure. Time is required for reflection, discussion and sharing of the work which has been carried out. These discussions centre on successful and unsuccessful attempts at change, and the work which still remains must be explored. New personal growth of family members is placed into the context of their past, present and future lives. Feelings about the therapist are discussed. Entire sessions may be spent in an unstructured way, temporarily releasing family members from the stresses imposed by a goal-orientated approach which has emphasised the need for performance and change. In these sessions, feedback of information to the therapist by the family members is facilitated.

Ending Therapy

Family therapy need not generate the strong transference feelings and dependency upon the therapist that individual therapy necessarily entails, especially when family therapy is used in the manner described. Most family therapy treatments last for one to five sessions. The timing of the ending is determined largely by the disappearance of the presenting problem and the resolution of the underlying family quandary. The end point is reached when each family member is adjusted to the new state of balance in the family; no individual is being blamed for the daily aggravations of life together; and the family members are feeling more comfortable in their lives.

The family sessions end with a summary of where we have been in the past, how the present is altered from that past and what the future holds. I try to maintain a follow-up contact of one year or longer in order to evaluate my own work. I rarely need to wean family members away from the sessions, if they have only attended between one and ten sessions.

In family therapy which has extended over a period of one to two years, ending the sessions may require more delicate handling. Transference of feelings from the family, real dependence and countertransference issues might need to be explored. Such families, whose adjustment may have seemed satisfactory, create a new family crisis as soon as the termination of sessions is mentioned. The new crisis, if it is designed to prevent the ending of the sessions, can be useful in illustrating that the family members have the ability to cope with such crises on their own. Emphasis throughout therapy on homework allows the family's real capabilities to be separated from whatever feelings of loss are present. I share my own feelings of loss during termination as well.

Families which have grown as a result of successfully negotiating a difficult transgenerational obstacle course are a source of satisfaction to me.

Family therapy sessions may end without effective relief of the quandary or may even result in increased pain and distress to a family. A family therapy treatment may end without complete resolution. An impasse can be reached when the crisis which precipitated the cry for help has ended and the family members settle back into old patterns with no further stimulation for change. Families may cancel further sessions with little explanation, make excuses about missed appointments and simply disappear, neither answering letters or phone calls. For the therapist it is important to acknowledge failures of treatment as well as successes.

The sessions may end on a realistic if incomplete note. After having worked with a family of five for one year, two tasks remained which were acknowledged by the husband and wife. Neither of them had been able to approach their own parents to form new relationships. The sessions ended when neither party was able to carry out the remaining work. The truce arranged between them remained and their relationships with their own children had altered. They have been in contact again two years later and have returned for more help.

Failures of treatment are failures of the therapist as well as the family members. There are cases in which I have chosen family therapy incorrectly as the vehicle of treatment; I have had cases which illustrated my failure to discover the underlying family quandary; I have chosen some families whose motivation for therapy was lacking; and I have had some families for whom my task-setting was inept. Many of these families have taught me more than I was able to impart to them.

Summary

The family therapy process begins with the exploration of the family quandary after the initial evaluation of the appropriateness of the referral. A detailed exploration of presenting symptoms and precipitating causes precedes the decision to use family therapy as the focal intervention. The family members are engaged in an education process in which they are taught the difference between traditional individual intervention and family therapy. Transgenerational concepts are introduced, using the geneogram during history-taking and analysing the germane transgenerational material. A tentative working plan is conceived based on the analysis which includes corrective emotional and educative experiences designed to change the relationship structure of the family. The successful conclusion of therapy is heralded by the increased ability of each of the family members to deal with each other and the crises in their lives. Some families fail to respond to family therapy. These failures are the shared responsibility of the therapist and the family members.

Notes

1. F. Hatfield, *Understanding the Family and Its Illnesses,* 1978, privately printed manuscript.

7 FAMILY THERAPY STRATEGIES

The cure for this ill is not to sit still
And frowst with a book by the fire
But to take a large hoe and a shovel also
And dig till you gently perspire.

R. Kipling, *Just So Stories*

The Structure of the Sessions

Within a discussion of the structure of family sessions I include their timing, location and content. In timing family sessions flexibility is required.
Although I would prefer monthly family or marital sessions lasting one
and a half hours, or monthly hourly sessions for individual family
members, the length of a session must depend on the needs of family
members and the tasks ahead of them. Some sessions may last for thirty
minutes while others extend for two hours. The first sessions may occur
weekly with later sessions spaced bimonthly; sessions may occur at
regular fortnightly or monthly intervals. Flexibility of timing in sessions
accentuates the importance of work done outside the sessions. Regularly
timed and spaced sessions provide a routine practice which creates
dependence upon the therapy sessions rather than encouraging the development of the family's resources outside the sessions.

Family therapy sessions are usually located in my office, a ten foot by
twelve foot room. There is enough room for individuals, couples or small
family groups. A blackboard, videotape and audiotape facilities are
readily available. Larger family groups are seen in a room which is thirty
feet by ten feet and has similar facilities. The larger room is used when
activities requiring more space are planned during the session, such as
sculpting or other experiential exercises. Home visits may be done at any
time during the therapy.

In my practice of family therapy using a transgenerational model,
work may begin with an individual, a marital couple, or any conjoint
combination of family members. During the course of therapy there are
often changes in the combination of family members who attend. The
patient originally referred may be seen once and excused from further
attendance while other family members become the focus of family
therapy sessions. Nuclear families may be seen occasionally while intensive work is done with one individual or a marital couple. Extended
family members may be invited to attend the sessions and may become
the primary focus of therapy. Marital couples may be split and seen on

their own before bringing them together again. The choice of participants in a family session is dictated by the needs of the family in resolv-
ing their quandary.

The presence of a family member in a session or his calculated
absence from sessions is linked to an understanding of those areas of
family dysfunction in which that family member is involved. If a family
member was being blamed or labelled as ill in the presenting crisis, excus-
ing him from the sessions removes the stigma and dissociates the presenting crisis from the family quandary. Later that family member can
attend sessions as an ordinary family member, able to help his relatives
and be helped in return. Following clues about the transgenerational
influence of the extended family brings decisions about which family
members should be invited to attend later sessions. A family containing
a teenage enuretic son revealed belatedly that the paternal grandparents
lived next door. The father had had a similar problem which had
resolved without professional help. Since the grandparents were living so
close and had solved the problem one generation previously it made
sense to ask them to attend the next session. Family members may wish
to be seen on their own; some must be seen alone before they will agree
to reveal material which they feel is too destructive, embarassing or painful to be shared in conjoint sessions. I use these individual sessions to
gain a clearer understanding of the gravity of these communications
while aiding family members to judge the potential for harm of secrets
if they were revealed in a conjoint session. For the above reasons I
respond flexibly to the needs of the family when deciding which family
members attend the sessions.

The structure of the sessions may also be classified by their content.
In general terms, I would divide the emphasis of content into investigative, planning, activity or reflective sessions.

Investigative sessions are planned when new family members are introduced in a session, when added information is required by family
members or therapist, or when therapy is foundering for no obvious
reason. These sessions are often explorations of transgenerational
influence. Time is spent delving into the way in which the activities and
interactions of family members relate to the bonds, collisions, replacements and patterns which have been previously discovered and traced.
Areas of secrecy are further examined to discover information which
may be hampering change in the family system. In investigative sessions
nothing should be assumed, nothing taken for granted. Documentary
evidence of births, deaths, marriages and other relationships are sought
whenever suspicion exists. For example, in a family session an alcoholic

woman, the identified patient, swore that her father had died of a heart attack. Her mother instantly confirmed this story while the woman's ten-year-old daughter seemed bored and uninterested. In an investigative session, the woman and her daughter returned with a newspaper clipping which claimed that the father had committed suicide. The clipping brought a new shared relationship between grandmother, mother and child which was previously lacking. Grandmother no longer needed to keep this secret from the other members of the family.

Planning sessions are used when investigation has turned up enough information to plan for change. These sessions often require complex negotiations between family members and therapist over what is a necessary, desirable or possible task to induce change. Explanation, persuasion and practice through role-playing may occur before the task is accepted and accomplished. Mrs Blue and her husband were advised to set aside one hour each week in which they would discuss their differences. At first they resisted by claiming the task was an artificial way of achieving better communication. I left them in my office for half an hour to discuss their differences and when I returned they were arguing fiercely over their son's education. The experience broke down their resistance to the task and they went on to achieve their goal.

Planning tasks for family members can leave each family member with separate assignments, some of which may interlock. In a family of six, the four children were to pick the location to which their father would take them on a Sunday morning while their mother was cooking the Sunday lunch. Mother was to spend the afternoon with the children while father listened to his stereo headphones. Father had to plan a weekly evening out with his wife. These tasks were all negotiated by the family members with each other and were generated from the needs of the family in a planning session.

Some sessions are devoted to activities such as role-playing, sculpting, videotape recording and feedback, gestalt games, or sexual instruction. These activities address the family quandary by providing instruction, corrective emotional experiences or diagnostic projective tests of the family dynamics. Sharing of common experiences such as a family pillow fight or sharing of common emotions as in forced mourning provides family members with new experiences within the session which generalise in the family home. The diagnostic use of activities can lead to insights and unblock therapy, enabling further progress to occur. For example, a sculpting session revealed the annoyance of the father towards his wife for 'wearing the pants' in the family. He placed his wife centrally but revolved around her bumping her out of position. He became consciously aware of his role in disturbing his wife.

Reflective sessions coincide with the occurrence of a significant change in family structure. Structural changes in families may be comparable to the allomorphic changes in chemical structure such as the change from lampblack to graphite to diamond. The changes leave the family to view its new and unfamiliar self with anxiety as well as pleasure. Reflective sessions consolidate and explain changes prior to continuing work towards further change.

Most sessions are spent between investigation, planning, activity and reflection in combination rather than devoting entire sessions to each particular emphasis. At times a planned session may have to be abandoned in response to the family need in order to explore events outside the session.

Task Setting: Work Outside the Session

Tasks in transgenerational practice aim towards the separation of past influences which haunt the family from the present reality of existing relationships. The work outside the session will accomplish desired relationship changes through task setting.

One common task assigned is that of gathering information about past and present relationships with and between relatives. For example, George Graham was a family member who was asked to describe his parents' relationship with each other. He was unable to do so because his mother had died giving birth to him and he had been raised by his stepmother. My interest in his mother was that he had chosen his wife as a replacement for the mother he had lost when he was born. The evidence for this included a similarity in names and physical resemblance with a photo of his mother. His wife failed to match the idealised image George had of his mother, so that his marital bond was based consciously on an idealised image while unconsciously determined by the model of his stepmother. A task was set for him to discover as much as possible about his mother.

The task could have been accomplished in several different ways. A direct approach would involve him in discussing his mother with his father. This task might prove a difficult or impossible one involving a confrontation with his father. It might be accomplished.by asking him to set up a structured interview with his father with specific questions set by the therapist conveyed to the father. A less direct approach might involve the task of finding any existing documents relating to his mother. Newspaper articles, birth, marriage, and death certificates, old photographs, diaries, or her letters might still exist. Another indirect approach might involve the task of seeking out his mother's relatives and speaking with them; or discussing his mother with other relatives who had known her, such as his father's siblings or grandparents.

Information gathering is a task which may reduce the fantasies upon which many family quandaries are constructed. The conflicting details of these fantasies can be investigated by family members while filling gaps in the transgenerational information gathered by geneogram.

By seeking out information from relatives outside the session, significant family patterns, family losses and replacements, moulding, transgenerational passage and the derivations of marital choice may all be investigated and clarified. Information gathering breaks down secrecy and boundaries between family members. When one member seeks previously withheld information there is a general lowering of the continued classification of painful material as secret among family members attending sessions. Gathering information involves each family member in the therapy process. They are engaged outside the sessions by devising methods of obtaining information as well as actively seeking it from relatives and other sources. Family members can communicate through telephone calls, letters and visits to informants, whether relatives, friends or strangers.

Gathering information about important family facts and relationships is the easiest of tasks to explain to family members; the tasks are also the least difficult to accomplish. The use of the geneogram increases the ease of setting this type of task since many questions normally arise out of the diagramming of family structure.

During the process of gathering information from relatives, new ways of interacting, discussing, asking and approaching relatives must occur. Long-abandoned or disused lines of communication with relatives must be reopened; old relationships are reopened and new links made with other relatives. In this way, relationship bonds are altered. The very act of gathering information for clarification leads to this alteration of relationships between two family members.

Relationship bonds may be altered by direct task setting. The task may be a simple one, asking one family member to share new emotions with another outside the session. This differs from setting an information gathering task which results serendipitously in sharing of new emotions. The intent of bond-altering tasks is either to increase bonding, decrease bonding, or reorient the bonding into a new framework. Minuchin's concept of helping enmeshed families disengage describes the situation in which overly intrusive bonds have become a family pattern[1] which must be altered. But family quandaries may result from weak bonds, distorted bonds, or lack of bonding, as well as enmeshment.

An example of a task set to affect directly the bonds between family members is that of John Village, a 29-year-old single bus conductor. He used to phone his mother every day and shared all of his emotional problems with her including his sexual fear and fantasies. The task set him was uncomplicated; he was to reduce his phone contact with his mother to one call each week. He realised that he had had an over-close relationship with his mother which had excluded his father. Through the task he established closer ties with his father and lost one of his major symptoms, an obsessive fear that he might be homosexual. This change in relationship with his father was generated from the first task of decreasing contact with his mother.

In another example of bond-related task setting, Martha Brown was asked to write and express her feelings of anger to her geographically distant father. Their previous relationship had been one of distant admiration punctuated by incestuous fantasies. Mr Brown responded to the letter by visiting his daughter. Both family members were invited to attend a therapy session. Their relationship altered to a more realistic one through thorough exploration of their incestuous fantasies. Sharing the incestuous feelings reduced their boundary functions which had prevented the two family members from forming a closer relationship.

Quandaries involving bonding may become apparent through use of the geneogram or through direct observation of interactions within the session. One couple who were endlessly discussing decisions without reaching conclusions displayed these interactions in the offices. Their vacillation had paralysed them into inaction and was a symptom of the over-close bonding between them. They were asked not to talk to each other unless they had individually made a decision. This task provided one month's peace at home in which their marital bond seemed to have little substance beyond their chronic indecision. The original marital bond had been forged from sibling rivalries within their families of origin. Removal of that rivalry through task setting revealed a relationship only weakly bonded by love and mutual sharing.

Some bonding tasks aim to establish new relationship with distant relatives or relatives with whom relationships had been severed. Parents, grandparents, uncles, aunts, cousins and other relatives may be made the object of an information quest aimed at establishing a new bond. The quest for information is used to overcome resistance generated by fantasies existing between relatives. New bond formation can result in the weakening of other bonds and a disengagement in other relationships. This natural consequence provides the rationale for a task designed to decrease pathologically-engaged relationships. The resulting emotional distance allows individual family members greater freedom. Setting the task of forming new relationships with a relative serves as a method of diffusing the intensity of existing ones. This task is especially attractive in family quandaries where family members have put all of their emotional eggs in one basket. This type of task must be set after close study of the existing relationships in a family. Mr McTavish was asked to contact his father's oldest brother who was living in Dubai in order to establish certain details about his father's upbringing. Mr McTavish was the oldest son in his family but was over-involved with both his father and mother to the detriment of his marital relationship. His uncle and he had much in common except that his uncle had managed to escape over-involvement in his own family of origin. I felt the task would provide Mr McTavish with a new relationship, model a new relationship with his parents, and allow him to separate by forming the new relationship. His uncle wrote a warm reply to his initial letter and suggested that they meet when he returned to England for a visit. When they met they found that they enjoyed each other's company and conversation. The relationship between them grew while his relationship with his parents became less intrusive.

Bonding tasks accomplished outside of the therapy sessions through decreasing, increasing, establishing or re-establishing new relationships are natural outgrowths of a transgenerational practice. This technique of changing family relationships through tasks set outside the session uses present and past relationship patterns in the planning and achievement of future alterations in relationships.

Outside tasks may also be assigned to follow on behaviours newly learned within the session. Sexual instruction is an example of this use of outside tasks. A range of techniques taught within sessions which are then practised at home have been developed to deal with specific problems.[2] Outside practice sessions can also be assigned when using forced mourning procedures, or when argument skills have been taught. For example, after having shared feelings about a dead relative in the office, a family member will be assigned the task of sharing those feelings at home with the same or different family members. Couples may be given the task of planning a one-hour argument session at home after having practised in the office using role-playing and simulated situations. The tasks are necessary because they directly oppose transgenerational influences which are evident as resistances to the tasks. In order to survive, marriages require argumentative skills of great sophistication. These skills may be inhibited in the spouses whose moulded experience with their parents was never to argue. Alternatively, when parents, presented a model of constant argument and bickering, their children may have determined never to do the same. The choice of a task to be practised outside of the session is tailored to the needs of family members through exploration of the family quandary and its trans-generational background.

Techniques within the Family Therapy Session

There has been a creative explosion of new techniques for use in the family therapy session. These techniques have been developed in response to the redefinition of the goal of therapy in family-oriented treatment. They are aimed at producing changes in the constitutive properties of families as well as generating new insights for the family members. Most of the techniques assume active and directive participation by the therapist. Specifically, they are used to increase the sharing of emotions or information, for developing interpersonal skills among the family members or for increasing motivation for change.

The use of the geneogram has already been described in Chapter Four. It is a major technique used in the transgenerational practice of family therapy but there are many other techniques which I have found useful. A few have developed out of the theoretical postulates of family therapists but most have developed pragmatically in response to the changed clinical goals in family therapy.

Paradoxical Intentions and Prescribing the Symptom[3]

A paradoxical intention is an instruction given by the therapist to one or more family members which *proscribes* the very result, reaction, behaviour, or resistance which the therapist wishes to occur. For example, if a family member is known to resist the therapist's instructions he might be told to argue forcefully with his mother at home with the intention that he ceases his destructive arguments. This technique must be used judiciously and accurately or the intention may be taken at face value by a co-operative family member, thereby causing greater suffering and pain.

Prescribing the symptom is a special form of paradoxical intention in which the therapist focuses on the original, identified symptom, either individual or interactional, and asks that the family member continue the symptom behaviour with even greater intensity. The result of this paradox is that the symptom, which was previously seen by the family member as outside control, becomes controllable. The family member or members gain control of the offending behaviour either by carrying out the prescription or by resisting it and decreasing the symptoms. An amusing and instructive case using this type of technique describes the treatment of a marital couple, each of whom suffered from lifelong enuresis.[4]

Both members of the couple were instructed at bedtime to kneel side by side on the bed and 'deliberately, intentionally and jointly wet the bed'. They were then told to go to sleep and repeat this behaviour every night for two weeks. If after one night's respite the bed was spontaneously wet the following morning, they were to continue the prescribed behaviour for a further three weeks. The couple obeyed the prescription with increasing discomfort and dread for two weeks and following their one night's respite they never wet the bed again.

In transgenerational practice, the paradoxical intention is a useful way of instructing resistant family members to recontact estranged relatives. A thirty-year-old actor had been out of contact with his parents for three years. His wife and daughter had been unable to tolerate his increasingly aggressive behaviour. The behaviour arose at the time of his daughter's birth. His wife had become more involved with her daughter, shifting some of her interest from her husband. Since she constituted his only strong emotional bond he responded with anger and frustration. He was estranged from his family of origin and would not initially consider contacting them despite my explanations. Finally, I stated that I had reconsidered his objections to contacting his parents or siblings. Since he clearly felt that they were not interested in him he must know his family better than I did. His feelings that his parents had never loved him or cared for his welfare must be true. I asked him to formally address the issue that to him his parents were as good as dead, and that no further contact should or would ever be necessary in the future. We were to begin working on his position of being alone and isolated in the world. The following session he returned to proclaim defiantly that he had spoken to his parents on the telephone and arranged to visit them. He recanted his previous negative feelings towards them and expressed instead his anger at me for having attempted to permanently sever his relationship with his family. A sense of bewilderment and relief was present in him throughout the session. His aggressive behaviour at home disappeared.

Prescribing the symptom may also be used to good effect in transgenerational practice in the attempt to loosen, strengthen, or alter bonds. In marital couples who have been referred because of their constant quarrels, increased arguments at home are prescribed. Families complaining of an over-closeness are asked to do more together. One particular example of prescribing the symptom is the 'divorce session'. In some couples one partner uses threats to leave the other as a way of maintaining dominance. These couples are involved in a session in which all possible routes to the achievement of a divorce are explored in great detail. The effect of this procedure (if correctly chosen) is that objection after objection is raised to each aspect of divorce until both partners are fully aware that neither of them really wishes to carry out the threat. The resulting relief is often considerable and sometimes provides a singular resolution of the family quandary.

Reversal[5]

The reversal is a technique used to alter family patterns by asking that one family member reverses the way in which he deals with another family member. It differs from the paradoxical intention in that the underlying goal of the reversal is to accomplish the task which the therapist has devised rather than its opposite. The family member is asked directly to reverse their behavioural interaction in order to express the silent and disregarded aspects of their relationship. Since most family members in a quandary try harder and harder by using their familiar patterns of response, they create a spiralling feedback of ever-increasing problems. For example, a husband responded to his wife's quarrelling by withdrawing from the argument and physically leaving the house. She interpreted this withdrawal as a lack of love and quarrelled increasingly with him because of it. He was normally a solicitous, kindly, passive man and these traits had originally led his wife to choose him as her husband. Her increased quarrelling increased his solicitude and kindness as he desperately tried to use his every trait to help his wife. When I proposed a reversal of his behaviour so that he began to argue rather than retreat, to be 'cruel instead of kind', the balance in their relationship changed and became less tense.

Similarly a woman who complained that her husband never took her out in the evenings was asked to take him out instead. The result was a closer bond between them, followed by an equitable sharing of the task between them. The reversal is a difficult technique to employ without thorough explanation to the family members involved. They must first begin to realise the destructiveness that trying harder in the same familiar ingrained way entails.

The Use of Humour

Because of the serious nature of the quandaries which family members bring to therapy sessions it is all too easy to allow sessions to become unbalanced in the direction of serious, sombre discussions with an over-emphasis on the gravity of the situation. This overemphasis towards the darker side of the problem serves to detract from the valuable use of humour, lightheartedness and play in placing problems into a more balanced perspective. A humourless relationship or family is an unhappy one and the introduction of humour into sessions may serve a valuable function. Most family therapists whom I have watched at work have used humour to ease tension within a session, sidestep resistance to their suggestions, point out absurdities in family situations or simply model a less sombre approach to relationships. Ackerman[6] cites the use of humour on eight separate occasions either to ease tension, soften a blunt interpretation, provide support or as an ironical comment. For example he asks a man about his father's penis size and when he denies having seen it, Ackerman wonders aloud at the man's short-sightedness, a reference to his thick glasses. The man and his wife laugh and the point is made.

I feel that humour should be an integral part of the therapeutic process, not only permitted but encouraged as a part of the full inter-play of human emotions. An example in the exploration of the geneo-gram of a married couple occurred when I came across a clue to the possible replacement connection between the husband and his grand-father. The husband was a drummer in a pop band, and after he had described his grandfather in words similar to his description of himself I smiled and raised the connection by asking him if his grandfather also played drums. Similarly while exploring the past history of the mother and father of an anorexic girl (see Chapter Four) the following dialogue took place:

Therapist Is that when the two of you met?

Mother Yes, I worked in the bank and I suppose he thought I had unlimited funds.

Father She was a very popular woman and I was passing through.

Therapist You were passing through and she hooked you.

(Parents laugh.)

Father She was good-looking, a good dancer, good fun, very sociable.

Mother The compliments are flying now. See what you've done to me, look at me now.

Therapist (smiling) That's the trouble with marriage. It ruins great romances.

Mother (laughing) It does. It should be abolished.

(Father and mother both laugh.)

The final laughter was in response to the realisation that a point of great importance had been made about the passage of time and its ravages upon a romantic relationship.

At another point in the interview the following exchange occurred:

> *Therapist* (to mother) And your periods stopped three years ago?
> *Mother* Yes.
> *Therapist* (to daughter) And yours never started?
> *Father* (answers for her) They started.
> *Therapist* They started and then stopped when her periods stopped?
> *Father and Daughter* (together) Yes, they stopped about the same time.
> *Therapist* (smiles) So ... you are going through the menopause with your mother?

Roars of laughter from the entire family followed and the daughter relaxed considerably. The laughter acknowledged the importance of the connection as well as its absurdity, while the tension which had been building in the session was released.

Whitaker[7] formulated several tongue-in-cheek rules which apply equally to therapists as well as the families we treat. Among them are injunctions to 'develop the benign absurdity of life, develop your own craziness, learn to love by flirting with any infant available, and be childish with your mate'. The judicious use of humour will keep both therapist and family from going stale and maintain within them a greater spark of enthusiasm and life.

Forced Mourning[8]

Forced mourning is a technique first described by Paul[9] as operational mourning. Operational mourning was a procedure designed to provide a belated mourning experience in those families which have developed a pervasive defence against losses and disappointments as a result of incompleted mourning. This defence is passed from generation to generation unwittingly and promotes a fixated family pattern and equilibrium. Operational mourning was developed to weaken the fixed equilibrium allowing family members to develop. Forced mourning is a similar procedure designed to unblock the pathological bond which one or more family members may maintain with a deceased member of the family. Forced mourning is based on the application of recent ethologic and behavioural concepts as well as specific work on aspects of morbid grief. The procedure may be used individually or conjointly depending on the needs of the family members involved.

During the use of the geneogram to explore family losses and replacements the family's reaction to losses is explored. The need for a forced mourning procedure to be undertaken arises out of this exploration.

Table 7.1: Principles of Bereavement Counselling in Normal Grief

---

1. Initial comfort during the stage of numbness allowing the bereaved time to take in what has occurred.

2. Acceptance by the helper of the pain of bereavement with concomitant attempt to do nothing to inhibit the expression of grief.

3. Review of the relationship which the deceased shared with the bereaved including:
   (a)   verbalisation of guilt;
   (b)   working through of hostility;
   (c)   expression of sorrow and loss;
   (d)   attention to the fear of changes in feelings towards the deceased.

4. The counsellor must help make real the fact of the loss without forcing at an early stage.

5. Reassurance that the process of grief is normal and that the feelings, dreams, hallucinations are expected and accepted.

6. An acceptable formulation of future relationship with the deceased must be a goal.

7. New pattern of conduct must be acquired through people around the bereaved.

In normal bereavement counselling various precepts have been developed in order to help prevent morbid grief reactions from occurring (See Table 7.1). Individuals receiving this type of assistance are aware of their loss and its impact on their lives. Morbid grief and forced mourning are distinct from bereavement counselling in two main areas. First, there is a need to justify and explain the connection between the family quandary or individual symptoms and the loss. Family members with morbid grief reactions often present with symptoms which have been isolated from the loss that stimulated their reaction. The connection of the loss and its resultant production of symptoms often requires persistent and patient explanation of events which may have occurred many years before the family member has been seen in a session. The second area lies in the primary goal of forced mourning, the conversion of a morbid grief reaction into a normal mourning which is then followed to completion. The therapist must actively stimulate and direct the family members to explore and experience the avoided and painful feelings and remain tolerant of the strong expressions of those feelings when they come.

In forced mourning, grief becomes a conjoint experience in the office and at home as photographs, letters, and other memorabilia are used to provoke feelings and memories about the deceased. Visits to the grave are encouraged and letters written to the deceased may be an assigned task designed to uncover hidden feelings. Any stratagem which will aid the exploration of buried emotions is encouraged. The feelings which are shared between family members are both negative and positive. Resolution occurs when family members have reviewed their relationships with the deceased, acknowledge both positive and negative aspects, put aside all avoidance behaviour, and have readjusted existing relationships while placing the deceased into a realistic perspective.

The following clinical description presents an example of the use of forced mourning in a transgenerational family therapy. Mr and Mrs Chislehurst were referred for marital therapy following complaints by Mr Chislehurst of marital problems related to his wife's anxiety at home. During the first three sessions Mrs Chislehurst appeared alone. At the fourth session both husband and wife were present and during the course of that session a geneogram was constructed which revealed that their firstborn child had died at the age of nine months while being treated for a severe congenital abnormality. Mr Chislehurst became deeply withdrawn and tearful for two years afterward while his wife had accepted the child's death with remarkable composure. She was advised to have another child immediately. The resulting second child was born both physically and mentally handicapped. Both parents felt guilty, upset, but were unable to communicate these feelings to each other. Two further children were born and were normal in every way. The initial therapeutic work involved an exploration of their constant quarrels, his brooding depression and her overreactive anxieties. This work moved on after a directed investigation of their firstborn child's death. Throughout the two years of the husband's gloom and depression, neither spouse had been able to share feelings about their daughter's death. They had never since allowed any discussion about her or the impact of her loss on their relationship. At this time I introduced a forced mourning procedure. The first phase involved a detailed history which continued into all major losses sustained by each of the members of the Chislehurst family and their reactions to them. A thorough explanation of normal reactions to loss was followed by an explanation linking the symptoms which they had suffered together following the death of their daughter to the morbid grief process. The second phase of forced mourning required the exertion of an implacable pressure to initiate normal mourning. I verbally recreated the scene of the last moments of their daughter's life and death until Mrs Chislehurst began to cry. Mr Chislehurst showed his annoyance at her until he was directed to examine his own feelings. He began weeping and the couple were able for the first time to share and expose their feelings about their daughter's death. They were instructed to share their more negative feelings as well as their positive ones both in the office and at home. Their remaining children were included in some of the following sessions. During the course of the forced mourning they were asked to visit their daughter's grave, view her photographs, relive her final illness, share with each other their shameful feelings of anger and discuss openly their hostility towards their daughter for having subjected them to these painful feelings. Throughout, my job as therapist was to stay with the painful feelings and tolerate their expression. The resolution phase was heralded by a change in relationship patterns in the family. The parents became less protective of their children; Mrs Chislehurst began learning to drive; and a photograph of their dead daughter was hung in their living room along with that of their other children. At the end of the forced mourning their marital relationship had improved although further work remained.

The use of forced mourning in family therapy is reserved for those families whose quandary involves a transgenerational pattern of grieving which is morbid and has stifled the growth and development of the family members. The forced mourning procedure should convert a morbid reaction into normal grief which is followed to its resolution phase. The conversion is stimulated by the therapist actively. By sharing the strong feelings which are generated a new family communication pattern is modelled while revealing replacements in the family, altering bonds, and providing a greater tolerance for the minor losses and tragedies of life.

Videotape Recording and Playback

I often use videotape recording in my sessions with families. I value its unique ability to electronically capture verbal and non-verbal communications which can be studied at leisure after the session. The playback of a session provides me with feedback of my own errors, reveals

missed, unheard or covert communications and provides a record of
associations in the session. As a therapeutic tool for the family members
the gift to see themselves as others do is a powerful one. The first
objective look at themselves in action enables the discrepancies between
their own internal perception and external reality to starkly contrast. In
this way a model is provided to develop a family member's objectivity
about himself as well as other family members about whom perceptions
are distorted. The videotaped session also provides a record of the
progress (or lack of progress) which has occurred since the initial session.

Alger has written most extensively on the use of videotape recording
in family therapy.[10] He describes its use in the session in three different
ways. An entire session may be recorded and then played back, either
immediately afterwards or at the beginning of the next session. Alternatively, a small period during a session is recorded and the remainder of
the session is used to examine the tape in detail. Lastly, during the course
of a recorded session any of the participants may call for an instant
replay and it is played back and discussed. Alger has also described the
use of the video image in self-confrontation. The family member talks to
his television image and other family members are allowed to join in
talking to the real person or the image. But like any tool, videotape
recording and playback is limited by the technical limitations of the
equipment and the creativity of the therapist. Many other uses may be
found in the future.

In my use of videotape, I rely on simplicity of equipment, needing
neither technician or cameraman. I use a one camera, half-inch reel-to-
reel recording system with a wide-angle lens, which enables me to carry
out the entire recording session myself. The camera is placed in such a
way that the entire family and the therapist are captured on the tape. I
have also mounted the camera on a tripod with a zoom lens sitting next
to me and operated it during the session. I only record occasional
sessions and delay playback for at least one week in order for the
immediacy of the experience to fade. Since objectivity is the goal of my
use of videotape feedback, the same tape may have to be viewed by
family members on several different occasions before they can feel
sufficiently detached from their screen images to gain objective understanding about their behaviour. Videotape provides an opportunity to
reveal to family members the pathological nature of the bonds formed
between them, some of which are based on the replacement phenomenon
in the family. Conventional explanation which provokes fierce resistance
will be accepted if the replacement phenomenon can be shown. Videotape may capture those moulded traits which have passed from one

generation to another and show the way in which a member of the
junior generation in a family has taken on characteristics of a senior
member.

An illustration of the use of videotape to generate objectivity in
family therapy is provided by the following case. A 32-year-old nurse
had been treated for depression for four years following the death of her
maternal grandmother. Treatment with various drugs, group therapy and
marital therapy had little effect. She maintained an over-close relationship with her husband who received the brunt of her anger and helpless-
ness. After an initial session with her I became aware that her marital
choice and her feelings about her maternal grandmother were inextricably involved with the relationship maintained between herself and
her parents. She was asked to invite her parents to a session which would
be videotaped, because they lived so far away and could only attend
sessions rarely. During the session she appeared hostile, angry and bitter
at the way her parents had treated her grandmother and herself, but
denied any feelings of anger towards them, nor did her parents acknowledge the non-verbal communication of anger which was present. Her
fear of her parents remained unspoken despite its obvious manifestation
in her inability to tell them of her depression or her marital problems
until the session had been arranged. After the session her parents were
asked to return in several months' time and she was asked to view the
session on videotape. It required four viewings before she could accept
that the angry feelings she saw on the playback were her own. When the
next conjoint session occurred she was able to reveal directly her bitterness and anger towards her parents. They reacted with apologies at first,
then with matching anger of their own. The session ended in some confusion but her parents agreed to return for further sessions. She viewed
the videotape of the second session and quickly realised that the expectations she had of her parents would never be fulfilled. She felt isolated
and abandoned by them, feelings she connected to her anger about their
treatment of her grandmother. But her relationship with her husband
and parents improved subsequent to these two sessions. The videotape
had allowed her to gain an objective look at herself, her parents, and
their relationship.

The husband of a marital couple were set the task of arguing in a
session which was videotaped. When the session was played back, the
husband was able to perceive the intense competition between himself
and his wife which he had denied for so long. He immediately connected
it to the rivalry he had established with his elder brother. This insight
led to his enthusiastic participation in further sessions. Previously he had

been stubbornly certain that his wife was the problem in their family. The videotape had provided an objective learning experience for him and had helped him trace the transgenerational origins of his behaviour.

Videotape playback can capture an emotional moment which provides the family with a permanent record of their warmth and involvement. A family living in fear of fragmentation attended a conjoint session in which they were asked to play a game which they had invented when their children had been younger and much smaller. It involved a song, 'familamilamilies', sung while jumping up and down and holding on to each other. This warm and moving display of togetherness, captured on tape, was played back and broke through the feelings of fragmentation that threatened to engulf the family.

The previous examples illustrate the contribution this new technology can bring to family therapy. When emotions are running high and long-standing family patterns require exposure and alteration, an objective view of themselves may now be provided to family members and therapists. Videotape feedback captures a segment of family life and interactions for later viewing and reviewing until necessary insights into present behaviour lead to a motivation to change. Family members may dislike what they see but they cannot totally ignore or deny that they are doing or acting as their screen images reveal.

Audiotape

I also use audiotape for recording sessions, for feedback and in order to allow family members to listen to sessions at home. Audiotape recording is inexpensive and uncomplicated. The sessions may be recorded and played back in the same way as videotape is used, providing insights and objectivity. The loss of visual material is offset by the ease of recording and the ready availability of cassette playback facilities in many family homes.

Recordings can be done in sessions attended by selected family members. These tapes are later shared by the total family at home. In this way open communication is fostered between family members and the dimension of secrecy between family members may be breached even if family members were originally reluctant to reveal secrets in full conjoint session.

For the therapist, audiotape recordings provide an inexpensive method of reviewing family therapy sessions. The recording allows a leisurely replay of the session with special attention to therapist errors, missed communications and points to raise in the next session.

Experiential Techniques

Experiential or action techniques differ from the parts of sessions in which words are used as the main therapeutic tool. The use of action teaches the family the value of experiential learning in establishing new behaviour, emphasises non-verbal communications between family members, as well as providing new experiences through doing rather than talking about doing.

Experiential learning is the earliest form of learning. Before we learn words and symbols, we learn as infants and children through watching others, through experiencing, through trial and error, and through our body movements. This earliest form of learning eventually enables us to form words with the musculature of our vocal apparatus. But the non-verbal, experiential learning model remains with us as a powerful tool in effecting changes in behaviour and relationships when words are inadequate. Action can speak louder than words provided that the action is judiciously applied and based on the needs of the family.

The importance of experiential learning may be illustrated by considering the difference between reading about sexual intercourse and experiencing it. The metaphor is appropriate; sexually there is a great deal of individual apparatus which works without the need of a relationship (masturbation). A sexual relationship may consist of two partners engaged in mutual masturbation or it may involve a great deal more of the interactive, mutually-dependent responsivity which defines a different level of practice and experience. The latter requires practice in the organisation of the sexual relationship physically and emotionally. No amount of reading or talking can replace it. The practice is experiential learning and similar practice is involved in the establishment of new behaviour in other spheres of family life.

Which experiential technique to use is dictated by the transgenerational analysis and its resultant theoretical solutions to the family quandary. The methods may involve the simple movement of seated positions in a conjoint session, elaborately planned games or family sculpting sessions.

I often use changes in position, posture or movement in family sessions. For example, in a session including five family members — Peggy, the identified patient, her parents, brother and maternal grandmother — the seating was as pictured in Figure 7.1a. Peggy was seated between her mother and father while the therapist, grandmother and her brother were more peripherally located. Both mother and father revealed that they had been dependent upon their parents with bonds which were only partly severed by the death of their respective parents. The strong influence grandmother exerted during the sessions confirmed the nature of the relationship. Peggy had fallen ill when she briefly left home for the first time in her life. During the session while her parents described their dependence, she became agitated. Her mother and father then attempted to parent her; this only stimulated rapid and increasingly incoherent speech in her. A 'white noise' enveloped the session with all three family members talking at once, followed by Peggy getting up and walking out. The parents then knowingly gazed at the maternal grandmother and the therapist as if to say 'She certainly is mad, isn't she?' On her return the sequence of events repeated itself several times. Finally, Peggy was asked to sit next to the therapist who placed himself between her and the door. The parents were moved to face each other in confrontation while their son and grandmother were seated together in the room as in Figure 7.1b. The move was initially intended to counteract parental dominance of Peggy by getting her to sit with the therapist. The moves actually changed the experience in the session in three different ways. First, the tension between the parents could not effect Peggy as much, due to the support of the therapist's closeness; second, the separation from her parents in the session modelled an experience that Peggy required and wanted despite her guilt. Finally, the position of the therapist near the door inhibited Peggy from leaving; she would have had to walk out in front of him and he could prevent this if necessary. The result of the change in position in the session went as expected. Mother and father responded to their confrontative position by expressing differences of opinion instead of presenting a united front. Peggy felt more relaxed with lowered anxiety. The relief in the session generalised to all participants. The simple change in position was later used to explain the family quandary and set tasks to deal with it, while providing a simple experience of active change.

Role-play is a more complex activity than simple position change. Role-play in a session is illustrated by the following portrayal of emotional bonds which occurred in a marital session. While quarrelling the wife began to weep. Her husband, paralysed by her tears, did nothing to acknowledge or assuage her distress. He turned to me and began discussing his job. I asked him if this was his usual reaction to his wife's distress and he admitted that he was unable to console his wife. I asked them to stand up and embrace each other. His wife tolerated the embrace briefly and then pushed him away. I asked him why he had so easily let go and entreated him to hold on to his wife despite her moves to the contrary. When he accomplished this task, his wife began deeply sobbing in his arms and allowed him to comfort her. This sequence of behaviour was used as a model for work at home which enabled them to share their distress with each other. I knew that the husband's timidity in approaching his wife was representative of the cold relationship he had had with his parents. He needed to learn to comfort and be comforted through touching. When his wife pushed him away he felt rejected and was helpless to deal with her distress. By holding on to her long enough his persistence was rewarded.

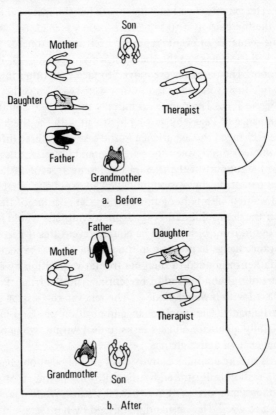

a. Before

b. After

Figure 7.1 Change in Seating in a Family Session

A more elaborate activity was the dominant-submissive game in which a family of three were involved. Two parents and their eight-year-old son were seen together. They were each asked to take a turn standing on a table looking down on the other family members. The person on the table was dominant and in charge of the other family members. The family quandary was the result of parental democracy which gave each member of the family an equal vote. Endless wrangling and avoided decisions resulted from split ballots until their son was born. He was given a vote and each of the parents attempted to woo him to their side. The game was designed to give each of the family members absolute dominance over the others. When the son was ordering the parents around the room the natural order in the family was revealed. The son, and only child, was relaxed while ordering each of his parents, who were two youngest siblings in their families of origin. His parents spontaneously recalled how they had been constantly told what to do by their older siblings. The husband realised that he had abdicated his responsibility for decision making in the family. He agreed to work on that task at home. He was to make decisions over his wife from a standing position while she was in a sitting submissive posture. Their son's neurotic traits ceased after the session.

In other forms of role-playing I have asked family members to replace each other or play the role of a dead or absent relative. For example, in a marital session Mr Blair was asked to play the role of his wife's dead father. She was asked to talk to her father as naturally as possible. The discrepancy between his acting and her memory of her father was so great that she was able to distinguish her husband from the replacement role for which she had been using him since she married him. In other role-play sessions I have asked family members present to exchange roles. The over-exaggeration which often results creates freedom and novel experiences for each of the family.

In family sculpting,[11] relationships are pictured without the use of words by placing family members in various positions and using their expressions and postures in order to represent the bonds and constitutive properties in the family. A scene from the past or present may be represented as well as hypothetical scenes or relationships based on emotional states. A tableau of distance, responsibility, or domination might be constructed for example. Transgenerational input may be depicted or the sibling position portrayed.

I used one sculpting session to enable each of the family members to portray their feelings of closeness. The family, consisting of father, mother, son and daughter, were each asked in turn to do a sculpture of their feelings of closeness. The mother's sculpture (see Figure 7.2a) shows an alliance between her and her daughter with some distance between her and her husband and son. The next sculpture was done by her husband (Figure 7.2b) who portrayed his family in a planetary model, measuring closeness by the distance from the centre of the model where he placed his wife. He represented himself as the closest

a. Mother's Sculpt

b. Father's Sculpt

c. Son's Sculpt

d. Daughter's Sculpt

Figure 7.2 Family Sculpting

planet followed by his daughter and finally his son in a distant orbit. The son placed his father and mother in opposite corners of the room facing the wall while he and his sister occupied the middle of the room facing each other (Figure 7.2c). The last sculpture was done by the daughter who placed her parents together while her brother stood next to her. All four were placed in a line (Figure 7.2d). The four tableaux revealed the differing attitudes of each of the family members and enabled each to experience themselves from a different point of view. The tableaux were later used in an experiential exercise. The family members were asked to change what they were unhappy with and the changes were acted out. The sculpting session provided them with insight, new experience, change and eventual growth as they were finally able to compromise and allow each family member the space they needed in the family.

Family sculpting is an example of the creative formal activities devised for use in family therapy sessions. But all experiential techniques, whether spontaneous, structured or formal, can provide experiences which are informative, cathartic, or confrontative to the family members, increasing the repertoire of response to life. Their successful use depends on matching the experience required to the family needs. Creative use of experiential techniques provides a powerful tool for family therapists if they are rooted in care and concern for the family members.

Sexual Instruction

Within the ambit of specialised techniques, sexual instruction is one limited to the marital subsystem. Many marital problems contain within them an element of sexual dysfunction so that the family therapist must have some ability in this field. Instruction in sexuality follows the model of the pioneering work done by Masters and Johnson.[12] Often couples referred specifically for sexual dysfunction treatment have major relationship problems concomitantly which are affecting their lives. Even such sexual dysfunctions as vaginismus or premature ejaculation may have roots in transgenerational influences which will require analysis. The use of sexual techniques in family therapy is illustrated by the following case. Mrs Edwards, a thirty-year-old social worker, was referred for marital therapy with her husband. She had previously been admitted on many occasions suffering from phobic anxiety, chronic depression, and had made multiple suicide attempts and abused psychotropic drugs. The ward staff and her psychiatrist had reached the limits of their skill and patience. Her referral was in the hope that a family approach might help.

It was noted in her medical history that she had three surgical vaginal dilatations for vaginal constriction. The couple had a poor sex life due to painful intercourse, according to the history. The marital therapy was undertaken and her symptoms were traced to their transgenerational source. Geneograms were used in several conjoint marital sessions in which Mr Edwards's contribution to her symptoms was explored. One family session with Mrs Edwards and her mother was also undertaken. Both she and her husband were so naive about sexual matters that they had assumed the marriage was consummated. In fact they had not actually experienced penetration during their four years of marriage. The transgenerational influence from both sides was one of intense naivety and secrecy regarding sexual matters.

Both Mr and Mrs Edwards felt that their sexual education was inadequate from family, friends and school sources. They had attempted to read books but found the words difficult to connect with their anatomy. Sexual work seemed necessary and was undertaken at this point in the therapy. The treatment involved six sessions. Sensate focus, a technique in which the couple explore and massage each other's bodies, was taught to them. Mutual exploration and verbal feedback sessions were prescribed to be carried out at home. Attempts at sexual intercourse were prohibited to relieve stress caused by pressure to perform the sexual act.

The nature of the sexual problem was her vaginal tightening (vaginismus) combined with his inexperience and fear of female genitals which prevented him from consummating the marriage. These factors were explained and anatomy lessons were given using diagrams and photographs. The entire course of therapy for vaginismus was explained. Mrs Edwards was given a vaginal dilator and instructed in its use. She was asked to insert it within her vagina. While leaving it there she was to imagine that it was her husband's penis. Following the completion of the sensate focus and dilator tasks an instruction session was planned. During the session Mrs Edwards explored her genitals. Her genitals were explored by her husband while I showed them the correspondence between the diagrams and the actual anatomy and feelings of the body. Her husband was encouraged to penetrate her vagina with his fingers. He was fearful of hurting her at first, but eventually was able to insert three fingers and was convinced that his penis would be able to fit. Following that session penetration was successfully achieved. Much of the marital disharmony disappeared as it became clear that they both felt cheated of a normal married life and the possibility of having children which had not materialised. Mrs Edwards was able to continue working for her qualifications and required no further treatment. She and her husband now have one child with a second one on the way. No further psychiatric or therapeutic interventions have been necessary.

The point I wish to make is that sexual instruction does fall within the province of the family therapist although it requires additional specialised skill and knowledge. Sexual anatomy, physiology, awareness of physical pathology, and the interaction between hormonal regulation and emotions must be studied. Frank, informed and open discussions of sexual relationships must be part of the armamentarium of the family therapist even if the couple are to be seen by a specialist sexual therapist. Since sexual feelings play such an important part in the establishment of marital bonds and serve as a unique distinguishing feature between the marital subsystem and the other family subsystems, it is a vital area for the family therapist to master.

Home Visits

Family home visits may be time-consuming and wasteful of resources, but they are equally essential as Bloch has described.[13] I use home visits when I am puzzled by the discrepancy between reported behaviour and behaviour which I experience in the session. Home visits are also valuable in assessing the environmental influence on the interactions between family members. Finally, home visits have enabled me to meet family members who were unwilling or unable to attend sessions at the office. Home visits increase understanding of the difficulties which clients feel when they attend the familiar territory of the therapist's office. The therapist unaccustomed to visiting in the homes of his families may feel de-skilled and de-roled as the family envelops him. An increase in therapist anxiety and puzzlement may result. The visit may turn into a social occasion rather than a working session. An ability to work while in the territory of the family will increase the therapist's ability to work in his office.

A home visit done to the Bond home was undertaken to discover why there were discrepancies between the family stories about the state of the home. The family arguments centred on the wife's inability to cope with her housework or her two children. Mrs Bond had a long history of suicide attempts and had been treated for endogenous depression. Her husband denied that things at home were as bad as she believed and the children's description of their home life was at variance with hers. I offered to visit the house to see for myself. I arrived to find a home immaculately kept, well decorated and maintained. The other family members were very uncomfortable as I confronted Mrs Bond with her misrepresentations. She broke down and wept as she turned to the emotional difficulties which had bothered her. Mr Bond had withdrawn from her five years ago after his father died. Their sexual life had stopped then. Their youngest son was in trouble with the police for truanting and theft and their oldest son was heavily overeating. The other family members admitted the truth of these facts although they had denied that there were other problems in the family during the sessions. The home visit had led to a confrontation which opened the family members to new issues in therapy.

In another family the discrepancy between the living conditions of a family as reported by the family doctor versus reports by the family members led me to visit the home. The home environment was substantially as the family had reported; the damp which had come through the ceiling had indeed caused the paper to peel off the wall. Otherwise the house was neat and tidy. The parents were rightly concerned about the health of their children and the family quandary involved the provision of basic needs for the family rather than a relationship problem.

Some of the home visits which I have done were required in order to engage family members who would not otherwise be included in the sessions. The children of a couple were of primary importance in the marital disharmony. The youngest child was autistic and brain-damaged. The parents had refused to allow their children to be seen at the hospital and had objected to their eldest son being involved. By planning a home visit I was able to gain their agreement and trust. The home environment was one of 'treading on eggshells' and emotional strain which was infectious and stifling. The over-control which was a feature of the family setting at home was an important factor in the marital dilemma.

Similarly a home visit was made to the home of the mother of the wife of a marital couple in treatment. The mother had refused to set foot in the hospital but agreed to a home visit. She was very bitter about the way in which she had been treated by previous doctors over her daughter's illness. The visit allowed reparative work to be done between the two which would otherwise have been impossible.

Before leaving the home visit I would like to call attention to the work of Scott.[14] He has organised and developed a community psychiatric service in which family-oriented home visits form the bulwark of the primary intervention to the request for psychiatric help.

Notes

1. S. Minuchin, *Families and Family Therapy* (Harvard University Press,

Cambridge, Mass., 1974).

2. W. Masters and V. Johnson, *Human Sexual Inadequancy* (Little, Brown, Boston, 1970).

3. P. Watzlawick, A. Beavin, and D. Jackson, *The Pragmatics of Human Communication* (Norton, New York, 1967).

4. M. Erickson, 'Indirect Hypnotherapy of a Bedwetting Couple', in J. Haley (ed.), *Changing Families* (Grune and Stratton, New York, 1971), pp. 65-9.

5. E. Carter and M. Orfandis, 'Family Therapy with One Person and the Family Therapist's Own Family', in P. Guerin (ed.), *Family Therapy* (Gardner Press, New York, 1976), p. 200.

6. N. Ackerman, *Treating the Troubled Family* (Basic Books, New York, 1966), pp. 6,15,29,118,123,145,146,271.

7. C. Whitaker, 'The Hindrance of Theory in Clinical Work', in P. Guerin (ed.), *Family Therapy* (Gardner Press, New York, 1976), pp. 154-64.

8. S. Lieberman, 'Nineteen Cases of Morbid Grief', *British Journal of Psychiatry*, vol. 132 (February, 1978), pp. 159-73.

9. N. Paul and G. Grosser, 'Operational Mourning and Its Role in Conjoint Family Therapy', *Community Mental Health Journal*, vol. 1 (1965), p.339.

10. I. Alger, 'Audiovisual Techniques in Family Therapy', in D. Bloch (ed.), *Techniques of Family Psychotherapy* (Grune and Stratton, New York, 1973), pp.65-75.

11. F. Duhl, D. Kantor, and B. Duhl, 'Learning Space and Action in Family Therapy: A Primer of Sculpture', in D. Bloch (ed.), *Techniques of Family Psychotherapy* (Grune and Stratton, New York, 1973), pp. 47-65.

12. Masters and Johnson, *Human Sexual Inadequacy*. Books which can be assigned to clients to be read at home include the following:

(a) P. Brown and C. Faulder, *Treat Yourself to Sex* (J.M. Dent & Sons, London, 1977). A self-help manual which provides simple explanations and 'sexpiece' exercises.

(b) A. Comfort (ed.), *The Joy of Sex* (Quartet Books, London, 1974). A book which describes lovemaking in detail, readable and easily understood.

13. D. Bloch, 'The Clinical Home Visit', *Techniques of Family Psychotherapy* (Grune and Stratton, New York, 1973), pp. 39-47.

14. R.D. Scott, 'Cultural Frontiers in the Mental Health Service',*Schizophrenia Bulletin*, issue 10 (Autumn, 1974), pp. 58-73.

8 FAMILY THERAPY WITH ONE FAMILY MEMBER: A CLINICAL CASE STUDY

No man is an island,
entire of itself

J. Donne,'Devotions'

That classical psychoanalysis forbids contact between analysts and their analysand's family has led to a feeling amongst some family therapists that contact with only one family member could not be considered an 'orthodox' family therapy. This polarised position grew from a dialogue between individual and family therapists which has also generated a wealth of creative thinking. The clinical reality often bears little resemblance to the polarised theoretical position. An individual, couple or family seek help from a therapist with problems in their lives. Defining or labelling their problem will not solve it. As practical therapists we must help in the solution of the problem brought to us. If one theoretical framework brooks no solution the framework must change.

Bowen introduced the concept of family therapy with one family member as an effort to modify the family relationship system when only one family member was available to attend therapy sessions.[1] Since 1960, few articles have been written about this particular method. Those which have, have tried to explain the work in the language of the Bowen Theory.[2] The rationale for this method of therapy resides in the interlocking relationships between family members. Any family member who changes a relationship between himself and other family members will change the entire pattern of relationships which has previously existed. Bowen coached family members to change their relationships with others in their family, thus altering the entire family system.

In the following detailed case report I hope to present an example of the use of transgenerational practice in which I treated only one member of the family. This type of work is similar to a case already described in chapter four, where only one session was required to alter existing relationships. The difference between this type of therapy and a more traditional individual therapy is that at no time do the intrapsychic mechanisms or psychology become a focus of treatment. Neither does the relationship between the individual and the therapist. Rather than encouraging a transference relationship to develop so that it could then be analysed and resolved, it is the real and imagined relationships between family members that are explored. The therapist uses the therapeutic alliance to act so as to generate a change in family inter-actions.

I shall present the case as it was presented to me and describe my work session by session. I have summarised my thoughts during the session in italics and include my analysis and afterthoughts of each session in separate sections. This format will be used in the two succeeding chapters.

The Referral

Glen Tucker was a 32-year-old photographer referred to me by his general practitioner. He had been referred to a social worker after a suicidal gesture had been treated by his GP. She was unable to form a psychotherapeutic relationship with him and was instrumental in asking that he be referred to me.

The referral letter read as follows:

Dear Doctor,

Mr Tucker is a very intelligent young man who suffers from lack of confidence and anxiety. His parents live in Sussex and though he described his father as perhaps a bit neurotic, there is nothing abnormal in the family history. He has always been a bit shy and introverted but has managed to conquer this fear in recent years and his social life is adequate. He has had difficulties in his sexual life for he has had a number of girl-friends, most of them involving short-lived romances.

He has more recently been subject to fits of despondency when he has had thoughts of suicide which culminated in a minor overdose (eight aspirin tablets) last March. He was visiting his family at the time and I wondered if there was some difficulty between them. Since then he has continued to feel depressed despite a small dose of amitriptiline. I wonder if you would see him and undertake some form of psychotherapy.

I began to analyse the referral by questioning the difficulties which might exist between the family members. He was a single 32-year-old son unfulfilled in his formation of relationships with women – possibly trouble in breaking or attenuating his bonds with his mother? He was unfulfilled in his work, lacking in confidence with a possibly neurotic father – trouble with authority? Identity crisis? I wondered why he had become despondent now – no mention of losses but something to look

*out for. Actually very little to go on in this referral letter. Could be any-
thing from an organic condition or incipient schizophrenic episode to a
family relationship problem. The GP seemed to settle on the family
influence and a need for psychotherapy. No transgenerational data at all.*

First Session

Mr Tucker arrived late. He was a short, bearded man, casually dressed.
During the first minutes of the session I read the referral letter to him
and he agreed substantially with its contents. *I did this in order to share
what little I knew. It was also a response to non-verbal cues of sus-
piciousness on his part.* The session proceeded along traditional psychiatric lines thereafter until I had satisfied myself that no organic or
psychotic illness was present.

I asked him to share as much of his family background with me as
was possible and introduced the idea of doing a geneogram. He was both
interested and relieved. The tension which was building in him receded.
He grasped its use as a visual aid readily.

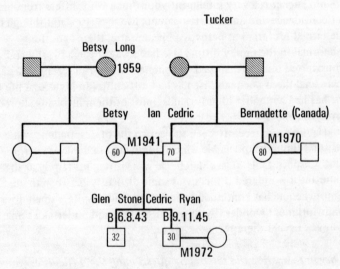

Figure 8.1 Geneogram of the Tucker Family, I

The information obtained is shown in Figure 8.1. Glen was the oldest of
two brothers. *I wondered why his character seemed not to fit that of an
oldest sibling.* His younger brother, Cedric, had married two years

previously and the period of his brother's engagement and marriage seemed to coincide with the overt development of Glen's symptoms. *Was this exit-entry-shift in family relationships the precipitating event in the development of his problem? Sibling rivalry? Their ages are close.* His parents married during the war in 1941. His father, Ian Cedric, trained as a lawyer. He had a sister, Bernadette, who was ten years older and lived in Canada. She had married recently after a long life as an eccentric spinster. *I noted that his mother couldn't have been pregnant when married unless there had been a miscarriage; also that his brother Cedric had been named after his father; and finally that his aunt had also married recently. Was there some moulding of his aunt's personality into him through his father?* His mother had a married sister who lived abroad. Glen didn't know whether she was the younger or older sister or whether she had children. He and his family had lost touch with her long ago. His maternal grandparents had died many years ago and he had no memories of them. The details of his mother's family background were ill-defined and sketchy. He showed little curiosity in pursuing his lack of knowledge. *I thought that some secrets must exist in this area but that it was not yet time to pursue it. Did it relate to his difficulty with his relationships with women?* Information about his father's side of the family was equally sparse. He had never met his paternal grandparents since they had died prior to his parent's marriage. The resulting geneogram was a very incomplete one. *I had in my mind at this point that his first task would relate to his lack of knowledge about his family.*

First, I felt more attention must be paid to the initial engagement in therapy. After a brief discussion about his lack of confidence at work he returned to his heterosexual relationship problems. I offered him an initial formulation of my view of his problems. I said that I felt he was drifting from moment to moment without a clear understanding of his own motivation. He didn't seem to know what he wanted from his life. His brother's marriage had triggered his restlessness and despair, perhaps as a loss of a close relationship and a symbol of his own lack of bonding with anyone outside his family. I explained that his lack of interest in his background showed how little he understood the influences in his family which had moulded him into the person he was and maintained him as such. I felt that there was a danger that he might drift into therapy with no commitment as he had previously with the social worker. Before I agreed to treat him and possibly other members of his family I would need his emotional commitment to the therapy.

He reluctantly agreed with part of my formulation of his problems. He was unable to accept that his family could be involved in his problems, but he felt that I understood his feelings of despair and confusion. He explained that since he had left home seven years previously he had hardly seen his parents. He mentioned out of context that he had had little to do with his father since he had beaten his father in a game of chess when he was eight years old. His father thereafter avoided playing with him and they drifted apart emotionally. *I felt at the time that he was steering me away from any task involving his family.* As we talked he became more intrigued by the idea of therapy involving his family. *I sensed underlying reservations but decided that he was making enough of a commitment to work. He had also given me an opening for his first tasks.* I instructed him to sit down with his father and discuss his father's past with him. I asked him to seek out those sensitive and secret areas of the family past which might be present as barriers between him and his father. The areas included the courtship between Glen's parents, the deaths of his paternal grandparents and their effect on his father, and some information regarding his father's sister, especially her relationship with his father in their childhood. I suggested that he could write to his aunt requesting information about his father's early years from her memory. Finally I instructed him to challenge his father to a game of chess. *I gave him this instruction as an intuitive response to his previous disclosure. I felt it was a self-generated task from him.* We both laughed about this instruction and broke through his reservations. The session ended after one hour and he was given an appointment to return in one month. I expected that it would take one month to complete the tasks and realise some of the emotional impact which would result.

Afterthoughts and Analysis of the Session

I recognised a feeling of indefinite boundaries common to adults in an arrested adolescence. I was alert to issues of identity, maturity, and the growth of adult relationships. I wondered as the session proceeded how well I had explained a family-oriented view of his problems. I avoided pressing him to involve himself with his mother and her side of the family. I sensed his reluctance. His view of her was of a perfect but unapproachable person. I mentioned that she would have to be involved in the future and noted his coolness to this prospect.

The tasks were intended to catalyse an adult relationship with his father by exposing secrets. I also wished him to develop a peer relationship with his father's sister. I hoped that this step in altering relationship bonds would prepare him for work with his mother. I recognised afterwards that playing chess with his father was a task set by Glen. It was his declaration of motivation and a test of my willingness to treat him as an equal participant in the therapeutic situation.

His family's background was a mystery but I speculated that Glen's father identified him with his eccentric older sister. His brother was identified with his father by similar names and sibling positions in their families. Glen was an eccentric without knowing why, and his relationship with his father had turned sour at an early age without logical reason. This would partially explain his difficulty with his own identity.

I felt that Glen was loosely engaged in therapy and that the tasks assigned him would be carried out eventually. I was aware that neither he nor I knew the source of his problems. The family quandary involved an arrested transition from adolescence to adulthood in at least one child, the eldest child in the family.

Session Two

Glen returned and appeared more relaxed. He was early for his session and was enthusiastic in his greeting. He immediately launched into a description of his session with his father. He found that his father was surprisingly willing to talk about his family. Glen had used his request for a return chess match as an entry into a discussion with his father about his father's family. They spoke hesitantly about his family until the game ended. Glen won the game and his father asked for a return match. *I felt that this was a signal of the altered reaction between him and his father.* To his amazement his father then took a monograph from his bookcase and showed Glen a complete family geneology which his father had researched long before marrying. His father informed him that Cedric had seen it. He had wondered whether Glen would ever become interested. Glen was given a copy which he proudly displayed to me in the session. We were side-tracked into a discussion of his family's remote past. *I felt that the family geneology was an important document for Glen but that it ignored the more immediate, recent emotional issues.* I asked Glen what secrets he had learned about his father or his father's family. His father had revealed that he had been married twice. The first marriage ended tragically when his wife had died on their honeymoon. Glen was emotionally involved as he spoke. His father had remarried late in life. He had met Glen's mother while she was nursing him in hospital. *I noted that the courtship was mentioned perfunctorily. Anything relating to his mother was avoided.* He learned that he was named after his father's father. His father felt that his sister had drifted throughout her life and noted some similarities between Glen and this sister. Glen believed his relationship with his father was better. They would have more contact although the relationship was still cooler than he would have liked. He was more relaxed in his father's presence and they had been phoning each other more often since his visit. *I felt that the bond between them was reactivated but changed from a child-parent bond to one between peers.* He had written to his aunt three days before the session but had not yet received a reply.

When asked how he felt in himself, he was still confused. Glen felt no better about his work or his ability to develop lasting relationships with women. He was less unhappy and despondent but such temporary improvements had occurred in the past. *It was time to turn to his relationship with women, leading to a discussion of their links with his mother. His statement about temporary improvement reawakened my fear that he would drift in the therapy.*

In the remainder of the one-hour session we discussed heterosexual relationships and bonds. He described an intense ambivalence towards his girl-friends. If they became attached to him or interested in him he was repelled. Women who were uninterested in him proved a challenge. As soon as he had gained their attention and interest he left them. With one girl-friend who argued with him over trivialities he unemotionally disagreed with every third remark she made. This confrontation satisfied his girl-friend and she stopped arguing, but he lost interest in her. *A conflict was moulded into him from some transgenerational influence. There was a heterosexual bonding quandary. His father had a traumatic first marriage, his aunt only married late in life, and his symptoms began when his brother married. Perhaps he can't contemplate marriage while he remains in a child-parent bond with his mother?* A comparison of the similarities between his mother's relationship with him and his relationship with other women was made. His mother's contact with other family members was fraught. His brother argued often with her and his father did the same. Glen was the only immediate family member who did not argue with her. He often sided with her in her arguments with the others. He felt that he kept a distance from her which enabled him to keep his independence without arguing. He felt his mother would be easy to talk to and more understanding than his father. Yet, he shrank from engaging in close conversation with her. He revealed that his middle name, 'Stone', was his mother's maiden name. *He must have been named for some reason. Replacement? Some secret on his mother's side of the family?* He mentioned his annoyance at his mother's continued use of an infant nickname, Pooba. This fleeting comment was quickly covered over with further accounts of his mother's kindness to him. *I felt he had given me the clue to another task.*

I explained that naming him after his grandfather might mean that he replaced some aspect of his grandfather in his father's eyes. I asked him to continue exploring his father's family of origin. I explained that this task should keep him in some contact with his father and help establish a new affinity with him. I asked him to request that his mother stop using his baby name. His adult name was Glen and she should call him that. I asked him to talk to his mother about her family of origin and her past. He was unsettled by both suggestions despite a full explanation of the reasons and the connection between her and his problems with girl-friends. *I felt that he might fail in these tasks with his mother but hoped that he would make the attempt.* He was asked to return in four weeks.

Afterthoughts and Analysis of the Session

I was pleased with the work that Glen had done with his father. He had taken steps to balance their relationship and in the process had learned more about his own roots. I had hoped that work would increase his motivation more than it had. The intensity of his avoidance of tasks relating to his mother puzzled me. Either there were some family secrets around which his mother held a boundary, or my initial formulation was in error. I hoped it was the former. His ambivalence towards women certainly included his mother. Since my own family had included an analogous problem I hoped the similarities hadn't affected my ability to judge the tasks necessary for him to change. I wondered if he would return for the next session and I worried that I had rushed him into tasks for which he was ill-prepared. I hoped he would accomplish the tasks he had suggested, that of being addressed by his adult name.

Session Three

Glen arrived late to the session. He looked unhappy; his clothes were scruffy and his beard and long hair were dishevelled. He had dark circles under his eyes. He started by explaining that he had had several severe crying spells since our last session. He was feeling more troubled and unhappy than he had for several months. He had been home to see his father and mother and had asked his mother to stop calling him Pooba. He felt that he had hurt her by his request but that she reluctantly agreed to honour his wishes. She said little during the remainder of his visit. He did not feel able to approach her about personal matters after he had just injured her. He spoke at length with his father but despite the increasing intensity and interest generated within this new relationship he ended his visit home feeling increasingly despondent and lonely. One week later his mother phoned him on his birthday and used his baby name while wishing him a happy birthday. He was intensely annoyed but unable to correct her on the phone. Since then he wondered whether it was wise to delve into these matters since they only seemed to make him more miserable. He had become increasingly aware of the anger he felt towards his mother but felt extremely guilty about it. *We had come to the turning point of the therapy. If I could explain the task more clearly and motivate him sufficiently, I felt that he could break through the barriers erected between himself and his mother. I was pleased that he had realised some of the negative aspects of that relationship.*

I spent most of the remainder of that session confronting Glen with the task that faced him. I pointed out my own speculations about the cause of the secrecy which existed between him and his mother. I explained that he must be a replacement for someone in her family but that there was no proof yet because of the lack of information. I pointed out the similarities in her relationships with each of the men in her family. She was attracted to her husband when he needed nursing and protected him still. Her relationship with Glen and his brother was over-protective. Because of the collision of the two family cultures, Glen was less able to break away from the over-protection. I redrew his family geneogram on the blackboard to enforce an objective view of his family on him. I explained that the task facing him must be done. His main problem was fear of his mother and of the effect a change in that relationship might have on him. He responded by admitting that his relationship with his mother needed changing. But his first attempt had failed and he felt much worse since the effort had been made. I pointed out that it was the failure of the task which had made him despair. He finally realised that his failure had deeply affected him. His motivation was stimulated by this obvious connection between the task with his mother and his emotional state.

We had been involved in a therapeutic relationship for three months. The remainder of the therapy was clear to us both. He fatalistically agreed that he would return home and ask his mother about her past and her family background. He more firmly resolved not to allow his mother to call him Pooba. *This resolve seemed the start of an inner change from adolescent to adult.* He departed admitting that he was frightened of what might happen over the next four weeks but his strength of purpose had asserted itself. He seemed more agitated but less depressed than when he had entered the office.

Afterthoughts and Analysis of the Session

By the end of the session I felt considerably relieved. I was certain that the session marked a turning point, not only in the therapy, but in the life of Glen Tucker. In order to change a relationship, one of the two people involved must take the first step. I felt that Glen had done that during the session. The task assigned would lead him to a confrontation with his mother which would alter their relationship. I was not certain that the task I had chosen for him was a correct one. I hoped that he would learn the reasons for his mother's over-protective concern, but the boundary between himself and his mother would shift and change. I was sure that he would return. On his return he would undertake and complete any further work required. I felt the entire family would ultimately benefit from the shift in relationship. His next session might be the last one required.

Session Four

Glen arrived early, appearing relaxed and happy. He moved with an assurance and confidence which I had not seen in him before. He started the session by informing me that the weekend after his session with me he had returned home for a visit and spoken to both his parents. He related with pride that he had firmly told his mother that he did not want to be called Pooba any more because it was degrading. He asked his mother to spend some time going through old photo albums with him. Although she was startled at the strength and forcefulness of his request, his persistance was rewarded. While looking through old photographs she described the story of her life and that of her family (see Figure 8.2).

Glen told his story with a depth of feeling which he had previously rarely shown. His maternal grandfather was born out of wedlock. He was the bastard son of English nobility. Throughout his grandfather's childhood he had been an embarrassment and a well-kept secret to the family which helped support and educate him. When he married he was encouraged to emigrate to Ghana. There his first-born son died after contracting malaria at seven years of age. He had also had two daughters; the younger was Glen's mother. The loss of their eldest and only son was a tragedy which hung like a pall over the household for many years. Glen's mother recalled that her father blamed himself and was a broken man thereafter. They returned to England shortly after their son's death. They refused to contact their noble relatives and secrecy enshrouded the connections with their extended family. *Now it was clear to me; Glen was the first-born son who had taken the place of his dead uncle, the dead older brother of his mother. She had become over-protective of her son, following an unconscious moulded concern about ensuring the survival of her son. The avoidance of discussion was moulded into Glen's mother from the secrecy which his maternal grandfather possessed within him.* Glen was surprised to discover that his younger brother had already known most of these details about his mother's past. Cedric had questioned her about it in his early teens. She hadn't wanted to worry Glen with the details of her life and so had never volunteered the information. He spent over two hours in conversation with his mother, during which he felt emotionally strained. By the end of their talk he was exhausted. He reported that when he took his leave of his parents at the end of the weekend he had felt alive and at peace with himself.

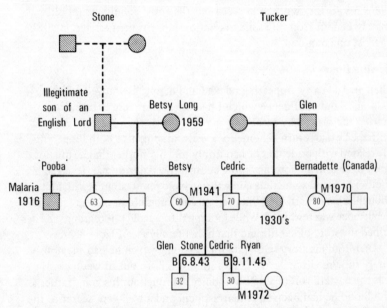

Figure 8.2 Geneogram of the Tucker Family, II

During the following weeks he felt a new sense of freedom and responsibility. His mother contacted him several times and was careful not to call him by his childhood name (a name which had also been his dead uncle's). Concomitantly he noted an alteration in his relationships with women at work and on dates. As a result of his discussions with his mother he found that he was much less worried when getting into intimate situations with women. He found that he was more direct in dealing with his photographic models and colleagues. He had no recurrence of the feelings of despair or lack of drive which had plagued him previously. *I felt that he was almost euphoric in his sense of accomplishment. He was perhaps floating at an unrealistic level.*

The remainder of the session I explored the impact of his new growth on the rest of his life. Since only three weeks had elapsed, he was too close to the alteration in dynamics within his family. I felt that a follow-up period would be necessary. He incidently reported that the arguments between his parents had decreased and that he was in closer contact with his brother than he had been previously. The only task which had failed to develop was that of involving Glen with his father's sister. She had failed to reply to his letter.

The session ended with a discussion of the need for further work. He felt that he had no further need to continue. After some discussion I agreed with him and asked that he return in six months for a follow-up appointment. *I felt that he was asking for necessary time to consolidate his feelings and the alteration in the family relationships which had resulted from his work.* He thanked me for my help and left the office.

Afterthoughts and Analysis of the Session

My immediate thought after this session was that it all seemed too good to be true. I was suspicious of this 'instant relief'. From his account, the transgenerational analysis had become clear. His mother had singled him out as the especially vulnerable child who must be protected from any form of physical or emotional harm. She was unable to prepare him for separation from the family by taking the initiative. In the collision of family cultures, his father had identified him with his older sister, an eccentric and uncommunicative sibling. He had cut Glen off emotionally at an early age and was unable to provide the help Glen might have valued in his adolescence. Secrecy was a strong and common feature on both sides of the family, which created difficult boundaries for Glen to cross because of his vulnerable position. His therapeutic work involved uncovering the secrets, forging a new relationship with his parents and integrating himself within his nuclear family as an adult instead of a child. As a result of this alteration he gained a stronger sense of identity, increased confidence and supportive adult relationships with his parents. Nevertheless I felt uneasy when he left the office. I hoped that he would return for follow-up if only to confirm that his new-found status was not temporary.

Follow-up

Mr Tucker did not return after six months for his follow-up appointment. Neither did he answer written requests suggesting that he attend at an alternate date and time. Attempts to contact him by phone and letter were to no avail. I wondered what the ultimate result of my interventions in his family were to be. Although vaguely disquieted I was reasonably confident that none of the work we had done together would have damaged Glen or his family members. As time went by with no word from him I gave little extra thought to this family therapy which I had provisionally classified as successfully concluded.

Two years following the completion of the therapy, I began a pilot study on the outcome of my patients. With help and some detective work I managed to trace Glen. He apologised to me for having missed his final appointment. He had felt that the last session was sufficient for him and events in his life overtook his resolve to keep the follow-up appointment. He had moved from his original flat several times during the six-month period and as a result both his address and telephone number had changed. His relationship with his parents and brother had blossomed, and he was now married and expecting the arrival of his first child. He had received several promotions in his work since the therapy sessions and he was very happy and content with his life. I was satisfied that the family therapy sessions had been instrumental in the change in his life.

A Treatment Failure

In this chapter and the succeeding two chapters I intend to provide synopses of cases using similar transgenerational practices and techniques to those used in successful cases in order to illustrate the failures of this approach. In this way I hope to provide a balanced picture of my work. I believe that no one theory or method of therapy can provide a universal method of dealing with family quandaries.

The following case report briefly describes the unsuccessful use of transgenerational family therapy methods with an individual family member.

A 26-year-old writer was referred to me by his general psychiatrist. He had requested the referral because the patient wished a psychotherapeutic approach to his problems which included an obsessive preoccupation with sexual matters, free-floating anxiety and guilt.

In our first interview I established that he had a mild obsessional neurosis characterised by ruminations. He also suffered from multiple discrete phobias, including a public-speaking phobia and a telephone phobia. His original referral coincided with the exacerbation of symptoms while preoccupied with his feelings about a new girl-friend of whom he was unsure. She had recently emigrated abroad. His family background was remarkable for its paucity of married siblings or uncles on both his father's and mother's side of the family (Figure 8.3).

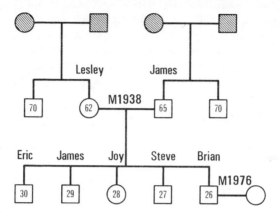

Figure 8.3 Geneogram of a Treatment Failure

Neither of his uncles had married nor had any of his four older siblings. His parents came from widely divergent religious backgrounds and religion played a major role in the patient's development until the age of eighteen when he rejected the teachings of the church and became an atheist. Despite this break with his parents' orthodoxy, his parents continued to accept him and welcome him into their home. His mother was his major confidant to whom he would detail his every problem.

My analysis of the transgenerational influences led me to conclude that he was unable to become an adult member of the family without a major battle with his parents. Since his parents were so accepting they could not be induced to fight with him. This situation may have been similar to that which had prevented his older siblings or his uncles from separating from their respective parents. As the youngest son, he was the most over-protected by his family and he reacted to it by over-compensating. His attempt to stir up conflict by rejection of his parents' beliefs had failed to free him from their influence. His obsessional symptoms had been present since his early teenage years but were increased in severity when his girl-friend left and he realised that he was in love with her. Since the only model of marriage he had was that of his parents he had rejected marriage as an institution. Because of that model, he had become paralysed by indecision. A part of him wanted to follow his inclinations to propose and marry.

The therapy involved this patient in several weekend sessions with his parents, attempting to confront them with his inner feelings and needs. Further transgenerational information was obtained and finally a confrontation that was engineered between himself and his father occurred. The resulting conflict split the family and the patient became totally estranged from his parents for six months while his siblings polarised and wrote letters to him taking sides. He proposed to his girl-friend and married her without inviting any of the family to attend. An uneasy rapprochement occurred between himself and the family. His problems at work and his phobias had disappeared as the result of some behavioural work.

At two-year follow-up he had begun to attend a private therapist for guidance and help with his obsessive ruminations and marital difficulties. His relationship with his parents remained strained but cordial.

Notes

1. M. Bowen, 'Family Therapy after Twenty Years', in *Handbook of Psychiatry*, unedited draft.

2. E. Carter and M. Orfandis, 'Family Therapy with One Person and the Family Therapist's Own Family', in P. Guerin (ed.), *Family Therapy* (Gardner Press, New York, 1976), pp. 193-219.

9 FAMILY THERAPY WITH A MARITAL COUPLE: A CLINICAL CASE STUDY

If a man loves you he will marry you
and never be mad at you and always smile;
and you will be happy ever after.

Paul, *An American Fairy Tale*

Sing and dance together and be joyous,
but let each one of you be alone
Even as the strings of a lute are alone
though they quiver with the same music.

Gibran, *The Prophet*

A man may not marry his grandmother.

Book of Common Prayer

Marital therapy is often treated as a discipline separate and distinct from family therapy. For example, leading textbooks in the field of family therapy separate 'marital' from 'family' therapy in their titles.[1] The position of marital therapy as a separate discipline, requiring its own strategies and techniques, acknowledges real differences. The heterosexual bond upon which marriage is based differs from other bonds in important respects. Sexuality is the first of these distinguishing features. The physical relationship between a man and woman joined through their lovemaking adds a new dimension to emotional attachment and cohabitation. A second feature is the peculiarity of the marital choice. Marital relationships are newly-formed; spouses do not grow up together nor do the partners accept each other from birth, as occurs in almost every other family relationship. Two comparative strangers choose to share their lives together. Transgenerational influences in the family collision affect this marital bonding. Finally the marital bond differs from other bonds through its future potential. The marital partnership can be and often is a prelude to parenthood and the production of children. This procreative function creates unique problems as new families develop.

For the above reasons alone, the marital relationship is subject to immense stress. It is all too common in Western societies to isolate this stress within the marital subsystem. Even when requiring treatment, the marital couple are regarded in isolation, without consideration of the

175

extra-marital sources of the stress. In his attempts to solve the marital puzzle, Paul[2] offers a model with a transgenerational perspective to marital therapy. He incorporates marital therapy within the framework of the extended family, analysing the marital quandary to determine whether there are unsolved problems which relate more properly to pre-existing relationships.

In the following clinical case study I have attempted to illustrate the type of marital therapy which can be done through the use of the trans-generational perspective. This brief case provides a model in which only the marital couple attend the therapy sessions, but their extended family members become involved in the therapy.

The Referral

Mrs Susan Yardley was referred for individual treatment to a general psychiatric clinic by her general practitioner. She was a 21-year-old married Canadian secretary, with a history of depression for several years which had recently worsened. She and her husband were referred after the psychiatrist treating her in the outpatient clinic found a link between her major problems and symptoms and her relationship with her husband. She had refused medications; her referral was an alternative to admitting her to hospital for voluntary electroshock therapy.

The referral was a verbal one initially. I spoke with my colleague and examined the case notes before my first interview.

Case Note Summary

Mrs Yardley was accompanied by her husband at her first interview. She had been depressed for three years, with increasing intensity since a visit by her mother and sister, Linda, four months previously. She had suicidal thoughts but had not attempted suicide. Her depression began in Toronto where she attended Art School. Her relationship with a boy-friend ended when she became pregnant. She had an abortion and then visited England hoping to enroll in an Art School but was turned down. She met her husband at a pop concert in England six months after arriving in the country.

He was a guitarist in a band. They lived together for a while and married eighteen months later. She felt that her relationship with her husband was deteriorating as had many of her previous relationships.

Her family background was recorded as unremarkable except that her father died when she was eight years old. She was the middle daughter of three sisters. She felt that her younger sister received attention that was rightfully hers. Mrs Yardley argued frequently with her mother. She felt her mother had a wicked streak. After their rows she would leave home. After her elder sister left home there was a relatively happy period in her life at home.

Mrs Yardley had been treated briefly for depression in Toronto when she was sixteen. At the end of this first interview, the psychiatrist diagnosed a neurotic depression and prescribed tricyclic antidepressants.

In the following interview, the psychiatrist listened to the husband's view of the problem. He seemed an inoffensive man, concerned for his wife's welfare. He added little to her history and his background was unremarkable. He was an only child with no psychiatric or family problems. She complained that medications hadn't helped.

After missing one further appointment the couple attended four weeks later. Mr Yardley felt his wife was much improved. He rambled on until his wife interrupted and asked to see the psychiatrist alone. She admitted to a great marital unhappiness. She couldn't bear his touch, couldn't communicate her feelings to him. She felt they had little in common. If she was critical of him he responded by looking and acting hurt so that her guilt increased. Their sexual relationship had been a good one until they were married. She had made the decision to marry him after returning to Canada on a visit. She had missed him desperately. She now regretted returning. She felt that nothing was shared and that they were leading two independent lives. The psychiatrist asked her husband back into the office and shared this information with him.

The next session four weeks later she attended alone. She and her husband had had a dreadful row. She was depressed and tearful. She stopped her medicines because they were ineffective. Her eldest sister had visited but the visit increased her misery. The psychiatrist prescribed phenelzine and agreed to see her in two weeks.

She returned alone and told him the medication had been useless. She felt worse and her relationship with her husband was poor. The psychiatrist offered her the choice of marital therapy or admission to hospital and she chose the former.

My discussion with her psychiatrist added his conviction that the relationship between the husband and wife was a crucial precipitant. Although the couple had been living together before their marriage, their sexual and emotional relationship had deteriorated immediately after their marriage.

Afterthoughts and Analysis of Referral

I found myself with more questions than answers. Was this a case in which marital therapy would help? My thoughts skipped about. Do these two love each other? From all the present information they remained together despite their unhappiness and the bond was strengthened during a separation. Their family backgrounds must incorporate essential and important national differences as well as family cultural ones. The transgenerational influences must clash in ways not yet apparent in this 'hybrid' marriage. I drew my version of their family tree (see Figure 9.1). Her father's death was the most important of the life events which required exploration. I wondered if her husband replaced her father in several important unconscious attributes. What was her reaction to his death? What happened to her family afterwards?

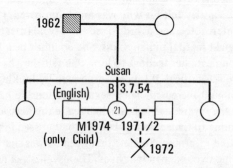

Figure 9.1　First Geneogram of the Yardley Couple

She was the middle of three girls and her husband was an only child. Perhaps this was the root of his communication problem with her. She expected that he would know how to communicate with peers the way she had learned to communicate with her sisters. Neither of them had experience of other sex siblings, however. His parents would have moulded him to a greater extent as an only child. I wondered why he was an only child. I felt that his extended family might be more necessary as a resource than hers. I wondered why he married her. He knew about her past background. Did he tend to pick women who needed him for his own compulsive reasons?

Session One

Videotape recording was used in this session. The couple were told that the tape would be available for them to watch. It would also provide me with a record of their interactions for later study and for teaching purposes if they agreed. *I wanted a tape which would show the geneogram technique.* The couple agreed to the use of the equipment and subject to its review they agreed to its use as a teaching aid.

They sat opposite me and Mrs Yardley began a long, tedious monologue about her depressive symptoms. Nevertheless, she was more animated than her husband, who sat silent and looked brooding and miserable. I asked about his feelings but he defended himself. He argued that he did his best to cheer his wife up when she was in her moods, but she seemed to get worse when he did it. *I felt that they were both too wrapped up in their own feelings and thoughts.* I explained that I'd like to learn a bit more about their family background.

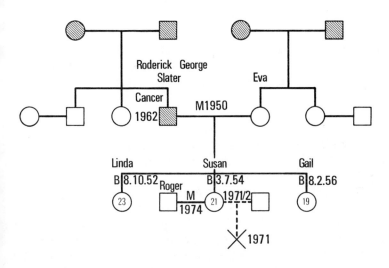

Figure 9.2   Geneogram of Susan (Slater) Yardley's Family

I began with Mrs Yardley and drew the resulting geneogram on the blackboard (see Figure 9.2). We quickly entered into an exploration of circumstances leading up to and including her father's death. She felt that her father had favoured her eldest sister, Linda. Susan had loved him or his character. She felt warm and loving towards her father and denied experiencing angry feelings towards him. *Idealisation of her dead father?* He developed cancer of the stomach when she was six years old and died slowly at home after refusing an operation. Her mother reacted badly to the death. She withdrew from her children, becoming bad-tempered, irritable, and depressed until she received private psychiatric care when Susan was sixteen. Susan was receiving psychiatric help herself at this time. *The death of her father had not been worked through by her mother or herself. I felt that Roger was a replacement for him. I was fairly certain that family therapy was the correct approach for this couple. My reasons for this certainty were unclear.*

I asked if Roger resembled her father in appearance or character. After some hesitation she compared their fastidiousness and artistic abilities. She also felt that his face resembled that of her father. I explained that people fall in love with partners who may represent the image of a person whom they loved in the past. The frustration which occurs in the resulting relationship owes much to the discrepancy between expectations and the reality of the other person's nature. *I'm leading up to an explanation of the way she replaced her father with her husband.* We discussed the details of her father's death more fully and I found out that she was the only member of the nuclear family who had not attended the funeral. She had avoided it and had stayed home with her maternal aunt, but she could not remember why. *The first signs of a morbid grief?* She could recall little of her reaction to her father's death but as I continued probing she began to cry. Her husband looked uneasy and moved to comfort her. He told an amusing story but she became angry at him and her tears dried up as they began arguing. *I wondered if this was their usual pattern of disturbed interaction. But how did marriage precipitate the depression in her?* I interrupted to explain the way in which an unmourned loss can remain dormant and reappear to haunt a person for years after the event. I pointed out that her tears had flowed while discussing her father. I introduced the idea that she might need to discover more about her father. I wanted to explore painful feelings originating with his illness and death. I connected this task with the fact that I felt she had placed some aspects of her father in Roger without being consciously aware of it. *I wondered if marrying him had put her in the position of repossessing her father only to paradoxically await a new loss. Had this reawakened her grief at her father's death?* I explained that she must discover what her buried feelings towards her father were and work them through rather than using Roger as a replacement for those feelings. Roger was NOT her father, came from a different family background and culture than her father and reacted to her differently than her father. I then suggested three tasks to her. Since she idealised her father, I asked her to write to her mother and ask about the negative aspects of his character and personality. *I hoped this task would allow her to obtain a more realistic view of her father while establishing an adult relationship with her mother.* Her second task was to list the similarities and differences between her husband and her father. Finally, I asked that she write separately to each of her sisters and ask them about their memories of her father and his death. *She seemed to be the only child in the family who had been adversely affected. I wondered whether it was due to her sibling position. Her mother was the second child of a mother whose own mother had remarried after her first husband's death. Identification with mother? Loss of a father would have been a very sensitive issue. Had her mother's psychiatric work involved this issue?*

The session was drawing to a close. Roger had been fairly uninvolved personally, acting as an observer. He felt that his wife prevented him from successfully dealing with her feelings of loss, depression or anger, I asked him why he had married Susan. He knew she had been depressed intermittently in the past and had accepted her despite this. He admitted that he had always had a tendency to put himself in situations with people who were basically unhappy and needed to be loved. I asked him to consider seriously from whom in his family background this particular tendency might originate. I told them both that their marital therapy was linked to their own respective past experiences rather than the present problem in their relationship. I asked if they were willing to work with me in this way and they both agreed. I admitted to Roger that I had neglected him and his side of the issues and that our next appointment in one month's time would be devoted to him and his family.

Afterthoughts and Analysis of the Session

After they departed I studied the geneogram. Roger was included as an appendage to Susan's family. Neither of Susan's sisters had married yet. Her mother came from a home in which her own father had died. Her mother had also lost her husband. This fortuitous transgenerational pattern suggested a focus for the current quandary, derived from Susan's family system. Childhood bereavement was a focal issue. It had occurred in her mother's childhood as well as her own. Susan needed to learn to deal with loss in a less disabling way. I hoped to get her to achieve this by balancing her positive memories of her father with her repressed negative ones while encouraging the sharing of her feelings with her sisters and mother. Marrying Roger had set up a situation in which she awaited his death. It was as if a time bomb was set to go off. His attempts to cheer her up actually increased her agony. Roger would achieve more if he allowed her to suffer. A spiralling negative interaction was set up between them. After their display of a developing argument in the session, I felt it would be pointless to set them a task related solely to their arguments. The content was trivial, not unlike those of most married couples in their beginning. The background context was significant.

I felt that the Yardleys were satisfied with my approach to their problems. I was confidant that they would return for their next appointment and that they would work on the tasks I had set for them. I was convinced that they were strongly bonded together; the work required was related to transgenerational influences. Future problems in therapy would depend on the material which came from Roger's side of the family. I guessed that his family might be more secretive and that his inability to penetrate this secrecy was related to his sibling position as an only child. His repetitive choice of unhappy women who needed him indicated some replacement aspects to his choice of a partner.

Session Two

The session was again videotaped. We began by reviewing the tasks which had been set during the previous session. Susan had written to her mother and sisters. She received a reply from her mother which had been informative and revealing. She learned that her mother had needed help in dealing with the aftermath of her father's death. At the time they had both attended psychiatrists; her mother had continued with the treatment. The mother's psychiatrist had involved her in an exploration of her feelings towards her husband, and the treatment had helped her overcome her grief. Her mother admitted that there had been several negative features to Susan's father which created difficulties in the home. He was a very stubborn man; he had been too stubborn to seek medical treatment when the first symptom of his illness occurred. Later, her parents had dreadful rows while considering the operation recommended by his surgeon. Her mother wondered why Susan was raking over the past in this way. She hinted that she had been thinking of visiting England in the near future. Susan reported that she had been more relaxed at home but she was still intermittently unhappy. She was often very angry with Roger since the last session. *I felt that her anger reverberated to her angry feelings over the loss of her father.* She had found it difficult to list her father's unpleasant traits. She found it difficult to think about him without getting depressed. She admitted that it served to confirm that her depression was directly related to her father. This understanding gave her hope for the future. The letters she had written to her sisters had not yet been answered. *I felt that she had done some useful work and was pleased with her mother's response. Susan no longer felt that Roger was responsible for her unhappiness.* I asked that she continue her correspondence with her mother about her father's death. I suggested that Susan trace her mother's reaction back to her own upbringing. I pointed out that her father's brother had died tragically in a car accident, her mother's mother had remarried after the death of her first husband. Death and loss were particularly sensitive issues in her mother's family background. Some of Susan's reaction to her father's death was certainly determined by moulded reaction patterns to loss derived from that heritage. I noted that her loss of her father might be translated within her into a fear or dread of the loss of her own husband. Finally I added that her mother's middle name and sibling position in her family or origin were similar to Susan's in her own family of origin. *Susan and her mother had more in common than she realised. I released the information gleaned from the geneogram in a blunderbuss fashion. I hoped she would be receptive to it. I was conscious that Roger was anxiously waiting and I felt that I must keep my promise to explore his background with him.*

Roger had been sitting patiently while I was speaking with his wife. I turned to him and asked for his impression of our last session — how he had felt and what he had remembered and understood. He had given the session a great deal of consideration and thought. He learned a great deal about his own response to Susan. He had been particularly intrigued by the idea that he picked people to befriend who were unhappy and in need of love. Susan agreed that he tended to date girls who were sad and depressed. I suggested that if she sorted her problems out, their relationship would have to change or it would probably disintegrate. *Roger needed to understand the need for himself actively to change his reactions. If she didn't need what he gave to her any more because she had become a more integrated person, then he would be unnecessary.* I asked if he had discovered the source of his tendency to pick unhappy women. He could find no one in his family who had been so unhappy that he had cheered them up and helped them in the way we had discussed.

At this juncture in the session I turned to the blackboard and began to construct his family tree (see Figure 9.3). He admitted that he had questioned his parents many times about their past and their backgrounds but neither of them had been very forthcoming. His parents had consistently refused to bring out any information related to sexuality or childbirth. Painful matters that may have occurred in the past were brushed aside. I pointed out that secrecy was a way of putting boundaries between the generations. Those on both sides of the boundary were

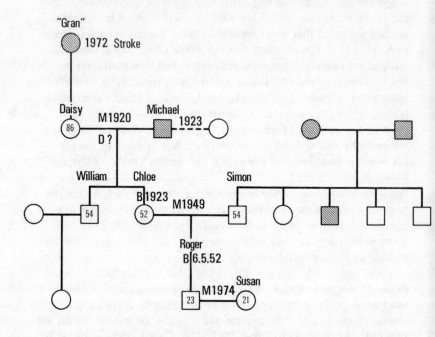

Figure 9.3   Geneogram of Roger Yardley's Family

responsible for maintaining it. He felt that his parents were basically happy although his mother often argued with his father. He described his mother as being very temperamental and thoughtless with her tongue, while his father was honest and caring. His descriptions of his parents didn't fit his description of his wife's character; I led him into a discussion of his extended family. We examined his grandparents in great detail, especially his maternal grandparents. His mother's father had abandoned his grandmother shortly after his mother was born. His grandfather then went to live with another woman. Roger had no idea whether his grandparents were divorced. He had tried his hardest to find out details about his grandfather when he was younger, but when he asked his grandmother she would become upset and tearful. *I began to wonder if there was a parallel between the relationship with his grand-mother and his relationship with his wife.* Roger believed that his grand-mother had never stopped loving her husband despite his desertion of the family. She still cried over him and felt bitter to the present day. His grandmother criticised his mother because of her arguments with his father. She would point out how lucky his mother was to have such a good husband. Here Roger passionately said 'She's a lonely old lady, my grandmother, and she had nothing but a hard time all her life. It's a shame!' *I felt that the link between Roger's grandmother and his wife was definite.* I asked Roger if he had had much contact with his grand-mother during his childhood. He recalled that as a child he visited his grandmother and great-grandmother nearly every day. His parents lived nearby and there was a great deal of contact between family members. Even when he grew older he would visit two or three times a week. He went to have a laugh with them; they would cheer him up when he was down and he would do the same for them. *I now saw the origin of the pattern with Susan.* I explained to Roger that I knew his grandmother was a crucial influence in his life and that his grandfather had been a crucial, if absent, influence on her life. I detailed my growing certainty about the parallel between his relationship with his grandmother and his relationship with Susan. I thought that these parallels needed to be further explored. Both Susan and Roger denied strongly that Susan was anything like his grandmother. *I wondered why they protested so strongly.* I suggested that his relationship with Susan was at least partly based on one established with his grandmother, but he felt there was no connection. *Was I wrong or was the resistance due to taking his defences on directly? I decided to outflank him.* I asked Roger why he had been unable to find out more about his maternal grandfather and the circum-stances surrounding his disappearance. He admitted that he had asked his uncles, his grandmother and his mother, but they had kept the veil of secrecy firmly drawn. He had not been able to pierce it. *I felt that he had established a useful task for himself.* I pointed out that he didn't know how to ask his family about these matters so that they would give him the answers. I challenged him to return to the members of his family of origin to discover the cause of this secrecy. I asked if perhaps he didn't feel adult enough to discuss these matters with them? *Cross the generational boundaries and become an adult was the message. His reluctance and inability to pursue the matter was a major factor in his lack of information. Why had this particular task assumed such import? The answer glimmered on the threshold of my thoughts but eluded me.*

After this confrontation with Roger I spent further time establishing other facts about the extended family background on both sides of Roger's family. He had always wanted a grandfather and had envied his school friends because they had one. His paternal grandfather had died when his father was young and his paternal grandmother had died when he was a child. The reactions to these losses were explored and seemed to have been appropriately mourned by the family members. I finished the geneogram by adding Susan to the Yardley family as an appendage. In order to add some conviction to the need for Roger to undertake and complete his task with his grandmother, I played back the section of the videotape which had captured his intense feelings about his grandmother. He watched a scene during which I had speculated about the effects of his grandmother's death upon him. He was able to detect that his outward appearance was incongruous with his inner feelings at the time.

The session ended with Roger promising to contact his relatives. Both Susan and Roger were pleased with the work that had been done so far. The session ended with assurances that they would continue their work.

Afterthoughts and Analysis of the Session

The session was a highly successful one. Not only was Roger engaged into the therapeutic process, he became a wholehearted and eager participant. He departed eager to pursue the task which he had suggested. I realised afterwards what I had glimpsed in the session. For Roger to complete his task with his grandmother he would have to refrain from cheering her up and cause her some pain during the process of finding out about his grandfather. I was worried that the task might alienate him from his grandmother. But I was reassured that there was no evidence in family patterns of this type of reaction. His capacity to tolerate his grandmother's unhappiness would increase. By forming a relationship based on empathy and tolerance he would establish a new model for his relationship with his wife, breaking the negative feedback in their relationship. If he no longer needed to entertain and comfort his grandmother he could talk more openly about the distressing and unhappy feelings which his wife possessed.

Susan had actively pursued her tasks. As a result of her work she seemed somewhat brighter than in the previous session. I felt especially encouraged upon hearing that her mother might visit her. The visit would provide a personal encounter which would be superior to the effect of communications by letter. I was certain that Susan would continue her work on her tasks.

I was confident that the therapeutic outcome would be a beneficial one for both marital partners and their families. I believed that their mutual understanding would increase and that their bond would be strengthened. There were areas of family life which remained untouched. The Yardleys had no children so that the collision of family culture might in future be activated by the occurrence of children. The familial pattern of absent male figures was a mutual one and seemed compatible, but socio-cultural backgrounds might cause conflict in child-rearing practices. But very little marital work would remain if the Yardleys were able to accomplish the work which we had mutually set out.

Session Three

Mr and Mrs Yardley returned for their appointment in a relaxed and cheerful mood. Mrs Yardley was beaming. The session was videotaped once again. Susan had received an unexpected visit from her mother. The visit was preceded by one day's advance notice. *A confirmation of the strength of the effect that her letters had in opening new communication channels.* Her mother discussed her letters on the way home from the airport. She noticed the change in her daughter's attitude from her letters. Her mother was both curious and pleased that Susan was at last asking about those difficult years in their lives. Her mother shared many personal feelings and thoughts with Susan during the short visit. Susan learned that she had always been her father's favourite daughter. He was a strict, unbending man however, dealing out punishment in the family when necessary. When his illness developed, he became very depressed and considered ending his life if the pain became too severe. Susan related with great feeling that she and her mother had cried together for the first time in her adult life. *This was a significant alteration in their relationship.* Susan went on to describe her father's faults in greater detail. She admitted to angry feelings about some of the punishments he had imposed. But she realised that the anger towards her father was related to his desertion of her when he died. *An acknowledgement that she accepted some of the facts I had taught her about the mourning process. She incorporated this information and it had changed her emotional reactions.*

Susan felt that her relationship with Roger was much improved. Recently when she felt unhappy, he allowed her space to be alone, he did not interfere unless she asked him for comfort. His changed reactions coupled with the work she had done on her father's death and the alteration of her relationship with her mother had considerably eased her depressive symptoms.

Roger entered the office with a new air of assurance. He explained

that he had left the second session determined to find out more about
the secrets in his family. During the following week, he arranged to see
his parents, his grandmother and his uncles. He visited and questioned
them about many different areas of their past. He forced himself to ask
questions at first, but found that he was much less frightened by the last
of his family interviews. He was able to find out a great deal about his
past and the family background. He learned that his maternal grandfather was a bigamist and might still be alive. He examined his grandfather's life minutely with his grandmother. Although she was reduced
to tears, he persisted, and when he had finished he felt emotionally
closer to his grandmother than he had ever been. He constructed his own
geneogram during his visits to his family. He proudly showed it to me
during the session (see Figure 9.4).

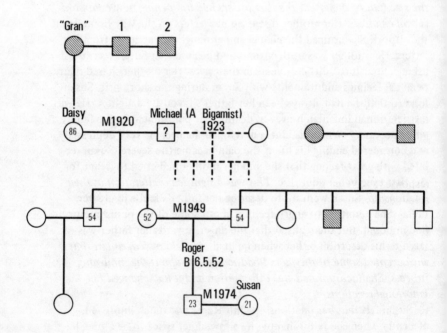

Figure 9.4 A Portion of Mr. Yardley's Self–constructed Geneogram

Mrs Yardley said that he was quite shaken after his visits with his relatives but that his attitude towards her had altered since then.

Their sexual relations had greatly improved; their daily interpersonal interactions were less sticky, warmer and more realistic. They both felt that their reactions with each other had improved to the point that they were better than before their marriage. *If their reports were true there was little work left for us to do.*

I questioned them about their plans for the future. Roger was considering a move to a new job in Scotland or Canada. They had recently discussed the possibility of having children although no definite plans had been made. Roger felt that the work we had done had benefited him considerably. He admitted that he had never before taken time to look at himself and his family. He valued the opportunity to let his true self show through the facade with which he had previously protected himself. I agreed to their request for several months' respite in order to let their new relationships settle. They would return in four months for a follow-up appointment.

Afterthoughts and Analysis of the Session

I was delighted with their achievements. Roger had done more family work than Susan; he had been ready and willing to attempt tasks which followed his natural inclinations (he had tried more than once to do the tasks on his own). Roger was now able to cope with Susan's unhappiness. The only remaining difficulty could be his ability to cope with his children, an issue which was too premature to contemplate.

Susan had done a great deal of work aided by her mother's helpful response. I was not as certain about the changes in her. My uncertainty stemmed from my experience with others suffering from morbid grief. Longer periods of time were required to recover. However, the morbid process had been converted to a normal reaction. Her mother was available as a family resource so that she could continue the necessary grief work in her family. I believed that they would both return without further need for therapy sessions.

My analysis of the family quandary was more coherent at this point. Roger felt responsible for his wife's happiness. He had to cheer her out of the depression which began shortly after their marriage. This need to help others was present in all of his previous female relationships and was rooted in his childhood relationship with his grandmother. He also gained the expectation that after marriage, husbands either die or leave home before they can become grandfathers. Susan's depression was a delayed morbid reaction to her father's death when she was eight-years old. Marriage symbolised to her the end of a relationship, not its beginning. The more her husband attempted to cheer her up the greater was her feeling of loss stimulated by his presence and imagined proximate loss. Roger's change of relationship with his grandmother produced an empathic tolerance for distress which he could apply in his marital relationship. The change in the marital relationship was aided by Susan's work with her feelings about her dead father. The replacement aspects of Roger were returned to their source, the unmourned loss of her father. The work they had done was sufficient to resolve their quandary.

Follow-up

Mr and Mrs Yardley appeared for their follow-up appointment on time and in good spirits. They both felt embarrassed about taking my time. They had experienced no difficulties since our last appointment. They had learned quite a lot about each other and about their relationship. They were especially pleased with being able to look into their family backgrounds and the way in which their families influenced their marital relationship. Susan still had patches of sad feelings, especially when reminded of her father, but she recognised and coped with them. *I felt that Susan had been working through her father's loss and would continue this work in a healthy manner.*

Roger mentioned that they were finalising their move to Scotland and that they would be leaving in a few months. I asked them to keep in touch, perhaps by postcard once a year. Two years following the start of their treatment they were continuing happily without further need of help. Their first child was expected soon. I was satisfied that the work had produced a lasting change in their relationship.

A Treatment Failure

The preceding case illustrated the use of transgenerational analysis and consequent therapeutic practice in a marital case study. Both husband and wife received major benefit by conceptualising their quandary as involving their families of origin. Conclusion of unfinished work with their family members improved their relationship. But not all cases involving this approach will resolve in such an agreeable manner. The following vignette describes a treatment during which transgenerational approach with a marital couple failed.

Mr and Mrs Derdle were referred following a three-year history of depression in Mrs Derdle, unrelieved by medications. Her husband's threat to begin divorce proceedings led to their referral for marital therapy. Three marital sessions were followed by one individual session each with Mr and Mrs Derdle respectively. During the first session Mr Derdle admitted that he had lost his job. He was so involved in looking for a new job that he was too preoccupied to work on his relationship with his wife. I took a short history and constructed a geneogram which revealed a sibling position mismatch, and major family collision difficulties. He was the youngest of three sons from a European lower-class immigrant background, while she was the youngest of two daughters from a well-to-do English family. Neither of them wished to take on a task until the work situation was sorted out.

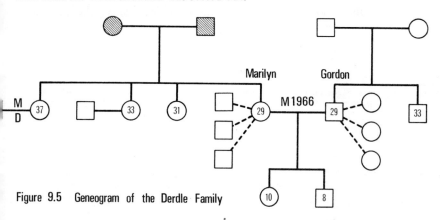

Figure 9.5   Geneogram of the Derdle Family

At their next two appointments, I carefully explained the transgenerational influences which seemed to bear on their marital conflicts. They discussed the extra-marital affairs they had during their marriage. Despite obtaining a job, Mr Derdle was reluctant to undertake any task at home or with a member of his family of origin. In their last marital appointment, Mrs Derdle felt that she was the one who needed help, not her husband. She wanted to be seen on her own. By this time the issue of divorce had disappeared. After a great deal of argument I agreed to see her alone if the session were audiotaped, and her husband was allowed the same option. I felt that they remained unengaged in the therapy. They were controlling the sessions with no investment in work aimed at changing themselves. I made my feelings about their lack of involvement clear. Their individual sessions were long vituperative catalogues of their partner's faults, interspersed with romantic descriptions of their various affairs. Neither partner understood their behaviour, yet they were curiously satisfied with the present state of affairs. I wondered if divorce had ever been more than an idle threat. No further sessions occurred after I asked them to listen to each other's taped individual session at home. They did as I asked, but prior to their next appointment I received a tear-stained letter from Mrs Derdle cancelling our appointment and requesting no further contact. She took me to task for my 'ludicrous' theories and castigated me for my calculated attempts to break up her marriage. She had talked to her husband's parents and found them a much greater help than my attempts to separate them. On follow-up of her case notes three years later, Mrs Derdle continued to be seen by a psychiatrist. She had made several further attempts to engage in marital therapy but they proved as unsuccessful as her individual visits to psychiatrists. She and her husband remained together despite her complaints about their relationship.

Notes

1. R. Skynner, *One Flesh, Separate Persons: Principles of Family and Marital Psychotherapy* (Constable, London, 1976); I. Glick, and D. Kessler, *Marital and Family Therapy* (Grune and Stratton, New York, 1974).

2. N. and B. Paul, *A Marital Puzzle* (Norton, New York, 1975).

10 FAMILY THERAPY WITH A NUCLEAR FAMILY: A CLINICAL CASE STUDY

Each unhappy family is unhappy
in its own way.

    Tolstoy, *Anna Karenina*

Children begin by loving their parents;
after a time they judge them; rarely,
if ever, do they forgive them.

    Oscar Wilde

Family therapy is popularly known as an intervention defined by the inclusion of children and parents in conjoint family sessions. Many professionals and most laymen use family therapy and conjoint family therapy synonymously. In fact, limiting family therapy to conjoint sessions can be as restricting and stultifying as any other therapeutic method. The intervention used should ideally flow from the family's needs rather than from the therapist's prejudice.

The nuclear family is most often the correct unit of therapeutic intervention when young, dependent children are referred as identified patients. The parents and siblings of a young child are inextricably involved in the child's daily life. They will have immediate and overpowering influences on any individual therapy attempted. Since these influences are omnipresent and the child cannot gain complete independence from his family, involvement of the nuclear family in the treatment process is a logical step. But conjoint therapy can begin with any family member as the identified patient.

Many family therapists work with various subsystems of the family at different times during therapy. Skynner,[1] in his treatment of a fourteen-year-old boy referred for behaviour problems, moved from a predominantly child-centred therapy to a marital therapy with the child's parents. In his discussion Skynner clarified his reasons for this necessary shift in emphasis. He found that work with the marital subsystem was required in order to resolve the presenting problem. Minuchin[2] emphasises the usefulness of varying the subsystems upon which the therapist acts. He adds a further twist by allowing family members excluded from a family session to watch the session behind a one-way screen in the company of another therapist. In one family study, Ackerman[3] treats an eight-year-old boy referred for childhood phobias in conjoint family sessions, individual sessions, and in many different combinations of family members involved in the sessions.

In the following clinical case study, therapy progressed from an individual adult referral to marital sessions, to conjoint family sessions, to involvement of extended family members. During the sessions, I used many of the techniques previously described in Chapter Seven.

The Referral

Mrs Felicia Keats was referred to the clinic for guidance by her general practitioner. I received the following referral letter:

> Dear Doctor,
>   I shall be glad if you will send this patient an appointment to attend your Sexual Dysfunction Clinic if you might be able to help.
>   She formed a recent lesbian relationship which has since ended. She is married with two children and is quite sure that if she were to tell her husband her marriage would end.
>   She has been depressed and is in need of guidance and she is upset and worried over her lesbian tendencies. Hoping you can help her.

There was no further information forthcoming. I agreed to see Mrs Keats and sent her an appointment.

Analysis of Referral

I wondered if this woman would require a family-oriented approach for what had been presented as a problem of sexual identify. She may just require individual therapy aimed towards adjusting her self-image to her lesbian tendencies. But there was an immediate, potential family and marital crisis. She had fears about informing her husband. The effects of her affair on the marriage indicated at least one area in which family therapy might help. The referral did not mention the quality of her relationship with her husband or children. Nor was there any hint of the extent of the sexual satisfaction in either of her physical relationships. Guilt and secrecy figured prominently. I wondered if she possessed an underlying tendency to deal with emotional matters through secrecy and guilt. I was curious about Mrs Keats and wondered where her problems might lead.

Session One

Mrs Keats was a tall, well-dressed blond woman with a masculine face.

She was visibly anxious and drawn. I allowed her to talk freely to me about her anxieties and feelings of guilt. She gave a detailed account of her relationship with an older woman who had befriended her. Their sexual relationship began when the woman had tried to comfort her during one of her bouts of depression. She found the physical side more exciting than her dull sexual relationship with her husband. She had been treated for over five years by her general practitioner for a mixture of anxiety and depression and was taking various antidepressants and tranquilisers. *She unconsciously connected her current crisis with long-standing problems. I wondered what had started her original symptoms.* Attempts to reduce her medications by her doctor resulted in 'withdrawal' symptoms including gastrointestinal upset and insomnia. Nevertheless, the medications had not controlled her panic attacks or crying spells. Nor had they helped her to deal with the intense guilt generated by her sexual liaison. She felt that she was losing her mind and was fearful of becoming a lesbian.

I asked about her background and upbringing. Her mother had had many affairs and four divorces. She said that she had been sexually assaulted by one of her mother's lovers. She was especially bitter about her mother's sexual promiscuity. Mrs Keats feared that her mother might find out about her relationship and use it against her. Her relationship with her mother and her stepfather was not a very close one. *The family transgenerational influences could reveal a great deal if I pursued them. But I filed away this information for the future. It was too early to introduce a geneogram or family-oriented work. I felt I must first help with the crisis, then engage her husband in the therapy.* I listened as she described her husband to me. He was a grocer who was kindly and inoffensive. She was frightened that she had ruined her married life. He was not sophisticated and she feared his reaction if he found out about the affair. He accepted her current 'illness' but had no idea of the cause. Her immediate major fear was that he might discover her indiscretion. *I had sufficient engagement to begin working on her problem but a family quandary was looming in the background. At the moment she was desperately worried and willing to depend on anyone who might help her survive the present crisis.* The rest of the session was devoted to plans of further action.

Her most pressing fear related to her guilt and the underlying need for punishment from her husband to ease that guilt. Since her husband was described as such a kind person I explained that I might be able to help her in discussing the issue with him. The next session would be a joint marital session. The immediate cause of her illness would be discussed if I thought it would not end their marriage. She was visibly relieved when I proposed this. She wanted to work on the sexual side of her relationship with her husband, confessing that the lesbian affair had awakened her to new possibilities of sexual satisfaction. She also wanted freedom from her panic attacks. Finally, she wanted to end her dependence on medications if possible. I planned a schedule to reduce her medications and asked that she contact me by phone if any symptoms returned. I cautioned that she might face a few difficult weeks while her body readjusted. She seemed to welcome this. *Receive punishment from me as penance for her misconduct?* I arranged to see her and her husband in two weeks.

Afterthoughts and Analysis of the Session

While considering her problems in isolation, I was already mapping out in my mind a progression of therapy from her to the marital subsystem, possibly also including her mother. Her husband needed to learn to satisfy his wife's sexual needs. He may also need to learn how to confront his wife. Their two children were not mentioned in the session. I wondered what effect their mother's problems had on them. A transgenerational pattern was evident in her description of her mother. Two generations with sexual problems might be significant. Her attitude towards her mother was rooted in the sexual pattern. I felt it was right to work with her on her immediate crisis while tying in other issues as therapy proceeded. A great deal remained to discover before I could be certain about the causes of this quandary and its solution. I was confident that Mrs Keats would return and hoped that the next session would increase my understanding of the quandary.

Session Two

Mr and Mrs Keats arrived together. Mr Keats looked much younger than his age. They both looked nervous and the initial minutes were awkward ones, taken up by my introduction to Mr Keats. Felicia launched into a description of her physical symptoms since stopping her medication. Finally she admitted that she had told her husband about her lesbian affair. He had responded with reassurance and support as well as puzzlement. Mr Keats was surprised about the severity of his wife's reaction. *I felt that Mrs Keats wanted her husband to react with anger or resentment; he seemed too passive and accepting.* I asked Mrs Keats if her fears had decreased but she admitted that she felt increasing anxiety. I asked Mr Keats about his family of origin. He was the youngest of four boys and his parents were advanced in age when he was born. His family had never discussed sexual matters and he had not been able to talk to his brothers about sex. He said that he was very naive about sexual matters and would value help in this area. *Mrs Keats had been working on her husband at home.* He admitted that his wife had suggested that they could both benefit from sexual therapy. I tried to explore his feelings about his wife's lesbian relationship, but his responses were muted and embarrassed. *He was afraid of his wife and her reactions.* He started to explain that his two daughters knew nothing about the cause of their mother's upset, but I returned to his feelings about his wife's affair. He finally admitted that he might be angry; he was afraid to show his feelings in case his wife reacted badly. Here Felicia interrupted. She returned to the issue of sexual therapy and asked if I could help them with it. *I must stick to their immediate felt needs, specifically in regard to sexuality. Only through their struggles with these needs would they accept that other issues were involved.* I discussed the possibilities of sexual therapy with them and introduced the idea of sensate focus. They were both enthusiastic to try this technique. They agreed to practise sensate focus according to a programme given them as written instructions.[4] Other tasks were set. Mr Keats was asked to express his feelings to his wife more clearly. Mrs Keats was to continue to refrain from taking her medications. Before they left the office I briefly explored the beginnings of her depressive feelings. Although her youngest daughter had started school five years ago, no loss or other precipitating cause for her illness was uncovered. *There might still be some unacknowledged or secret precipitant five years ago, but I decided not to pursue it.* They were to return in two weeks.

Afterthoughts and Analysis of the Session

I felt more puzzled at the end of this session than I had after the first. Mr Keats had been drawn into therapy easily. He saw the need for his inclusion in a sexual therapy dictated by his wife, but I was startled by the ease with which she informed her husband of her affair.

Other matters were clearer to me. I expected Mr Keats to take my permission to express his feelings to his wife seriously. They would probably have a row which would relieve some of Felicia's guilt. She would feel that he had punished her and shown his love for her at the same time.

The geneogram that I drew for myself (see Figure 10.1) revealed that Harry Keats, the youngest son of four sons, had married the oldest daughter of three children. He had little knowledge of the opposite sex and no premarital sexual experience, while she was the eldest child with two brothers and a mother whose sexual promiscuity was an open lesson

in her family. Mr Keats was surrounded by women in his present family
since both the children were girls.

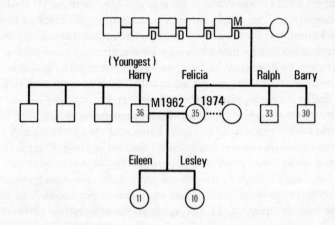

Figure 10.1   Initial Geneogram of the Keats Family

I wondered about Mrs Keat's choice of a lesbian affair rather than a
heterosexual one — perhaps an unconscious attempt to 'love' the mother
she despised? It certainly signified a breakdown of sexual control in a
way similar to her mother. The effects of this quandary must influence
the children in ways unexplained yet.

Mrs Keats had complied with all my suggestions and instructions. I
was certain that the couple would return but I remained uncertain as to
the final nature of real work in therapy. I planned at the next session to
explore both of their backgrounds in greater detail.

Session Three

Both Felicia and Harry seemed pleased to see me. They were anxious to
relate the events of the previous two weeks. They had returned home
and experienced several of the most intensely pleasurable lovemaking
sessions of their married life. These interludes had occurred shortly after
Harry had an angry argument with his wife about her affair. Two days
later, Felicia lost all sexual feeling for her husband. They attempted

sensate focus but Felicia experienced no response from the stimulation. They both felt that something was interfering with their sexual relations. *I guessed that Harry's ability to argue with and confront Felicia signified that he cared. He relieved her guilt long enough for her to respond to his lovemaking with abandon. She was then frightened by her responsiveness and lack of control.*

I explained that I felt she had great fears of her own sexuality and that he had been unable to confront her for many years. I asked if they knew the origins of these traits and at this point introduced the geneogram to them (see Figure 10.2). In drawing the geneogram I discovered that Harry's father died shortly before his wife had begun to experience anxiety and depression. He had turned inwards at the time and withdrawn from her. She became anxious and upset by his withdrawal; the lack of physical contact led to an increase in her sexual needs which were not met by him. *His withdrawal was coupled with her change in role from a mother with toddlers to one with schoolchildren. Increased time on her hands made her feel unwanted. She might also have been mourning her father-in-law's death.* Her increased sexual desire led to a fear of promiscuity that was intense. Her husband drew my attention to one of Felicia's guiding principles in life which was to avoid being in any way like her mother. Her fear led her to withdraw from her children so as to avoid contaminating them as her mother had contaminated her. She reached an unstable equilibrium in which her tension built up until the affair occurred. During this period she increasingly abandoned her children to her husband's care until she was an outsider in the family.

Felicia was attracted to her husband's naivety and boyishness when they met; she felt safe with him. She was able to draw emotional and physical comfort from him while remaining in control of the relationship. His withdrawal had threatened her control. When his normal mourning process receded she was entrenched in her pathological state and he was too weak to confront her enough to draw her out.

Neither Harry nor Felicia had much contact with their families of origin. Every Christmas Felicia's mother and stepfather would impose themselves by staying at their house. She had never been able to tell them not to make the journey from Exeter. Harry's brothers had moved away over the years and he had lost contact with them.

A pattern of sexual difficulties and conflicts over sexuality existed in Mrs Keats's family back to her maternal grandmother. Her maternal uncle and aunt had both found sexual relationships and marriage difficult. Her uncle had divorced and remarried, while her aunt confided to Felicia that she was frigid with both her husbands. Her maternal grand-

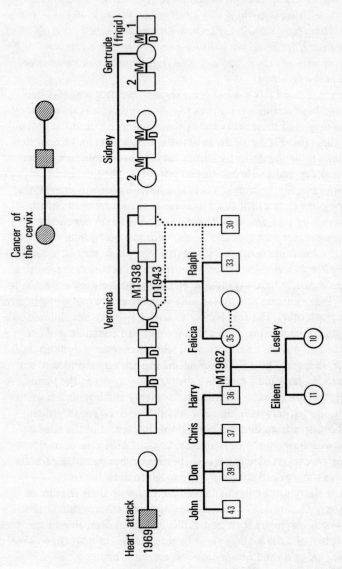

Figure 10.2 Final Geneogram of the Keats Family

mother died of cancer of the cervix and all three of the children were placed in foster homes after her death. Felicia's grandfather remarried soon afterwards but her mother, uncle and aunt remained in foster homes for two further years. They were all in their early teens. On return to the home of their father and stepmother no discussion was allowed about their mother or her death. *Felicia's fears of her sexuality and its control were more understandable in light of the passage of a family pattern.*

I ended the session by explaining to the Keatses that I would like to see them with their children so that I could assess the involvement that might be required of them in the therapy. I drew attention to the fear that Felicia had about passing on the family taint. With little further explanation they both agreed to a full conjoint session. *I hoped that a series of family tasks would grow from the session to initiate a process of change.* They left the office with no further tasks, to return with their children in four weeks.

Afterthoughts and Analysis of the Session

I believed that the lesbian affair had several meanings. It was a symbol of the loss of Mrs Keats's control of her sexuality. Poor control of sexuality was a family pattern, directly traced to her grandmother's disease, death and its aftermath. Sexuality, death and secrecy were intermingled in a family pattern. The affair was also a symbol of the similarity between Mrs Keats and her openly despised and resented mother. Finally, in her lovemaking with an older woman, she symbolically revealed her love for the mother who raised and moulded her. Her fears about the effects of her behaviour on the children were related to a fear of continuing the family pattern. Her husband's passivity and naivety were a result of his experience as the baby of his family of origin.

The family quandary was a serious one. In order to change, Mrs Keats must break a pre-existing family pattern. This would require her to establish a new position within her family of origin. She must also stop withdrawing from her family and her husband must learn to confront Felicia with greater authority. The tasks and techniques required to bring about these changes involved the entire nuclear family unit. They were living together and would be affected. I needed to see the family as a working unit.

Session Four

The children appeared at the interview with their parents. They were restrained at first with outbursts of occasional nervous giggling. I encouraged the children to discuss problems which they saw in their family. They both mentioned mother nagging too much and not playing with them. Later, a review of the family history was done in their presence. *I wondered why Mrs Keats was so reluctant to talk about her youngest brother, but I decided to ask about it later.* There was no information that the children hadn't known before.

Family role-playing was then attempted. The children played their parents' roles while Harry and Felicia acted as their children. *Both daughters assumed the guise of a distant and hostile woman when asked to be their mother. The children were intensely aware of Felicia's withdrawal but did not know its cause.* The children expressed the feeling that their mother must dislike them since she so often ignored them. Felicia played a very active role as one of her children. She proved that she could step out of her usual role and enter into a play situation with the children.

After the role-playing, we took stock of the tasks set previously. Felicia informed me that she was off her medications entirely. Harry complained that their relationship had not improved greatly over the past weeks. The children agreed that their parents weren't getting on with each other very well. I emphasised that the children were not in any way responsible for their parent's unhappiness. *Children often blame themselves for their parents' discomfort.* The session ended with two separate appointments being made. Mr and Mrs Keats were to return in two weeks while the entire family was to return for a videotaped session in four weeks.

Afterthoughts and Analysis of the Session

I felt that I could now plan family tasks for changing reactions and relationships in the family. Mrs Keats reacted to her children by isolating herself. I mapped out several possible exercises for the conjoint session which could be elaborated upon outside of the session and whose emotional impact might alter the present situation. But I needed concomitantly to deal with the marital relationship. Mr Keats still allowed his wife to dictate to her family and I felt he needed more support to assert himself. Mrs Keats needed guidance in order to alter her relationship with her mother. I hoped that if she succeeded, the resultant reaction would relieve her feelings about damaging the children and alter her feelings about her own sexuality. She might even come to accept her mother rather than avoid and fear her.

Session Five

After a brief catalogue of the current unchanging state of affairs in the family, a long discussion ensued about the last session. During the reflection and analysis which followed, Felicia spontaneously connected her self-imposed exclusion of her children with her feelings about her mother. *A flash of insight which I felt would make the solution to the family quandary easier.* She spoke heatedly and angrily about the tense and unhappy relationship with her mother and burst into tears. I asked if her mother knew of her inner feelings but she recoiled from any suggestion of revealing them. She remarked that her family was not an open one. *Here I remembered the hesitancy about her brother.*

I asked her whether her youngest brother was involved in the family secrecy and she revealed that her younger brother was the cause of her mother's divorce from her father. Her mother had had an affair with her uncle, her father's brother, and had become pregnant. She wept again and said that she was afraid that she was going to ruin her marriage as her mother had. Harry sat by helplessly, unable to comfort his wife. I challenged his passivity and asked him to make some positive effort to comfort her and I left the room. When I returned Felicia was being warmly and firmly embraced by Harry. *This instinctive move on my part grew out of my desire for Harry to take charge of his wife.*

I set Felicia a definite task to involve her mother in the therapy. She agreed reluctantly to consider inviting her mother to the sessions but only as a last resort. Instead she offered to write to her mother and express her inner feelings. I pressed her to make this letter a firm commitment. I explained that it was necessary for her to change her feelings about and her relationship with her mother, in order to change her relationships with her children and ensure that her relationship with Harry improved.

I set Harry the task of asserting himself in an argument with his wife before the next session.

Afterthoughts and Analysis of the Session

My feelings at the end of this session were mixed. Despite their reported lack of progress I detected that their relationship was improved and their marital bond strengthened. The lesbian affair and Felicia's fears about becoming a lesbian had receded into insignificance. I had weaned Felicia off medications unsuccessfully used for five years. I was especially pleased by Harry's ability to take charge in the session after my prodding in the office. I hoped it would generalise in the home environment. Despite her flash of insight, however, Mrs Keats had not yet effectively managed to change her underlying fears or alter her behaviour. I hoped that I had the right exercises planned for the next session and that my assumptions about her need to change her relationship with her mother were correct.

Session Six

This was a conjoint videotaped session. The family seemed relaxed despite the presence of the equipment. The first game which I had devised for the family was one in which Felicia was to be held forcibly within a circle created by Harry and the children. She relaxed and was held by the family at first. She felt that this was a supportive, comfortable and happy position. She was asked to break out of the circle and did so with some difficulty. The next exercise involved her in an attempt to break into the circle. She immediately removed her watch and glasses; she became aggressive, hostile and angry as she tried to break into the tightly knit grouping that her husband and children had constructed against her. She only succeeded by injuring her oldest daughter. *I felt worried by this. I had planned to follow a progression with these exercises but felt that I must now deal with the feelings aroused. Up to the injury things had gone as I expected. The second exercise revealed the way in which the family had closed ranks against Felicia.* I asked Felicia to comfort Eileen as she did at home. She took her daughter on her knee, and hugged her and patted her rump. The effect was to calm Eileen immediately and induce an intense rapport between them. *I thought there was an intense identification based on sibling position and personality traits. Felicia completely 'took over' her daughter at one point.* I asked Eileen to change places with her father. Felicia strenuously objected at first, saying that it was a ridiculous suggestion. I pointed out that there was no real difference. *This was a paradoxical statement intended to highlight the sexual differences.* My statement broke the tension and the family roared with laughter as Harry sat on Felicia's lap. I told her to pat his rump and the laughter redoubled. *With no explanation, I felt that the message got across; they would thereafter always know the difference between physical comforting and sexual relations.* There followed several attempts by Harry and Felicia to find a more comfortable way to cuddle each other. The children looked on with avid interest making suggestions as they watched. When a comfortable arrangement was found, I ended the games.

I asked them to tell me about their home work. Harry revealed that he had been very angry at Felicia one week previously, and the argument which followed ended when he threw Felicia out of the house. He still felt guilty about his behaviour and thought, at the time, she would ask him to leave the house. She related her version of the argument with a twinkle in her eye and seemed proud of Harry even while she related the details of his abuse of her. *Harry had accomplished his task. I hoped he would maintain his new position.* Felicia had not written to her mother yet and I asked her to bring a copy of the letter to her mother to the next session.

In order for the new experiences of the exercises to take root I set Felicia the task of going out with Eileen and Lesley to museums, beaches and other places. She was also to take part in activities with the children at home. I connected the feeling of being in the family circle with the task in contrast to trying to break into it. I asked the parents to return for the next session in one month.

Afterthoughts and Analysis of the Session

The activity session graphically portrayed a progression from family quandary to sexual problems. Resolution exercises helped prepare the way for homework tasks. One interesting transgenerational influence was uncovered when Felicia remarked that her aunt used to fondle her bottom when comforting her as a child. The children served as consultants during the session, apprising their parents of their needs and suggesting ways in which these needs could be fulfilled.

Harry had achieved all that I expected of him in his handling of the row with his wife. She was proud of his new ability to assert himself. I believed that he would maintain this new behaviour since no transgenerational influences directly opposed this new style. The following session was to be in one month. We might return to the sexual work, if Felicia succeeded in writing to her mother. I felt that if she did, there would be no more resistance to work on their sexual relationship. The transgenerational influences and passage of sexual anxieties would have been compartmentalised; the past separated from the present.

Session Seven

Felicia had written a letter to her mother. She showed it to me and the following is an excerpt from it:

Dear Mum,
    I have never been able to tell you about the way I feel about you. It has always been difficult for me. I am now seeing a psychiatrist who feels that my problems are partly due to my early life and all the things that happened at home. I always feel that you put me down

and take advantage of me. You may not know that when I was twelve I used to be so frightened when you and Uncle John used my bed.

I have tried to live my life differently from you and I still want to do that. Now that I've told you I don't expect you'll ever speak to me again but I had to write to you and it's no use hiding what I feel anymore. I still love you as a mother and can't blame you for everything. I hope we will be able to get along better in the future now that it's out.

Her mother quickly returned a short note.

Dear Felicia,
I hope to see you at Christmas as per our usual arrangements. I never treated you any different than your brothers. I'm sorry you hold a grudge against me. I enclose the children's presents.

Felicia wrote back to her mother and cancelled their normal arrangements. She asked her brother to house her mother and stepfather for the holiday period. When they arrived, Felicia spoke to her mother alone for a long time. She bared her more negative feelings and as a result of their talk she felt that her mother would never be able to frighten her or push her around as she had previously. Paradoxically, she felt an increased warmth towards her mother. *The concentration on Felicia's relationship with her mother had borne fruit.* Felicia reported an increase in communication and sharing between herself and Harry. Their sexual relationship had improved slightly as well. Felicia had no difficulty in carrying out her tasks with the children. The family outings to parks, museums and the beach had been enjoyed by her. *She lost her fear of contaminating them. The exercises had shown her that the children valued her.* Harry maintained his strength and had been able to take a more active role in controlling Felicia during her flareups.

Both Harry and Felicia felt that they were ready to work on the sexual side of their relationship. Felicia still had no orgasmic response to her husband. She found it difficult to find anything which would turn on her sexual feelings. Harry required specific education for his ignorance of sexual technique and female anatomy. They were both prescribed sex manuals and asked to resume their sensate focus exercises. The following session was scheduled as one devoted to sexual exploration.

Afterthoughts and Analysis of the Session

Several structural changes had occurred between the last session and this one. The relationship between Felicia and her mother altered; Harry took a more authoritative role with Felicia and the children; Felicia was more closely linked to her children; and the children had matured a bit by providing help for their parents. The children were now in a better balanced position between a relatively more distant father and closer mother. The balance between family members had been achieved but I was worried that it had been at the expense of Felicia's mother. I did not expect a total break in that relationship since nothing in the family history indicated that parents completely and irrevocably severed links with their children. I imagined that Felicia's mother was strong and would weather the storm. But I would dearly have liked to see her for my own peace of mind.

The sexual problem remained awaiting a solution. I hoped that a sexual exploration session would break through their naive fantasies about their bodies while their reading might increase the range of their sexual fantasies.

Session Eight

Mr and Mrs Keats were apprehensive and embarrassed. They were both asked to remove their clothes. An examination room of the conventional sort was used. I began by connecting Harry's genitals with the various words used for them in their assigned reading. Felicia was asked to examine Harry and touch his various private parts while she used these words. She blushed with embarrassment but she also became aroused. *Here was evidence that there was a sexually arousing stimulus for her.* Felicia was then asked to lie on the examination couch and a similar procedure was followed. I pointed out her anatomy and then asking Harry to do so. Both Felicia and Harry were surprised that they had been wrong about their assumptions of the position of the clitoris. Felicia found her husband's examination intensely stimulating.

The examination ended and after dressing we returned to my office. *They both seemed flushed; the examination had actually provided Felicia with an experience which she could use in her fantasies.* We first spoke about their reactions to the examination. Felicia had not found the reading material useful at all. They both seemed reluctant to discuss other aspects of their life although they admitted to a generally improved home life. They wanted to return home to continue their work on the sexual relationship. *The examination session had a profound emotional effect on them. They needed time to assimilate their new feelings. For the first time, I felt that they were reluctant to share their fantasies with me.* I asked them to continue practising their sensate focus exercises. They were reluctant but finally agreed. I asked them to phone me when they required further help on their sexual relationship.

Afterthoughts and Analysis of the Session

I felt that most of the therapeutic work had been done. Their responsiveness in this session showed that they were able to enjoy a sexual relationship. But when they realised their reawakened feelings in the session they began to exclude me. There was a great deal of follow-up data I wanted, but the session had plucked such deep personal chords that there was no room to talk about it.

They contacted me three weeks later, they reported that their sexual relationship had improved considerably. They both felt little need to continue treatment sessions. I suggested that they bring their children to watch their videotape sessions in two months. They could contact me if further problems developed. I was apprehensive because of the sudden cessation of treatment. My worry related to fears of unfinished business. I also experienced feelings of loss related to the effort I had put into the therapy sessions. I hoped for reassurance about the outcome of our work together.

Session Nine

The family which arrived for this session seemed a much more self-satisfied and complacent one than I had been expecting. *My fears were unfounded. Their assurance and poise told me that their family life was settled and improved.* After I greeted them, I asked them to watch the videotapes of their sessions on their own and left them in my office. *I wanted them to experience themselves as a family without the need for an expert to interpret what they saw. I was not confident that they would see the change in their behaviour since the earlier sessions.*

On my return the family had just finished drying tears of laughter. They expressed some disbelief that they had ever reacted as their images revealed. Eileen and Lesley felt older than their images. Felicia noted that she had been blaming everyone in her family for her behaviour in the videotape. She now realised that much of her behaviour was of her own doing. Harry was most aware of the passive way in which he acted and spoke. He felt that he had changed; he still avoided conflicts with his wife but not to an extreme. The parents admitted to a better relationship together, including their sexual relations. Felicia and her mother had been much closer since her letter and their talk. Her youngest brother recently took her to one side and praised her. He felt that she should have confronted their mother years ago.

I discussed with them my own feelings about the course of their treatment. The family had been in therapy for just under one year. I asked that they return for a follow-up session in one year or get in touch sooner if they needed further help. I discharged them to their general practitioner with the following letter:

> Dear Doctor,
>
> I am writing to tell you that Mr and Mrs Keats, who have been seeing me over the past year, have been discharged from treatment. Although Mrs Keats was originally referred to the Sexual Dysfunction Clinic, I have been seeing them and their children in family therapy. I feel at present that they have established a better relationship. Their sexual relations are improved, Mrs Keats requires no medications, and their children report a happier home atmosphere.

Afterthoughts and Analysis of the Session

Faced with the end of a difficult and complicated therapy I felt pleased at the final outcome and saddened at my loss of a good working relationship. I was surprised at the number of different techniques I had used. I believed that the effects of treatment would last despite the approaching adolescence of the children which must raise anxieties in the family.

The lesbian affair which had caused the referral had led us on to a tortuous pathway. It started with Mrs Keats and her feelings of anxiety, depression, guilt and disgust. Mr Keats was included when I understood how his inexperience with women and sexuality collided with Felicia's needs. The transgenerational passage of sexually-based conflicts were traced to Felicia's grandmother's disease, death and its aftermath. The children were included in the sessions when Felicia's fear of contaminating them with a family taint became clear. Finally, her mother was indirectly involved in the therapy when her continuing influence became apparent. The effect of the accomplishment of the various tasks was a removal of symptoms, an end to medications and a strengthening of the marital bond.

Follow-up

A two-year follow-up of this case revealed that the youngest daughter had become a school refuser briefly six months after the end of therapy. Mr Keats had dealt with this firmly without the need for outside intervention. No other unusual family or individual problems developed. The final outcome was a successful adjustment at this stage of the family's development.

A Treatment Failure

Conjoint family therapy sessions do not automatically provide solutions and favourable outcomes to family quandaries. Janet Clergy was referred as a fourteen-year-old school truant. Her mother attended with her at the first session. The problem was explored in relation to the other family members. Two years prior to referral, Mr and Mrs Clergy had lost their two-year-old foster child when his parents abducted him one weekend. Mr Clergy became depressed and simultaneously developed a morbid jealousy of his wife. Their relationship deteriorated after he struck her several times. She became pregnant and he denied paternity. He required his wife to pay for the private abortion and subsequent sterilisation, but his jealousy continued unabated. Finally his wife began fighting back, and Janet began staying home from school.

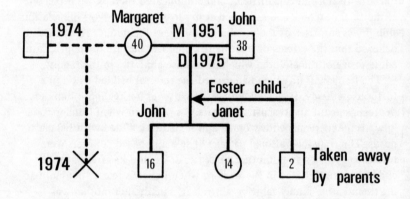

Figure 10.3   Geneogram of the Clergy Family

Her truanting was a minor problem, easily dealt with between her and the school, but the conjoint sessions which followed were difficult. Mr Clergy dated his jealousy to the loss of his foster son. He had also become depressed shortly afterwards when he had to clear the remains of a man from the railway tracks as part of his job. Several conjoint marital and family sessions failed to increase communication or improve relations between the parents. Mr Clergy was admitted to hospital following an overdose. When his wife found out about the admission she appeared at the hospital and signed him out against medical advice. Further treatment was offered but refused. He was much improved when taken off all of his medications. Home life seemed to have settled down. Six months later his wife went to live with her secret lover of two years' duration. Mr Clergy was seen by his general practitioner for help with his nerves, heavily in debt and facing eviction.

In this case family therapy seemed the appropriate form of intervention. But Mrs Clergy had consistently been deceitful in her dealings with the rest of the family and the therapist. The original symptom of truanting was easily resolved so that therapy may have been considered a success. But the family quandary was rooted in the loss of the foster child which destroyed the relationship between the parents. My failure to realise that the husband's jealousy was well-founded (accepting the wife's story without challenge) led to a poor outcome.

Conjoint family sessions were based on a false assumption and failed utterly to resolve the quandary.

Notes

1. R. Skynner, *One Flesh, Separate Persons* (Constable, London, 1978), pp. 329-60.

2. S. Minuchin and B. Montalvo, 'Techniques for Working with Disorganized Low Socioeconomic Families', *American Journal of Orthopsychiatry*, vol. 37 (1967), pp. 880-7.

3. N. Ackerman, *The Psychodynamics of Family Life* (Basic Books, New York, 1958), pp. 308-15.

4. M. Crowe and P. Gillan, *Training Program for Sexual Inadequacy,* privately published monograph, 1974.

11 A TRAINING ANALYSIS FOR FAMILY THERAPISTS

> The method of teaching which approaches most nearly
> to the method of investigation, is comparably the
> best; since, not content with serving up a few barren
> and lifeless truths, it leads to the stock on which
> they grew.
>
> Burke

> Self knowledge is best learned, not by contemplation,
> but action.
>
> Goethe

Psychological treatments requiring the development of a relationship between the client and therapist led to the need for a personal training experience for students which in some way mirrored the therapeutic process. To become a psychoanalyst, trainees now submit to a personal analysis; to become a group analyst, trainees are expected to take part in personal group sessions. This personal tuition is an early requirement in the process of becoming a qualified therapist recognised by various training institutes.

Such personal analyses have developed in order to meet emotional and educational objectives simultaneously. That the experience is akin to the therapeutic process the student will later employ, provides a unique understanding of that process. A recipient of therapy gains an empathic training which will stand any therapist in good stead in the future when dealing with his own clients. If the therapeutic procedure effectively induces change in the trainee, then his emotional investment and belief in the method will be strengthened. If the change induced resolves personal problems which would interfere with the therapeutic abilities of a student, then the experience is worthwhile for that reason alone. Finally, such a personal analysis exposes the trainee to an experienced therapist who is employing considerable skills and knowledge while in close contact with the student. Such an experience models the more subtle techniques of the therapeutic method for the trainee.

The discipline of family therapy faces an added dilemma when trying to provide a personal training analysis. Previous psychological treatments have been limited to the intrapsychic, interpersonal dysfunctions of individuals. The therapists, in order to gain a personal familiarity with individual or group therapy, needed only to commit themselves to the training experience. Family therapy involves a higher hierarchical level of organisation. In family therapy, the client is the family. Family therapists, in order to enjoy a suitable personal training model, might reasonably be expected to include their own family members (nuclear and extended). But it is impractical to require trainees to commit their entire family network to conjoint family sessions. Such an unwieldy model of personal training would be difficult to constitute or maintain in any training institute.

The ingenuity of family therapists has been taxed to devise alternatives to conjoint family sessions for the personal training of their students. Through the use of sculpting and the simulation of family sessions in groups of trainees, attempts have been made to bypass the need for any active participation of real family members. In a few training programmes the participation of the spouses of trainees has been encouraged. Other programmes content themselves with an insistence on the requirement that their trainees receive some alternative form of individual or group analysis. None of these alternatives fulfil necessary emotional and educational criteria for a training analysis for family therapists.

I wish to describe a model which does involve students in experiencing the rewards and difficulties of working within their own family system. It is a short step from the type of therapy described in Chapter Eight to the use of similar methods with motivated family therapy trainees. The use of geneograms and transgenerational analysis provides a way for trainees to be guided to work with their own families without requiring the presence of family members in conjoint sessions.

This model originates with Bowen. In 1967, he described his efforts to put his theories into practice by differentiating himself from his family of origin. Since that presentation and its subsequent publication,[1] several similar accounts have been written and presented by family therapists[2] guided by the postulates of the Bowen Theory. I have presented an account of work with my family of origin[3] using some of his techniques without adhering to his theoretical bias. All of these accounts have developed from efforts to coach trainees in work which involved changing their relationships within their families of origin.

Bowen[4] continues to use this model of training for his student family therapists. He describes the training technique as follows: A detailed family history for multiple generations in the past is drawn up and a personal relationship is developed with all important living relatives.

Activation of old family relationships brings about old triangles. With the advantage of objectivity and knowledge of triangles the old relationships are detriangled as they are brought to life. This paradigm of a family training analysis is used in a group seminar of trainees with one or more experienced therapists. In these 'coaching' sessions, trainees report on the visits they have made to their family of origin and extended family. Problems with detriangulation are discussed and advice is given on how to deal with situations which might develop on their next visit home.

Framo has taken the use of the family of origin one step further by inviting them to attend family therapy sessions as a resource.[5] During my psychiatric training I watched a similar technique being used by Paul.[6] Neither are adherents to the Bowen Theory but they have borrowed freely from his therapeutic methodology. The training analysis which I favour would combine the different methods of using the family of origin as a resource.

A Search for Identity: My Transgenerational Influences

The following account describes work with my family of origin during my psychiatric training. It was motivated by a quest for self-knowledge rather than as a training requirement. During the three years of this work, a family therapy seminar led by Norman Paul helped bring the work with my family of origin to fruition. I include this material as an example of work which is possible as part of a family analysis. I hope it will also serve to illustrate certain principles of the training analysis.

Early in my psychiatric training I began to develop the use of family trees derived from genetic diagrams. As I began to plot the non-genetic influences on my patients, I was stimulated into an awareness of the position I occupied within my family of origin. It was a position with which I was unhappy.

I constructed a geneogram of my family as I then knew it. There were so many missing bits of information that I despaired of collecting them (See Figure 11.1). My younger brother had once prepared a family geneology, an occupation for which I had previously ridiculed him. I wrote and asked him to send me a copy, but when it arrived, I found it skeletal, lacking much of the information that I wished to obtain.

During the year that followed I searched for the missing information. At this time I was not motivated by a desire to change myself, my family members or my relationship with them. I wanted to develop specific character sketches of distant relatives or relatives who had died before I was able to establish an adult relationship with them. I was also

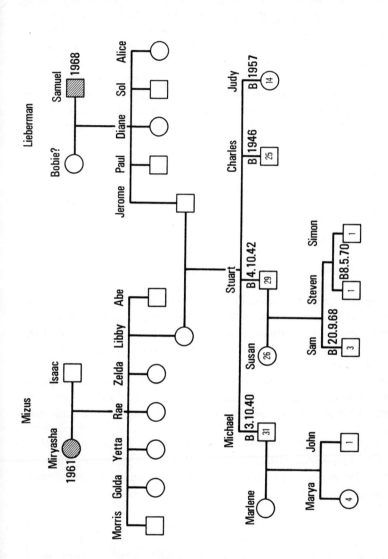

Figure 11.1   The Lieberman Geneogram   (First Attempt)

interested in any secrets that I might uncover. Finally, I sought information about the effects of significant life events upon my various
relatives, including their emotional reactions. I thought of this work as a
search for my own roots; it complemented my increasing interest in
family therapy but I did not consider this project as a part of my training, nor was our family therapy seminar available as a resource yet.

When my parents planned to visit with us in Boston I prepared myself. Upon their arrival from Miami, I had a list of questions organised in
my mind which I intended to press. I approached each of them separately and asked about certain areas in my life history or theirs which
were vague or poorly understood by me. For example, I asked my father
to share his feelings about our move from Chicago in 1951 when he first
separated entirely from his family of origin. I asked my mother to tell
me about her reactions to my maternal grandmother's slowly developing
senility.

Much of my probing was met by embarrassed silence or hesitant half-
statements. Some of the information awakened long-buried memories.
Some questions were side-stepped by my parents so that by the end of
their visit, I was in many ways no wiser than I had been about the details
of my family history. But, as I left the airport after putting my parents
on a plane, I was seized by an admixture of grief and happiness which I
had never before experienced. My eyes were filled with tears on my
drive back from the airport. In my mother's next letter, she described a
similar feeling which had filled her on the flight home. Several weeks
passed in which a feeling of freedom and sadness intermingled and prevented me from fully concentrating. Much later I realised the significance of those feelings. They heralded a change in communication
pattern between myself and my parents which was kindled during that
visit.

I soon began to gather detailed information about my family by letter
and telephone conversations. This long-distance communication was
necessary because I lived in Boston, most of my family of origin lived in
Florida (except for my eldest brother who lived in California), and my
extended family lived in Chicago.

I wrote separate letters to each of my parents and asked them to send
me the history of their lives — whatever they remembered which was
particularly formative to their character. I asked them for old photographs to be sent with explanatory notes about the more distant
relatives. I then waited expectantly for their replies.

My mother responded quickly with a nine-page letter. She started
with a history of her many medical illnesses during my early years which

had required that I board with uncles and aunts. She provided information about the characters of her brothers and sisters and told me of
some who had died in their childhood and whose existence was unknown to me. Secrets about the less reputable behaviour of my grandfather were revealed. He had been and still remained as a powerful
influence within our family.

  The following excerpt about my mother's birth and first year of life
reduced me to tears and it gave me a feeling of compassion and an understanding of my mother previously lacking.

Anyhow Isaac Mizus jumped the ship in New York, received help
from a New York organisation. How is this possible? Years ago when
you saw a man with a beard he was a jew. You spoke to him and the
jews always helped each other. They gave him a room, bath and
clothes and money to go to Chicago where Isaac had a brother. Isaac
got a job, borrowed money from his friends and got his wife and
children here to America (plenty of men never ever sent for their
wives and children). My mother and five children arrived on January
1st, 1916. January 1st, 1917 I was born. My mother developed 'bed
fever', infected ovaries from instruments or dirty hands from doctors
during my delivery (I was the first child that she had a doctor). I was
boarded out to a Dutch woman who was drunk all the time. Zelda,
Rae and Yetta went to an orphanage home. Morrie and Goldie were
home. My mother was taken to the hospital. She was operated on,
they removed one ovary. She almost died. She was in the hospital 6
months. Meanwhile, Zelda developed measles and almost died. Isaac
was called twice during the night, at different nights. This was the
cause of her heart condition. Plus, they say, she must have had
rheumatic fever. I was so badly cared for that when mother got well
and they took me home I was skin and bones. Mother said all she saw
in me was my big black eyes and running nose and ears.

  The deprivation and hardship in my mother's past contrasted starkly
with the life my parents provided for me. Her account led me to re-
evaluate my opinion of her. Some of the anger and resentment I felt
towards her abated. Simultaneously, buried feelings of loss were
awakened when I read her account of my grandmother's hard life in
Russia and France. The information in the letter added to my family
geneogram (see Figure 11.2).

  I decided to write to my Uncle Morris, my mother's eldest brother. I
wanted his account of events prior to my mother's birth. I asked in my

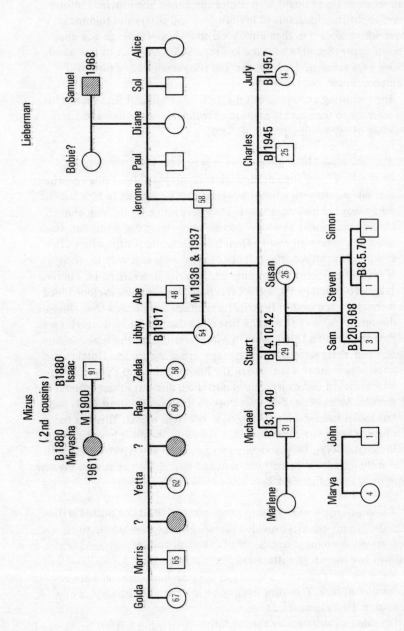

Figure 11.2 The Lieberman Geneogram, Mizus side completed

letter for his account of life in Europe as well as details about less distant events in Chicago. My intentions were to verify some of the stories written by my mother and to gain new knowledge. His reply was many weeks in coming and indicated the extent of the secrecy which pervaded my mother's family as revealed in the following excerpt:

Dear Stuart,

Now to explain of my late letter I must say that I should have wrote much sooner perhaps, but when I did get your letter I wrote to my father and your mother telling them about your letter, so not until the 10th of this month did I get an answer. My Pa told me that your mother sent you a letter with all the information which you might have wanted, but Stuart I must tell you that what you want to know is that which I must get and have more time to do it. I have gathered some notes so far. For I went back into my boy days to try and remember what went on in those years with my mother and the rest of the children. But I've been reading your letter and I am trying to figure out what you really mean to find out for yourself? I think if your mother did give you a history of my mother it could be up to a certain amount of years for her, but I do have some answers about my mother that perhaps she might have forgot to mention. But I am holding back. So — perhaps you might tell me just what information, or if any, she did give you?

By this time I was attending the family seminar led by Norman Paul. I discussed my work so far and mentioned this particular impasse. The way out of it was clear to my colleagues. Since my mother's letter was my property, I sent a copy of it to my uncle and again asked for his help. When several weeks passed, I telephoned him. He was able to tell me a great deal over the phone which he had found himself unable to commit to paper. He disagreed with several of the stories in my mother's letter and told me something of his past. He also mentioned peculiar behaviours of some of his siblings which were familiar to me through my psychiatric training. After our conversation I was elated. I felt as if I had become one with my mother's generation; I had altered my position in relation to my mother's family of origin.

My work with my mother's family emboldened me to turn my attention to my siblings. I copied letters that I had so far received and sent them to each of my brothers. I asked for their memories of our early years and for their feelings about me, past and present. My letter to Charles also contained some advice about his future. He sent back the following reply:

> I don't need any such advice from you or Mom. I know my own
> strengths and weaknesses better than anyone. Should you or Mom or
> *anyone* think that my judgement is faulty that is tough titty. I am
> not about to abdicate control over the major steps in my life to any-
> body.
>
> You know quite well my psychiatrist-brother that I have grown up
> under your shadow and Mike's and of course Mom's. And that all of
> my life has been a struggle to come *out* of that shadow, to overcome
> the passivity of my nature. I need not ask why Mike lives in California
> and you in Boston. Please don't think me ungrateful, brother, but I
> wanted to clear things up. Your interest in the family past I find
> somewhat mystifying. With a wife, 3 children and a mentally stimu-
> lating job, I do not understand your harkening back to the past. For
> my own self, I sought to fill in the great holes in my psychological
> foundation. But for Stuart it would seem not so.

His communication was a shock to me both for its content and its
confrontative honesty. I realised that my image of my brother had to
change. I had felt a need to protect him and ease his path while his letter
indicated that he had progressed far beyond me in some respects. My
respect and admiration for him increased.

I waited for eight months for a letter from my father about his
family. Nothing was forthcoming despite several letters and telephone
calls requesting the information. My own resistance to a visit home was
uncovered in my discussion in the family seminar. It was made clear to
me that I would have to visit Miami. In March 1972, the opportunity
arose to holiday with my parents. I stayed with my parents in their
home. We dusted off the family albums and discussed each relative as
their photo appeared. My father spoke freely about his family and
promised to put more of his thoughts on paper. I visited my grandmother's grave in order to recapture some lost memories and feelings
and I spoke with my grandfather for hours about his turbulent life. My
relationship with my parents was less strained than it had ever been. I
could move easily from being a child to being an adult in their presence.

When I returned to Boston, a letter arrived shortly containing my
father's account of several important events in his life. It was incomplete but explained some of the influences which moulded my father. It
also contained some information about his family of origin which was
of interest. The following excerpt includes a story which illustrates the

value of being a good neighbour as a transgenerational pattern.

> Samuel would go outside and look around for Jewish men who were killed by the Bolsheviks, the Russian communists. If found, he would make sure they were buried according to Jewish law. On one of these occasions, a dozen wagons were brought in with dead people fished out of the Boog river. Samuel went to the wagons to find Jewish bodies which the Russians killed during their retreat. A troop of Polish soldiers came riding up on horseback to the town square. The commanding officer saw Samuel with his Tallis and Tfillin looking at the bodies in the wagon. He took out his gun and said 'A Jew! I have one more bullet left, I will kill this Jew'. Thinking that he would be a hero in the eyes of the Polish people about him. The crowd cleared away from Samuel and I, Jerome the small son ran to his side crying with fear. Gittle ran to the commanding officer pleading for Samuel's life telling the officer what a good man her husband was. The Polish neighbours also ran up to the officer and begged for Samuel's life. They exclaimed 'he is a good Jew, honest, never cheating anyone and always ready to help a neighbour'. The officer said 'Jew, you are lucky, the Polish people like you'. Because of his goodness to people his life was spared.

Another story told of an incident in which my father had been tormented by a neighbour's son. He had hit back and fled in fear when the boy fell to the ground. The neighbours came looking for him in an ugly mood and he had to remain hidden in the manure pile for many hours. This story helped to explain the long fuse to my father's temper.

There remained much more of interest to me in my father's family. I heard that my father's younger sister was due to visit Boston. I contacted her and arranged to meet her. She revealed several gaps in my father's stories. She told me that my father was the second eldest in their family. The eldest child died in his first year from pneumonia; my father carried the same name as this child. She also explained that their family had emigrated to America from Poland shortly after the death of another brother in an artillery bombardment. Further details were supplied until my understanding of both of my parents' family influences were sufficient to satisfy me. I was able to add new information to the geneogram (see Figure 11.3). I felt comfortable with my family of origin. I wondered whether I could test my position in my extended family.

Two years after the beginning of my quest the opportunity arose for

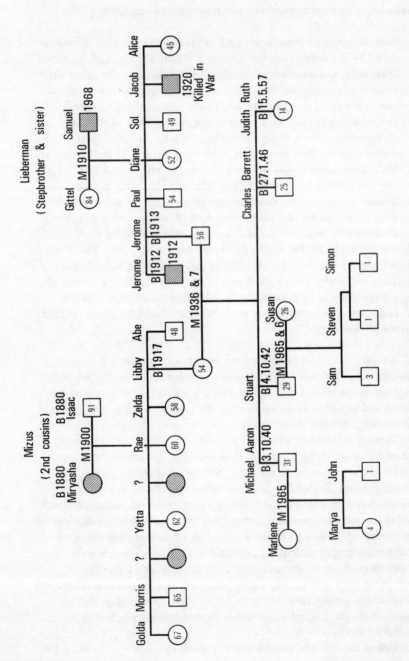

Figure 11.3   The Lieberman Geneogram Completed

me to visit Chicago for a gathering of the Lieberman clan. The occasion was the marriage of one of my cousins. I went with my cine camera, tape recorder and notebook in hand with the objective of revisiting the city in which I spent my first eight years of life and being again unfolded within a large extended family. It was to be a formative and nodal event since my mother's relatives planned a family gathering to coincide with our visit. I hoped to test out my ability to hold my new position within the extended family. Having weakened some bonds and strengthened others I intended to test the effect of my efforts on myself and my relatives.

One of my goals for the visit was to view the family cine films made between 1948 and 1956. The death of my paternal grandfather in 1968 had prevented the showing of these films ever since. Some of the films dated back before the death of my cousin in 1951 and had not been shown since then. Since the films had to be shown at a family gathering I found there was great resistance. Each person in turn whom I approached commented that they wouldn't mind but pointed to another relative as being unable to tolerate the memories that might be resurrected. Finally, by asking all of them and receiving assurances from each individually, I negotiated an occasion when the film show was held. I was able to see myself at six, eight and twelve; I saw relatives who had since died. More importantly, in the process of negotiating the film show, I maintained and extended my new position within the generational hierarchy of my extended family. I also managed to visit my old neighbourhoods, taped conversations with my grandmother and took cine film of much of my family. I returned to Boston pleased and satisfied.

The work which I did with my family of origin gave me confidence and the capability of dealing more comfortably with problems in my nuclear family. It also provided me with a resource and an understanding which have been invaluable in my clinical work. The experience provided me with an empathic awareness of the fears and difficulties involved in attempting to alter human relationships within a family system.

The meaning of much of the material added a great deal to my self-awareness and insight. For example, I discovered that I was named after my mother's grandfather. My mother's grandmother bears a striking resemblance to my mother in old photographs, a fact which partly explained the close attachment between my mother and grandfather. My older brother was named after my father's grandfather. My interpretation is that we each belonged to a different side of the family. Our sibling rivarly was a symbol of the family collision. It could also be seen as the competition between families and between my parents. Our close relationship as brothers mirrored the marriage of the two extended families through my parents.

My family history and the stories within it showed a repetition of patterns handed down from generation to generation along with the stories. Several recurring themes such as emigration, secret marriage and fixed emotional patterns such as extreme containment of anger existed in at least three different generations. Understanding these patterns and their origins led me to an acceptance of some of them and an alteration of those patterns which were less useful.

A Family Training Analysis

I believe that an experience similar to the work with my family under organised supervision would meet the criteria of a family therapy training analysis. If it were combined with a programme of didactic courses and live or recorded supervision, a balanced training for family therapists could be achieved.

The training analysis could be organised as follows. Applicants for formal training at a family therapy institute would be advised that they would be required to undergo a family training analysis as an integral requirement of their educational experience. Those individuals accepted for training would be assigned to a supervisor whose task it would be to help the trainee in work with his own family. The analysis would require ten to twenty one-hour sessions spaced over monthly intervals, and held in the supervisor's office. Family members who were interested could be invited to attend sessions although most of the work would involve the trainee only.

The content of such an exercise would be centred on the transgenerational analysis of the trainee's family background. An understanding of relationships between the trainee and his significant family members would also be included. The trainee should, as well, discover the reasons for his interest in family therapy. The discovery of the origin of motivation is important since it will help guard against the tendency towards becoming a compulsive therapist. Finally, any work involved in altering relationships within the trainee's family system could be planned and the alterations carried out.

The process of the family analysis would begin with the construction of a geneogram by the trainee with the help and assistance of his supervisor. Study of the results will provide an opportunity for tentative analysis and formulation of tasks. The significance of the trainee's sibling position may be important in relation to his parents or grandparents. The timing of the entries and exits within the family may prove significant. Reactions to loss, secrets and family patterns can be explored. This analysis of transgenerational influences would point the way toward the first tasks. The trainee would absorb an understanding of the way family therapy concepts apply to himself and his own family. Following the initial session, the trainee would be asked to construct his own geneogram and fill in missing details. Visits to relatives, letters, tape-recorded conversations, telephone calls and/or examination of family documents could be discussed and planned. The trainee would then consider which of his family relationships he would like to alter, if any.

The process of the analysis would continue in the following sessions. The supervisor would act as a problem-solving resource if the trainee was unable to work out a correct strategy for dealing with one of his relatives. The supervisor would also serve as an advisor who could spot blind-spots in the trainee's conscious awareness. For example, one valuable insight was given to me when the importance of my rivalry with my brother was pointed out. Since the alteration of a relationship in one's family might be an essential element of the exercise, the supervisor would be responsible for ensuring that the trainee accomplished this task without being destructive or malicious. The supervisor would ensure that no self-defeating moves were taken. The supervisor would also be available for family crises or visits by family members interested in attending a session.

A family training analysis would end when both trainee and supervisor were satisfied that the trainee had a comprehensive understanding of those transgenerational influences which moulded and continued to influence him. Concomitantly, the alteration of one or more relationships within the family would have been satisfactorily accomplished. The trainee should have experienced the emotional impact of a change in their own family.

If successfully concluded, the above process should meet the following criteria. First, the use of transgenerational methods will provide insight and increase self-awareness both of strengths and weaknesses. Since much of our character is moulded into us by our family, an understanding of that family inevitably leads to self-understanding and greater insight.

Second, the process of family therapy will be thoroughly understood by the trainee who has actually experienced it while working with his own family. A surgeon need not experience an appendectomy to do one, but in many psychological procedures, experiencing the effects – as

long as they are not noxious — can provide an education which no
amount of didactic teaching will provide. Because of the painful
emotions involved in psychotherapeutic procedures, personal involvement will provide much greater understanding and tolerance. Certainly,
before working with my family I had no clear understanding of the
resistances which I would experience and the emotions which were to be
raised, nor of the ways in which I would cope with them.

The third criterion for a training analysis is that it develops empathic
sensitivity in the therapist. The ability to put oneself in the position of
one's client should be enhanced by a personal training experience.
Accurate empathy is held to be one of the three necessary qualities for
any counsellor or psychotherapist;[7] the exploration of transgenerational
influences aids the development of empathy. The similarities between
my family and client-families from diverse backgrounds were more
apparent after my work increased my empathic awareness. Most families
have secrets, losses, recurrent patterns and griefs. Exploring one's own
family provides awareness of those elements of humanity which are
common to us all.

The fourth criterion for a family analysis is the provision of an
association with an experienced therapist who knows how to deal with
problems that arise during family therapy. Since a trainee's family
problems will be of the greatest importance to him, a supervisor will
have the opportunity to acquaint the trainee with techniques, methods
and strategies during first-hand experience. The training analysis could
be likened to an apprenticeship; the personal work involved is the most
difficult which the trainee might be called upon to face.

Finally, the training analysis can be a therapeutic experience for the
trainee and his family. Various of the personal insights and growth
experiences recommended by other psychotherapy disciplines contain
within them an element of therapy. My experience with my family was
a personal help to me, in my relationships with my family of origin and
more importantly in my relationship with my wife and children.
Therapy under the guise of a training experience has enabled many
trainees to mature and perfect skills which were held back by personal
problems.

Variations of the proposed training analysis could be equally effective. The analysis might incorporate a small group (six to eight trainees)
led by a supervisor. A training group would provide the support and
encouragement of peers. It would also supply cross-fertilisation from the
variety of family constellations represented by its members. The dis-
advantage of a group would include a lack of confidentiality and de-

creased time for the intricate discussion of each family at every session. The combination of a small group experience with individual sessions might prove a useful variation. Finally, the inclusion of the trainee's spouse and/or children might be an optional variant. The spouse could simultaneously do work on their family of origin and extended family.

Difficulties would arise when trainees with no living relatives in their extended family were accepted for training. Although the use of the geneogram and transgenerational analysis could proceed, experience of a change in relationship would not be possible. With those trainees engaged in a family analysis, any problems arising within the context of the work would necessarily be the joint responsibility of the trainee and supervisor. Relatives, unhappy with the trainee's attitude, could be encouraged to take part in explanatory sessions if they so wished. Complaints from relatives should be dealt with personally by the trainee and supervisor within the context of the family training analysis.

I believe that the format proposed would provide family therapists with a personal growth experience and insights comparable in most respects to individual and group analyses. This model would additionally provide trainee family therapists with a personal experience of working within and changing a family system.

Family Training Exercises and Structured Experiences

The use of the student's family of origin as a training resource is no longer as controversial as in the past. There have been many exercises and structured experiences devised so as to give the simulated feeling of involvement of family members. They can provide powerful emotional experiences and generate insight, but the exercises lack the feedback responses from relatives which are so necessary to test the effect of changes which occur internally.

Some of these exercises were used in the Family and Marital Course at the Institute of Group Analysis in groups of twelve to fifteen members. Many more family training exercises exist than are included here. I have outlined only those which provide some alternate experience of a trainee's own family system.

Geneogram Co-counselling

Goals:
1. To introduce and study the geneogram as a technique.
2. To provide practical experience of constructing a geneogram.
3. To explore the participant's family system in a co-counselling situation.

Time required: Approximately two hours.
Materials required:
1. Paper and pencil.
2. Blackboard and chalk.
3. Suitable writing surface.
Process:
1. The group leader explains the construction of a geneogram using his/her family as an example, and briefly points out the areas of interest (secrets, replacements, names, etc.).
2. The group leader pairs the participants by any appropriate method (for example: participants who don't know each other, alphabetically, alternately).
3. Each participant of the pairs is asked to construct the geneogram of their partner. After 30-45 minutes, the participants switch roles so that both have the opportunity to construct a geneogram.
4. The group re-convenes and discusses the results of the exercise.
Variations:
1. Each member of the pair may construct their own geneogram using their partner as a resource.
2. Geneograms are constructed with a particular goal in mind such as the discovery of a secret area.
3. Participants are asked after construction of the geneogram to pick one relative whom they would wish to ask unknown or forbidden material and to devise a method of doing so. They are not expected to actually carry out their plan.

Sculpting the Family of Origin

Goals:
1. To introduce and study family sculpting as a technique.
2. To provide practical experience in the use of sculpting.
3. To explore the family relationships of a participant.
Time required: Approximately one to one and a half hours.
Group size: Six to fifteen participants.
Process:
1. One member of the group volunteers to sculpt his/her family.
2. The participant is asked to choose a particular event or time in their family's life to sculpt.
3. The group leader acts as timekeeper and helps the participant to arrange the sculpture.
4. Other group members are chosen to represent the relatives. The sculpture is begun at the time of marriage of the participant's

parents. As each child is born they are placed sequentially into the tableau until the family of origin is completed.

5. The tableau is then arranged to represent the chosen time or event.

6. The group members representing the various family members are asked to discuss their feelings based on physical sensations and fantasies experienced while placed in their various positions and roles.

7. The participants are de-roled by asking them to state their own identity.

8. The group discusses the experience.

Variations:

1. Remaining group members not involved in the sculpture are asked to observe as if they were distant family members.

2. The participant whose family is sculpted takes his/her place in the sculpture instead of choosing someone else to represent him.

3. The group leader portrays various changes in the sculpture as a means of introducing the idea of therapeutic changes.

4. The group meets regularly giving each participant the opportunity to sculpt their own family.

Simulated Family Exercise

This exercise is similar to the sculpting exercise. The family members chosen from the participants to represent the family of one of them is allowed to act and speak in a form of psychodrama. The participants portray a particular scene and they are then de-briefed and de-roled followed by discussion of the exercise.

Notes

1. M. Bowen, 'Differentiation of Self in One's Family', in J. Framo (ed.), *Family Interaction* (Springer, New York, 1972).

2. F. Colon, 'In Search of One's Past: An Identity Trip', *Family Process,* vol. 12, no. 4 (December, 1973); anonymous, 'A Family Therapist's Own Family', read at Georgetown University Family Symposium, November 1973; anonymous, 'First Moves Back into My Family', read at Georgetown University Family Symposium, 1974.

3. S. Lieberman, 'A Search for Identity: Working With One's Own Family', unpublished paper presented to the Group Analytic Society, London, 17 March 1975.

4. M. Bowen, 'Family Therapy After 20 Years', unedited draft chapter for *Handbook of Psychiatry.*

5. J. Framo, 'Family of Origin as a Therapeutic Resource for Adults in Marital and Family Therapy: You Can and Should Go Home Again', *Family Process,* vol. 15, no. 2 (1976), pp. 193-210.

6. N. Paul, 'Personal Communication': I viewed a multiple family group for over six months run by him in which he included extended family members.

7. C. Truax and R. Carkhuff, *Toward Effective Counselling and Psychotherapy* (Aldine Press, Chicago, 1967).

AUTHOR INDEX

Ackerman, N. 16, 142, 159n, 193-4, 211n
Adler, A. 21-3, 38, 41, 42n
Alger, I. 147, 159n

Bateson, G. 43n
Beels, C.C. 17, 20n
Bell, J.E. 16
Berne, E. 19, 20n
Bloch, D. 157, 159n
Bowen, M. 17, 20n, 34-9, 40, 42, 43n, 160, 174n, 213-14, 229n
Bowlby, J. 26, 40, 42, 43n, 52, 66n
Brown, P. 159n
Byng-Hall, J. 43n

Carkhuff, R. 225, 230n
Carter, E. 141, 159n, 174n
Colon, F. 229n
Comfort, A. 159n
Cooklin, A. 67n
Crowe, M.J. 17, 20n, 197, 211n

Dominian, J. 53-4, 66n
Duhl, B. 159n
Duhl, F. 159n

Ellenberger, H.F. 21, 42n
Erickson, M. 139-40, 159n

Faulder, C. 159n
Ferber, A. 17, 20n
Framo, J. 214, 229n
Freud, S. 13, 22, 23-8, 42-3n

Gillan, P. 211n
Click, I. 192n
Grosser, G.H. 43n, 159n
Guerin, P. 94n

Haley, J. 43n
Hatfield, F. 115, 132n
Heard, D. 41, 43n
Howells, J.G. 16, 20n

Jackson, D. 43n, 159n
Johnson, V. 138, 155, 159n

Kantor, D. 159n
Kessler, D. 192n
Klein, M. 28-9, 42

Lidz, T. 43n
Lieberman, S. 59, 67n, 94n, 159n, 229n
Lorenz, K. 47

Masters, W. 138, 155, 159n
Minuchin, S. 136, 158n, 193, 211n
Montalvo, B. 211n

Orfandis, M. 141, 159n, 174n

Parkes, M. 57, 67n
Paul, B.B. 40, 43n, 176, 192n
Paul, N. 27, 39-40, 43n, 143, 159n, 175, 176, 192n, 214, 230n
Paykel, E.S. 67n
Pincus, L. 59, 67n

Satir, V. 16
Scott, R.D. 16, 20n, 43n, 158, 159n
Segal, H. 43n
Skinner, B.F. 65, 67n
Skynner, A.R.C. 16, 20n, 28, 42-3n, 192n, 193, 211n
Stein, J. 17, 20n

Toman, W. 23, 38, 42-3n, 96-102, 113n
Truax, C. 225, 230n

von Bertalanffy, L. 22, 30-4, 42, 43n

Walrond-Skinner, S. 16-17, 25, 42-3n
Watzlawick, P. 159n
Weakland, J. 43n
Whitaker, C. 143, 159n
Wynne, L. 43n

Yakovlev, P.I. 47, 66n

SUBJECT INDEX

acculturation 15
adoption 104
assortative mating 36
attachment theory 40-1, 52
audiotape recording 149

bereavement counselling 144
bond, caretaking 33 (Fig.), 52, 166
bond, heterosexual 33 (Fig.), 52-3,
  104-5, 165-6, 175
bonding 52, 59, 102
Bowen Theory 35-8, 160; detriangle
  36, 214; differentiation of self
  35-8, 213; emotional cutoff 37;
  family projection process 37;
  fusion 35-6, 38; integration of self
  35; multigenerational transmission process 37-8; nuclear family
  emotional system 36; pseudoself
  35-6; sibling position 38; societal
  regression 38; solid self 35;
  triangle 36

clinical examples: adolescent conflict
  106, 108, 111, 117-18; alcoholism
  133-4; anorexia nervosa 74, 85,
  86, 128, 142-3; anxiety state
  161-72; cultural conflict 116-17;
  depression 89-91, 109, 120, 123,
  148, 157-8, 161-72, 176, 190;
  eneuresis (bedwetting) 133, 140;
  family violence 103, 116, 125,
  140; frigidity 18-19; marital
  conflict 109, 118-19, 122, 134,
  141, 151-2, 158, 175-92; mental
  handicap 145, 158; morbid grief
  92, 103, 110, 145-6; morbid
  jealousy 210-11; non-consum-
  mated marriage 109, 156;
  obsessional fear 137, 172; premarital pregnancy 93, 103;
  schizophrenia 107, 125, 126,
  150-1; school phobia 13-14;
  sexual promiscuity 106, 116,
  194; stealing 93; suicidal 120;
  travel phobia 88; truanting
  210-11; vaginismus 155-6;
  wayward child 124-5

conjoint family therapy: definition
  13; example 193-211
constitutive 30, 32, 33 (Fig.), 35, 36,
  46-9, 60, 118
cross-confrontation 40

divorce: exploration of 104, 141;
  family pattern of 89-90, 110;
  threats of 116
double bind 41, 43

educating family members:
  geneogram and 88-9, 123; to
  family therapy concepts 119-26,
    conjoint family patients 124-6,
    conjoint marital patients 122-4,
    individual patients 120-1
enmeshed family 136
experiential (action) techniques:
  position change 150-203;
  rationale for using 150; roleplay
  151-3, 202, 204, 213; sculpting
  153-5, 213, 228-9
extended family: authors 221-3;
  collision of 108, see also family
  collision; definition 13; therapists' 214; therapy sessions and
  93, 176, 182

family: as a multigenerational system
  18-19; definition 13; existence as
  an organism 14-16
family collision: cause of family
  quandary 87-8, 109, 178;
  definition 55-7, 108-10; examples
  of 53, 85, 168, 187, 201, 224;
  exploration of 123; family
  culture and 108-10; Irish vs
  English 85
family constellation 23, 96, 101-2,
  110, 181, 197-8
family evolution 59-60, 65-6
family of origin: authors' 214-24;
  marital couples and 123-4;
  therapists' 213-19
family projections 26, 27 (Fig.)
family quandary: and family
  collision 87-8, 118; arrested